ALSO BY SARAH SUSANKA

The Not So Big House
Creating the Not So Big House
Not So Big Solutions for Your Home
Home by Design
Inside the Not So Big House
Outside the Not So Big House

the not so big life

the
not so big
life

making room
for what
really matters

SARAH
SUSANKA

RANDOM HOUSE   NEW YORK

Published in the United States by Random House,
an imprint of The Random House Publishing Group,
a division of Random House, Inc., New York.

RANDOM HOUSE and colophon are registered trademarks
of Random House, Inc.

LIBRARY OF CONGRESS CATALOGING-IN-PUBLICATION DATA

Susanka, Sarah.
The not so big life: making room for what really matters /
by Sarah Susanka.
p.   cm.
Includes index.
ISBN 978-1-4000-6531-8
1. Conduct of life. I. Title.
BF637.C5S87 2007
158.1—dc22   2006050435

Printed in the United States of America on acid-free paper
www.atrandom.com
246897531
FIRST EDITION

Book design by Carole Lowenstein

Not So Big® is a registered trademark
of Sarah Susanka.

With infinite gratitude for
The One Who Teaches Us

Watch the dust grains moving
in the light near the window.
Their dance is our dance.
We rarely hear the inward music,
but we're all dancing to it nevertheless,
directed by the one who teaches us,
the pure joy of the sun,
our music master.

—JELALUDDIN RUMI,
translated by Coleman Barks

CONTENTS

INTRODUCTION

One night perhaps a dozen years ago, I was lying in bed reading a light novel. This was my way of decompressing at the end of a stressful day in a very busy life. I'd been doing this every evening for years. It was a routine. It was usually comforting, but on this particular night I suddenly felt frustrated. I put down the book and started to listen to the thoughts feeding my irritation. "Is this really all there is?" came the thought. "Is this what my life has amounted to? I'm a successful architect, the managing partner of a firm of forty-five people. I have a lot of responsibilities, plenty of challenges to handle, and a to-do list that's a mile long. I work hard all day, answer innumerable phone calls, and attend a steady stream of meetings, all the while keeping up an incredible pace as I fulfill the dozens of obligations, both professional and personal, that I call daily life. Then I come home—usually well into the evening—to engage in a few mindless activities to help me change the subject from all the challenges of the day so that I can sleep sufficiently soundly to be prepared for another day of the same. Surely there's something more meaningful to life than this."

Once I'd allowed myself to really let that question sink in, I knew I had to make some changes. What I saw was the incongruity between the dreams of my early adulthood and the life I was actually living. As a high school student I'd always been full of ideas and ideals. I'd wanted to study the way the mind works. I'd wanted to explore what makes an object beautiful or an equation elegant. I'd wanted to design buildings that made people's hearts sing, and I'd wanted to work with individuals who cared about the places in which they lived and worked. But more than all of these, I'd wanted to write. I adored writing, no matter the topic or genre, and found that when I could still my mind and just let the words flow out of my fingertips, there was a palpable sense of magic as the meaning of what I was writing expanded my understanding of the subject at hand. I knew, in some deep place, that this was my true passion, and I longed to find a time and a place to fulfill it.

But alas, the life I had fallen into, although it fulfilled one or two of my early aspirations, had no room for anything else. It wasn't so much full of meaning and the pursuit of my heart's desires as it was over-stuffed—so jam-packed with obligations, in fact, that I felt almost suffo-cated on this particular night. Without some intentional shifting of priorities on my part, I now realized, this would be how things would con-tinue to the end of my days. I was asleep at the wheel while barreling down the road of life on cruise control, believing all the while that I was going somewhere important. But some instinct warned me that I was missing the most important part of the journey—the part that requires alertness, awareness, and full engagement. My life was so frenetic, so big, in the overwhelming sense, that the pace of it was its single most salient quality.

I felt as though I'd just been startled awake from a dream and was suddenly alive for the first time in my adult life. Now there seemed noth-ing more important than to learn to stay awake throughout each day's activities, and to figure out how to do so as soon as possible. Usually mo-ments like this seem to happen in the lives of people who have had a close brush with death or are facing serious illness, but I had experienced neither of these. It wasn't something external that had brought this to my attention; it arose from within, when I was relatively peaceful, and able to take the time to listen. Providence had simply tapped me on the head and invited me to look at what I was doing in an entirely new way.

That was the day I began to explore the possibilities of living my life differently. Although I continued to work as an architect, I also started watching myself and the way I engaged my life, observing the underpin-nings of its design. I started to question why I believed what I believed, and gradually all around me doors started to open that I'd never known were there. I began to simplify my life and focus on those things that were truly meaningful to me. Among other things, I made the time to write, that long-neglected passion. It was only by moving with my heart's desire—a key player in wide-awake living—that the Not So Big House series of books was born.

So, in fact, it was my living a Not So Big Life that gave rise to the idea of a house designed to inspire us daily, and it was by fully engaging in the writing process that the term "not so big" came to be—it flowed out onto the page without premeditation as I wrote that first book's introduction. That's how I came to understand something important through the process of writing that I hadn't realized I knew. But with the phrase committed to paper, I saw that it was exactly what was needed to explain our dilemma of scale, pace, and proportion, both in house design and in life.

I'm no different from you. Any of us can wake up from the overstuffed lives we are leading and make room for what we long to have time for. It's possible to take the blur that is modern life—the obligations, the messages to return, errands to run, and family and friends to squeeze in there somehow—and slow it down so we can actually be there in what we're doing. It's possible to start living a Not So Big Life of full, rich, vivid moments where everything that happens to us is experienced fully, and where spirit and connection have room to thrive. Just as I gave myself permission to explore beyond the normal boundaries of my particular career path, you'll discover that you too can pursue the aspects of your own nature that aren't being lived but that yearn for liberation.

Today I'm using the process of living in this new way as the *core* of my life, and not, as you might imagine, my career as an architect or my career as an author. Those are the content or story line of my life, but the process is what has allowed me to explore more and more of the potential I always knew was possible. That's the promise of a Not So Big Life, and it's accessible to anyone with a desire to live a more meaningful life with an increased sense of balance and harmony. If you are up for a life remodeling, follow the directions in the blueprint that follows and you'll discover that there really is something more to living than you currently know. I'm hooked. I hope I can infect you too.

PRINCIPLE
composition

Something that is well composed has a sense of integrity to it, both inside and out. No matter which way you look at a house that is gracefully composed, it appears balanced and has its own unique sense of beauty and harmony. Architects use the word "composed" to describe the interrelationships among forms, whether at the big-picture level (such as how roof meets walls and how walls meet ground) or at the detailed level (such as in the picture at left—how window meets surrounding surfaces, in this case, dropped ceiling and bookshelf).

With many newer homes today, although the façade has usually been composed somewhat—it has a fairly balanced and appealing "face" to the street—as soon as you move a few feet in either direction along the sidewalk, you discover that the sides could very easily belong to a completely different house. They haven't been composed in any way and in fact often look like an accidental assemblage of parts that have simply been thrown together. It makes the house seem insubstantial and inauthentic, as though it's trying to be something that it's not.

In our lives the same can be true. How many people do you know who have a face that they show to the world, while just beneath the surface they're feeling empty and frightened and not doing any of the things they yearn to be doing? A life that's well composed is one in which there is authenticity all the way through, a life in which the outer appearance and the inner substance match up. It is one in which you are living your passions and finding ways to express the beauty that you are. It is through this process of using your life experiences to continually explore your inner nature that delightful and vibrant composition comes into being.

A satisfying composition takes time, care, and introspection, whether you are designing a house, writing a short story, or living a life. This chapter is about the guidelines for composing your own Not So Big Life.

ONE

Blueprint for a New Way of Living

*Today, like every other day, we wake up empty
and frightened. Don't open the door to the study
and begin reading. Take down a musical instrument.*

*Let the beauty we love be what we do.
There are hundreds of ways to kneel and kiss the ground.*
—RUMI

What Are We Missing?

We are facing an enormous problem in our lives today. It's so big we can hardly see it, and it's right in our face all day, every day. We're all living too big lives, crammed from top to toe with activities, urgencies, and obligations that seem absolute. There's no time to take a breath, no time to look for the source of the problem. We are almost desperate for a solution. If we stop and consider what our lives would be like if things got much faster, we might feel overwhelmed by hopelessness and futility. We just don't have any more to give. We're at the end of our rope.

We need to remodel the way we are living, but not in a way that gives us more of the same kinds of space we already have; that would simply create an even bigger life. What we need is a remodeling that allows us to experience what's already here but to experience it differently, so that it delights us rather than drives us crazy.

Your life is a lot like the house you live in. It has some things that you like and some that you find irritating. It has rooms that are used constantly and others that you visit only once in a blue moon. It has features that need frequent maintenance and others that will last for decades without your attention. Almost all of us would engage in some remodeling of our house if we had the time and the money. In an ideal world all the shortcomings of our home would be remodeled to fit the way we'd like to live, with plenty of room for the things we hold most dear.

The real issue is that we want to feel at home both in our houses and in our lives, and we try to do this by tweaking the things we are aware of, the things we assume must be the problem, such as not enough space and not enough time. But some problems are less visible; they're about qualities rather than quantities, so they are more difficult to identify, articulate, and resolve. We can't create more of a sense of home if we don't understand where that feeling comes from. In your house, for example, if you feel upset every time you return home from work because you have to enter through the laundry room, pushing your way past baskets of clothes waiting to be washed, unfolded mounds of sheets and towels, and a miscellaneous trail of kids' coats and boots, you may require an architect to point out to you that yours is not a well-designed entry sequence. It's not the laundry itself that's the problem; it's that you have to pass through it to enter the house.

Our lives are just the same. We think the problem is our job or our boss or our child care arrangement or our spouse, and we keep trying to fix those things, only to find new frustrations popping up once we get free of the offending situation, making it impossible for us to feel at home in our lives. The problem isn't what we think it is. Like the process of identifying that it's the entry sequence that takes you through the laundry and not the laundry itself that's the problem, fixing the problems in our lives involves understanding what underlies these events. What's needed is a dramatic shift in perspective, and architecture and design provide remarkably useful metaphors for helping us to see what that shift might look like.

When you remodel a house, you don't need to change a lot of things in order to shift the character of the house, but you do need to evaluate what isn't working and determine what you would like to have room for but don't. Then you need to compose a good design solution that uses what already exists but modifies it here and there to accommodate the new functions. After that you must develop a thorough set of blueprints that record all the decisions made. And finally, to live the changes, you must build. This last step may seem obvious, but it's actually the easiest to miss. No amount of planning will bring about change. It's the actual implementation that allows things to shift.

In remodeling your life it's the same. You can read all manner of books and dream all manner of dreams, but only when you decide that you're really going to do something differently, and follow through with the implementation of those plans, will things begin to change. You have to start living what you've learned, and not just on Saturday afternoons when you have some spare time. The lessons have to be woven into your everyday life and lived just as reflexively as the acts of washing your hands and brushing your teeth. Solving the problem has two parts: first, we need knowledge in order to see things in a new way; then, we need to integrate what we've learned by being in our lives differently and doing things in a new way.

To accomplish a life remodeling, we need a blueprint, along with instructions for putting the plan into place in our lives. That's what this book offers you, the remodeler. When we're done, the contents of your days will still be quite recognizable to you, but there will be room to do what you've always wanted to do and the freedom to experience more of the potential you know is waiting within you to be revealed and realized. If you engage the steps prescribed, integrating them as suggested, there will be change, and you will experience things differently, and with new vitality.

So how do we get there? Let's take a look at the key ingredients that go into the making of a Not So Big Life. These will serve as a thumbnail sketch for each of the plans we'll develop more fully in the chapters that follow.

ONE • Developing a Blueprint for a New Way of Living

Because we tend to compartmentalize our lives—to see our working world as one thing, our home life as another, and our desire for connection with our inner nature as yet another—we don't really live in the way we know should be possible.

This compartmentalizing is similar to the way we separate room from room with walls. A house that's full of separate rooms that are connected to one another only by narrow doorways can feel claustrophobic no matter how large the overall square footage. What gives a sense of space is the extent of the connecting views between rooms. The more you can see of an adjacent room, by opening up a wall with an archway or an interior window, the more spacious you'll feel the house to be.

In our lives we need to make the same kinds of connections between realms, removing the barriers to flow so that we can feel as alive and whole at work as we do when we are engaged in doing the things we love. What is needed is an integration of what we long for and what we work for. We don't have to sacrifice one for the other. Both can coexist in deeply satisfying harmony if we learn to understand ourselves better from the inside out.

TWO · Noticing What Inspires You

When I first begin working with architectural clients, I ask them to show me pictures from magazines or from other houses they know that delight them, as well as their favorite places in their own house. These are the features that will make them look forward to returning home each day, so they are really important to a sense of well-being and a sense of home.

For example, I remember one woman, a mother of three active boys, showing me a picture of a small alcove off a family room, with a comfortable wingback chair positioned to look out across the vista of prairie beyond. When I asked her what in particular she was responding to in the photograph, she told me that it was the promise of a time when she could do nothing more than sit and look, without any obligations, and without her to-do list nagging at her. The picture captured a quality of being that she was missing in her life. Such a place, when designed into her remodeled home, would inspire her to find this kind of time for herself.

Another client, a man in his late fifties who was the CEO of a midsize manufacturing company, showed me a dog-eared photograph of his grandmother's summer cabin—a place where he'd spent many happy sun-drenched months as a child. For him, the character of the structure, a simple clapboard house with no frills or embellishments, spoke to him of the calmness and ease he had felt during those summers. He wanted to replicate the form in his new home to remind him of that simplicity, even when the events in his life seemed anything but simple.

We can use this same approach in our lives by identifying the activities and engagements that have made us feel most alive. Almost anything can provide raw material for inspiration and for an expansion of who we take ourselves to be. All we need to do is recognize the places where we are most susceptible to their showing up and build into our regular lives the elements to support them, just as an architect builds in places that make you feel at home in your remodeled house.

THREE • Identifying What Isn't Working

Once my new clients have shown me what inspires them, I'll ask them to show me what isn't working in their existing home. This is where they'll take me from room to room, pointing out the problem areas. Often they'll refer to the awkward configuration of work surfaces in the kitchen, for example, and the lack of room for an island where others can sit while food is being prepared; but they won't realize that the kitchen's isolation from the main living area is at least as big a problem as any of the smaller issues they've enumerated. An architect's job is to look beyond the obvious, beyond the stated problems, to the larger but often hidden issues underlying the overall configuration of the house.

Similarly, in our lives we can readily point to the things we'd like to have time for, and we can rattle off a list of ways to do more efficiently what we *have* to do, so we can theoretically find time for the fun stuff; but, like the kitchen's isolation, we can't see that the real problem is not a lack of time but how we engage time in general. We think the problem is the way we're sequencing or managing what we're doing, when in fact it's the way we engage the doing itself. Like the architect for the kitchen remodeling, I'll be showing you some ways to look at things differently so that you can recognize the real obstacles to living a meaningful life.

FOUR • Removing the Clutter

Almost every remodeling client I've worked with has had at least a handful of secret stashes of clutter. They're not always obvious on first inspection, but dig a little—open a closet, perhaps, or look under the bed—and you'll find all sorts of old stuff that's no longer useful and now just takes up space and gathers dust bunnies. Most of these clients also have a few more apparent piles of unused detritus taking up space and making it difficult to get around while giving the impression that there's no room for anything new. In a house remodeling, these out-in-the-open piles are easy targets for removal in order to make the house feel bigger. But to remodel successfully, you also need to identify and sort through the hidden piles to make room for what's really supposed to go into those closets and drawers—the stuff that's still useful and that plays an active role in present-day living.

In our lives we tend to see the frustrations with our jobs or our mates, but we can't see that the reasons we're frustrated with them emerge not from them but from some old conditionings from our childhood and early adulthood—patterns that might have served us once but are no longer useful. These are the life equivalents of the hidden stashes under the bed or the pile of miscellaneous papers on the kitchen counter. Old patterns keep you locked into the way things have always been, unable to imagine what a small amount of remodeling can do. Here we'll be engaging a little psychology and a significant amount of self-observation. You'll discover that when you are given the right tools to work with, the materials for the remodeling of your life are delivered right to your doorstep every day.

FIVE · Listening to Your Dreams

With my clients' lists of likes and dislikes clearly in mind, I'll ask them to tell me more about what they long for. I tell them not to worry for the time being about whether they can afford these things. If I am to help them make their existing house into their dream home, I need to listen to everything they are willing to tell me about their true longings. It's not that they will be able to build exactly what their dreams suggest, but with a little interpretation I may be able to design some features they'd never imagined possible on their budget.

For example, one client told me that in her dream house she would love to have a library, but she knew this was out of the question. Yet as I worked on the design, I realized that the wide hallway at the top of the stairs on the second floor could easily be lined with bookshelves, turning a space that was otherwise just for circulation into an ideal place for book storage. She was, of course, delighted. Had she never told me of her dream, the idea would never have occurred to me.

The same thing is true in our lives. If we tune out our dreams because we don't think they're possible, there's no chance they'll ever come into being because we won't be listening. Here I'm talking not only about the dreams we have for our waking lives but also about the dreams from the realm of sleep. Whether or not you believe that dreams have anything to offer you, in a Not So Big Life you start to see that everything that enters your life contains meaning. They're like signposts directing you in the process of waking yourself up more fully to what's right in front of you.

SIX • Learning to See Through the Obstacles

One of the biggest challenges for any architect working with remodeling clients is helping them envisage what is being proposed. I'll often use models, hand-drawn sketches, or computer-generated perspectives and animations to help show how the house is going to look in its newly re-modeled state. But learning to visualize the possibilities is usually an en-tirely new skill for the home owners, who are used to seeing their house the way it is right now. Imagining what it will look and feel like when a wall is removed or when the kitchen is relocated to the dining room's current position can test the visualization skills of even the most dedi-cated client. There are some tricks that can help the process, though, and when these are clearly communicated, it's possible to get a sense of the remodeled space long before the construction begins.

Looking at things in a new way is an important skill to master in the remodeling of our lives as well. To be able to see through the existing structure to the new shape that will gradually emerge can seem intimi-dating at first. But all it takes is practice. By learning to see through what appears to be absolute and permanent, you'll discover all sorts of flexi-bilities you'd never dreamed were possible in your life, and you'll quickly learn to see the potential that your life remodeling holds in store.

SEVEN • Improving the Quality of What You Have

Now comes the creative work of remodeling; crafting a new design out of what is there by looking at the whole house differently. Usually it's not more space you need but increased flow and the reconfiguring of rooms to make you feel comfortable and able to live more the way you'd like. People often ask me how the process of design happens, and there's ac-tually a secret that all artists and creative people know but seldom speak of. The fact is that when architects design or artists paint or composers compose, it isn't they who are doing the work. Their role is to collect all the inspiration and all the facts they need to execute the creative act and then simply get out of the way and let the art happen through them. It sounds mysterious, and in a way it is, but when it occurs, it's the most natural thing in the world.

This is the real key to a Not So Big Life. The creativity in crafting your life remodeling comes when you make all the preparations and then let go. This is how you improve the quality of what you have. You can't manage what you want into existence, but you can be the instrument of its creation by getting all the tools in place and then letting things unfold as they will. This kind of creativity is something we are all capable of, but in order for it to happen we have to be completely engaged in what we are doing, with no planning, thinking, or worrying about the exact form of what we are making.

It is possible to live much of your life in this state of creative flow. With the tools to start weaving this quality into the very fabric of daily existence, whether you are at work or at home, whether you are in pain or filled with joy, you'll find that the meaningfulness you've been looking for shows up of its own accord.

EIGHT • Creating a Place and a Time of Your Own

The people who make the best architectural clients are those who not only want a better house but also recognize that their home is a platform for living and expressing more of who they are becoming. The most powerful step you can take in making your house an integral part of your growth is to identify a space, however small, that is yours to retreat to when you want—a place where you can simply be quietly available to whatever is arising in your awareness at that moment. It can be a place for a hobby or a place to sit and read, as well as a place for contemplation and meditation.

This is where house remodeling and life remodeling intersect, because if you have the place, you are much more likely to make the time to use it. It is there waiting for you, with the promise of a new and more profound relationship with yourself as the reward for engaging in some quiet time to yourself. In many houses the amount of extra space is very limited, but this retreat place need not be available all the time. I've known people who have used a guest bedroom, the corner of the dining room, even a walk-in closet in a pinch.

In the same way, you can designate a time in the design of your life just to be still for a while or to meditate for a few minutes before your kids get up each morning. Or maybe you'll decide to leave work a little earlier so you can take a quiet walk in the park before heading home. Although we often believe there's no time for ourselves in our busy schedules, when we commit to making time, we find it's been there all along. We just haven't seen the possibility before.

Whether you call it quiet time, meditation, or contemplation, the point is to have a period each day when you are not thinking, socializing, or working. What you are really doing when you make a time and place just for you is inviting your inner nature to become a player in your outer life.

NINE • Proceeding Through the Construction Process

Whenever I advise clients of what to expect during the construction phase of their remodeling, I explain that you have to take things as they come. You can make all the preparations you want, but sometimes things just don't go the way you thought they would, so you have to hang loose and deal with matters as they arise. Lose your cool or get angry and frustrated by each unexpected wrinkle, and you'll drive yourself and everyone else involved in the project crazy. But if you don't panic and simply deal with what presents itself to be addressed each day, there's no problem.

When it comes to life remodeling, the same advice pertains. Enter the process knowing that there will be some unexpected plot twists and reversals but that you will be equipped with a set of tools that allow you to build with a composure you didn't know was possible. The construction phase of either a house or a life remodeling can be a remarkable time, because you can see the changes taking shape from day to day and begin to recognize the quality and character of the space that is being revealed through the remodeling process. If you focus simply on what is in front of you to do, everything else will take care of itself.

TEN • Moving into Your Not So Big Life

Once the building has been completed, it is time to move in and start living in the newly remodeled space. This can be a tremendously exciting time as the home owners discover how their lives shift automatically as a result of the new patterns of living that the remodeling allows. All the things that previously got in the way of flow have been removed, and now the house is much lighter as well, with a feeling of spaciousness that wasn't there before, even though no square footage has been added. Life shifts quite naturally, and every activity or interaction seems more alive because of the character of the new plan.

Our life remodeling offers the same magnitude of shift. By implementing the plans as the remodeler of your own life, you'll find that in only a short period of time the way you are living changes dramatically. There will be more light, more delight, more awareness of the beauty that surrounds you, and there will be more room to breathe and to engage in the things you really care about.

ELEVEN · Maintaining Your Newly Remodeled Life

The final step in any remodeling project is to pass along to the home owners all the manuals and directions for maintenance that will allow them to keep their new home in good working order. In its shiny new clothing, the house looks perfect, but without some long-term care and attention, it can easily slip into a condition of dishevelment not dissimilar to its preremodeled state. So I encourage the home owners to review at least once a year a checklist of mechanisms that require maintenance, as well as the intended functions of the various remodeled rooms and spaces in the house, to make sure they are all still working properly.

With all the effort you are about to expend to remodel your life, it would be a shame if there were no directions to help you keep everything working smoothly throughout the coming decades. So the final step in your life remodeling is the creation of an owner's manual, to be referred to at least once a year, that allows you to perform the routine maintenance that will ensure that the new form your life takes will continue to serve you and will continue to evolve as you shift and change. By making this review process an important feature of your year, as automatic as changing the furnace filter and as enjoyable as the celebration of a birthday or holiday, you'll be ensuring that you continue to live into the potential that you know deep down lies within you.

TWELVE • Being at Home in Your Life

The last and most delightful part of the whole process is that your life—all of it—will change as you engage your normal everyday existence in the remodeled structure. I can't tell you how often I've heard from clients that they'd never imagined when they began the process that just a small amount of remodeling could have such a huge impact on their lives. I remember one couple who'd lived for many years in a very average ranch house in south Minneapolis. After six months in their remodeled home, they invited me for dinner and told me that they were now living in the house of their dreams—a place they'd always imagined they'd have to build from scratch some time in the distant future, probably after they'd retired. It had never occurred to them that their current house had within it the potential to inspire them daily, as their remodeled home was now doing.

This is what I hope will result for you in your life remodeling. If you engage this material sincerely and intently, you'll discover that all that you need lies within you. You don't have to go to the top of a mountain. You don't have to travel far and wide searching for that certain someone who can touch you with a peacock feather and enlighten you. You don't have to desert your friends and family. You don't even have to get a new job. All you need is your full attention and an attitude of receptivity. Everything else will be delivered to your doorstep at exactly the right moment.

So what will life be like when you have enough room for what really matters—with sufficient time and space to express the whole of you? It's a reality that words can only point to, because its richness and vitality are its most essential qualities. But there are some physical attributes that we can recognize from this side of the doorsill.

With respect to what you do in your life currently, you'll be a lot less stressed than you are now, and no matter what is happening—whether it's pleasant or painful, happy or sad—you'll be able to take it as it comes and be in it with grace and presence. Things that in the past would have deeply disturbed you for days you'll deal with on the spot and move them out of your mind. You'll see in a new light people who have bothered you for years. They may do what they've always done (at least until they notice the difference in you), but they won't bother you anymore. And all those e-mails, voice mails, text messages, phone calls, meetings, and so on—you'll be engaging with them on your terms, and you won't be run ragged by them. In short, you'll be the director of your life, and you won't be afraid or on guard or waiting for the other shoe to drop anymore.

By making the time and the place to listen to your inner longings, you'll start to live them. You'll find that you are capable of a lot more creativity than you had thought, and you'll find opportunities falling into your lap that allow you to do what you've always wanted to do—not by your seeking them out but simply because you are ready to engage and able to be present in what you do. You'll find there's a lot more to you than you'd previously imagined. The remodeling will have opened up some room into which those features can now enter and take their place among your existing furnishings.

A quotation from the mountaineer William Hutchison Murray's *The Scottish Himalayan Expedition*, written in 1951 (often misattributed to Johann Wolfgang von Goethe), says it best:

> . . . the moment one definitely commits oneself, then providence moves too. A whole stream of events issues from the decision, raising in one's favor all manner of unforeseen incidents, meetings and material assistance, which no man could have dreamt would have come his way.

Murray understood that once you are open to the yearnings of your heart and soul, almost everything that shows up in your life can be used to help elucidate the things you are engaging in most passionately. Life prods us, cajoles us, and woos us in all sorts of marvelous ways when we are open to engaging. But you have to be willing to tune in to this channel of communication in order to be fed by it. Once you do, you'll never abandon it again because you'll know unequivocally that this is where the real nutrition resides, where the real wealth of living lies. This is what I mean by the Not So Big Life; it's a life lived wide awake, reading the signs along the way and engaging fully in what moves you.

Preparing Your
Not So Big Life Notebook

As you go through this book and engage in the exercises at the end of each chapter, you'll need a place to keep your notes. So at some point in the next day or so, as you are beginning the process of your life remodeling, it's important to find a notebook that can be dedicated to the task of recording what you learn along the way.

Over the years I've used all sorts of notebooks—three-ring binders, blank books, legal pads, computer hard drives. Because the exercises in this book are especially interactive, it may be easiest to use a notebook that allows you to introduce additional pages where they are needed. There are downloadable blank versions of the questionnaires in chapter 3 and chapter 10 on the Not So Big Life website, for example, that you may want to insert. But if your heart is set on a particularly beautiful blank book, go ahead. You can always paste in an extra page or two of paper in a particular section if you need to.

The important thing is that the format of your notebook allow you the greatest degree of creative freedom. You are about to embark on a journey into parts of yourself that you never knew existed, so make sure your notebook is up to the task of receiving all your thoughts and insights, allowing you to keep them together in one place and reasonably well organized.

As you read this book, you may be surprised at some of the undigested experiences from your life that rise to the surface. There will be wonderful memories that you'd forgotten, that will allow you to see how you came to be who you perceive yourself to be today. And there will probably be some sad, embarrassing, or frustrating memories that you'll recall as well. As you explore aspects of your inner world, there may even be things that scare you a little, things that have heretofore been hidden from view—the everyday-life version of the stash of forgotten treasures under the bed.

This is all part of the process of self-discovery. Being able to see that the monsters under the bed are only illusory is an important part of the process. These monsters are the old and no longer useful patterns of behavior that keep us from engaging in the things we long to do. They are what get us stuck in our lives. We're being run by old fears that make us believe there's no room for anything new and stop us from becoming aware of the diversity of experience that's available. If such unexpected deliveries arise as you read, you don't need to do anything with them. Just notice them, write them down if you like, and keep reading. Gradually the tools to process what you are recognizing about yourself will present themselves.

At the end of each chapter, you'll find a major exercise that is important to perform before you proceed to the next chapter. Although this means it will take you longer to read the book, if you don't do these exercises, you'll be accessing only a very small part of what this material has to teach you. Your notebook is for keeping your responses to all the exercises in order, so that you can refer to them later. By preparing your notebook now, you'll be able to keep it with you as you read, so that you can jot down your thoughts and comments as you go. In this way you'll be creating your own companion to share the journey with. Over time you'll also be able to refer to insights you've had in the past in order to help yourself better understand what is becoming clear to you in the moment.

Each exercise is self-explanatory and will require from 1 to 10 pages in your notebook, as indicated in the list that follows. But along the way there will be some other things you'll likely want to keep track of, such as strategies, phrases, questions, and behavior flags that can help you in both the life you are living today and the long term—the years to come. As you progress through the book, you'll be customizing your own owner's manual—the tool we'll discuss in chapter 11, toward the end of our journey together, that will allow you to conduct your maintenance checkup each year and ensure that your remodeling is functioning properly.

The following list contains the primary sections you'll need along the way. There may be others you'll want to add as well, to personalize your notebook so that it reflects your particular interests and proclivities. But for now use the accompanying list of section dividers to help keep track of the things you'll want to recall later. You don't need to do anything with these pages now, other than label them. I'll explain how to use them as we go, and after a while you'll be able to tailor what you are creating to fit your specific needs and insights.

These are the primary sections you'll need right away (allow at least 5 blank pages per section):

- Everyday routines to support my growth
- Strategies for engaging my everyday life differently
- Phrases to keep in mind
- Questions to keep asking myself
- Personal behavior flags to watch for
- Insights and "aha"s
- Issues that seem disturbing to me
- Subjects to inquire into
- Personal longings and aspirations
- General musings
- Surprising life events that seem related to what I'm reading

These are the sections you'll need soon for chapter 2:

- Significant Objects (allow 1–2 pages)
- Significant Moments (allow about 5 pages)

The other chapters will each require around 10 pages, though some you may want to complete more than once over the coming months and years and therefore will require more.

That's all you need to do right now. With your notebook in hand, you are ready to proceed. If some phrase or idea appeals to you or causes you concern, write it down on the appropriate page. As you'll see, everything that seems intriguing, exciting, or disturbing has the ability to help you see yourself more clearly. And through the process of this seeing, you'll discover more and more of your potential, and you'll find more and more tools to help bring that potential into being. When you look back through this notebook in a month or so, you'll be amazed at what you've discovered. Just like a photo album of a vacation, your Not So Big Life Notebook will help you remember where you've been and what you've discovered along the way.

PRINCIPLE
the process of entering

The way you enter a house provides a transition from public to private realms, so it's an incredibly important element in the design of a house. But the entry is not simply a door; it's actually a process—of first seeing the house from the street, then approaching the house along some sort of path, being received by the house as you stand beneath a porch roof perhaps, ringing the doorbell, and finally being greeted and welcomed inside. The entire sequence sets the stage for your experience of the interior of the house. A pleasant, well-designed entry sequence predisposes you to like the house. A discordant or unwelcoming entry sequence convinces you that you don't like the house even before you've set foot through the door.

So it is with the process of entering your inner life. It is important to set the stage. If you simply dive in without any consideration of the path you are taking, perhaps without even bothering to ring the doorbell, you may peer inside quickly, decide it's not for you, and beat a hasty retreat. The experience of entering your own inner world takes some time if it's done properly, but once you've set up the process, each time you enter, you'll be welcomed by the same sense of wholeness and integrity that you set in motion with your first explorations.

Like a well-designed house, a Not So Big Life doesn't shriek "I've arrived" from the sidewalk, but as you step into it, its richness far exceeds any exterior flourishes intended to impress the neighbors. This isn't about the neighbors. This is about receiving yourself. And just as a beautiful sequence of places that leads you to the door of your house can make you feel delighted to return home each day, so the preparations for the journey into your innermost self can endlessly delight you. If you spend the time now to weave them into your life's fabric, they will serve you for the rest of your days. So roll out the welcome mat, and let's begin the process of finding out what's inside.

TWO

Noticing
What Inspires You

We must be the change we wish to see in the world.
—MAHATMA GANDHI

Finding Inspiration

Whenever I begin working with clients on a remodeling assignment, I start by inquiring about what inspires them and by exploring what their dreams of home entail. If we were to dive into the nitty-gritty of construction right away, there'd be no room for envisioning what's possible and no place for imagination to enter into the equation. Our lives work the same way. Although there are a lot of things in your life right now that probably frustrate you and that you'd like to change as soon as possible, the first step in implementing the new blueprint must be to identify what inspires you.

In adult life, as we go about becoming what we've settled on in a career path, we often lose touch with what inspires us. It's important to reconnect with these capacities and enthusiasms because they can give us tremendous insight. And the best place to begin this search for meaningful moments is to look to your past, to the time when you were a child, before any well-meaning adults told you what they expected of you and before you were told who you were supposed to be. What inspired you then? What were the things that moved you most? And why? Those impulses and yearnings can provide clues to help you identify the things that can inspire you today.

To start this journey together into the essence of a Not So Big Life, I'm going to describe my own explorations into what inspired me early on and show you how that process allowed my daily engagements to become a far closer reflection of those early proclivities than would have been possible had I not started to listen to my inner longings. There's a natural functioning that each of us possesses—a delight in certain types of activities—that offers us food for a lifetime if we learn how to recognize it. Those passions can serve as a compass if you know how to observe, and they will steer you ever closer to the function you are best suited for.

What captured my attention most profoundly as a child were moments of epiphany. Every once in a while, without warning and given the right conditions, I saw that time would seem to disappear almost entirely, as if by magic, and what would open instead was beyond words. I loved these "aha" moments because they were times when I knew that I was completely alive. I wanted to know how they happened and why.

Early in my tenth year my father, an industrial engineer and product designer by trade, took me to see an exhibition in London put on by the Olivetti Typewriter Company. I don't remember much about the typewriters themselves, but the exhibition completely enchanted me. A temporary structure had been erected in a courtyard surrounded by stately old buildings. Within this enclosure the architect of the exhibition had created a maze of enclosed hallways in which every pathway was artfully designed to manipulate the visitors' senses. Many of the hallways leading from one typewriter display to the next had sloping floors or descending ceilings, so that as I moved through them I felt as if I were growing or shrinking in size, like Alice in Wonderland, when it was in fact the walls themselves that were changing the shapes of the spaces they contained.

One hallway in particular is indelibly ingrained in my memory. The space was quite dark and long, angled here and there so that you could never see far in front of you. The walls and ceiling were somewhat reflective—not as shiny as a mirror, but bouncing back what little light there was so that the space seemed softly luminous. There was an abrupt turn in the passage, and suddenly the darkness was transformed by a brilliant focal point at the end of the newly revealed hallway. There, under a sharply defined cone of light, sat—what else?—a typewriter. I was transfixed. Experiencing this sudden shift in orientation, combined with the dramatic increase in light level in an otherwise darkened area, was beyond description. I felt the thrill of absolute presence, of being totally alive with delight.

Over the next several years one of my favorite exclamations was "Ol-i-vet-ti!" I used it as a declaration of excitement and overflowing enthusiasm, sometimes sung, sometimes chanted. This series of staccato syllables meant much more than just the name of a brand of typewriters. To me it had become inextricably linked with a moment of epiphany, when time stood still as I balanced on the brink of a great mystery. The sheer wonder of being alive pervaded every cell in my body, and I really began to understand the power of space and light to affect my state of awareness. I remember that moment as though it is still happening, yet it occurred almost forty years ago.

Just like the symbolic meanings of images from our nighttime dream world, all of the symbols in the waking world have a fluid interconnectivity that can help to shed light on what's going on in your life. The above story seems to be about typewriters. But in fact, its hidden meaning reveals my fascination with both space and time. So every time I think of a typewriter, or a computer keyboard, I know to look for concealed meanings related to space and time.

Your Turn

This is the first exercise for you to enter in your notebook, under the section headed "Significant Objects." As you read, did any significant objects come to mind from your own life? Make a list of those objects that seem to have hidden meanings for you. Even if you can't yet identify what those meanings are, you may be aware of the recurrence of particular objects—objects that seem to be around when big things happen. If there are any, write them down, and if not, don't worry about it. They'll become apparent as you read on.

Making Room for Something New

Despite my early fascination with time's ability to morph and suspend a living moment as if it were a fly trapped in amber, I am also excruciatingly aware that all my life I've struggled with time—how to be in it effectively, how to engage it productively, and how to avoid being run over by it. For many years as a young adult, I was aware of my instant response when someone asked me how I was. "Too busy!" I'd say. Gradually it dawned on me that although I always thought the condition of *too-busyness* was temporary, it was in fact the most constant aspect of my world. And after a few more years of self-observation, I began to wonder if the condition was in fact my own creation. Was I somehow contriving my reality to be first and foremost too busy?

I noticed that although there were many things that had always inspired me and that I longed to do *when I had time*—such as writing a book, mastering another language, or learning to play the cello—these longings never got satisfied because I was . . . too busy, too busy, too busy. So I started to wonder if perhaps there was some way I could make enough time to accomplish one of the items on my wish list. Since I'd wanted to be a writer before I knew much about anything else, I decided to build into my week some time to write. I decided to put it on the calendar, schedule it in, just as I would a meeting with one of my clients, even though it seemed an outrageous act, given how busy I always was. I told myself I'd just have to live with the consequences; the one thing I wouldn't compromise was my writing time.

So began my Tuesday and Thursday morning meetings with myself and with my computer. Although I didn't realize it then, my life was about to change dramatically, and the keyboard would be a major player in that change. At first the purpose of these mornings was pretty fuzzy. I knew I wanted to write a book about architecture, my primary passion and career direction at the time, but I didn't know what form it would take. For several weeks I simply wrote to myself, in more or less a journal format, pondering the book's direction.

My father's early advice to me often echoed in my mind. He had wisely advised me, when I was a teenager and determined to become a fiction writer, that I should wait until I had something to say before becoming an author. During the past decade I'd frequently felt that I now had the appropriate level of expertise under my belt and was ready to say something, but paradoxically I believed that I no longer had the time to say it. My career was going full tilt, and I hardly had time to meet my architectural commitments, let alone do anything else. It was only when I decided to question my belief in my own "too-busyness" that I discovered the time was there, ready and waiting. An Olivetti moment if ever there was one!

I simply needed to clarify for myself what part of my expertise I wanted to commit to paper. When I spoke in public about the designs of our homes—the focus of my architectural career—audiences seemed fascinated. What I described, in terms that made architecture accessible to everyone, was the power of good design to inspire us and affect our sense of well-being. I knew that there was much more significance to a house than merely the provision of shelter, and I wanted to impart what I knew about designing in all three dimensions—not just the floor plan, but the heights of spaces as well. Over my years of practice, I'd developed some language to help explain the various principles that architects use in their three-dimensional designs. It occurred to me that this might be the material I should write about.

I'd entered the field of architecture because I had always been profoundly affected by spatial experience—by the way beautifully designed buildings and spaces could transport me into a state of rapture, just as the Olivetti exhibition had. Over my early life I had accumulated numerous memories of powerful spatial experiences that had moved me deeply and affected who I had become. And somehow, through describing my own passion for spatial experience, I'd been able to convey my enthusiasm to others.

After much deliberation, I decided to write down what I was already teaching in my public talks, describing in simple terms the principles I'd developed to help people of average means, who were not trained in design, make their homes into more comfortable places to live in, as well as truer expressions of themselves. As I started this process by making time for something I'd always longed to do, my world—all of it—started to shift in ways I could never have imagined.

The idea for the book led to my designing and building a new house for myself, to illustrate all the concepts I was writing about. I needed to show, in almost prototypical form, that it's possible to create a house for today by paring away the old, formal rooms, such as the living room, dining room, and foyer, so that the dollars saved can be put into the spaces we *really* use instead.

What I wasn't expecting as I went about the design process was the amount of soul-searching that went on as I tried to determine what spaces I personally desired. I'd designed hundreds of houses and additions for clients and knew that it was a pretty all-consuming process—almost like therapy, some people told me—but I thought it would be different for me because this was how I made my living. I already knew how to design a house. But I quickly found myself just as lost in the possibilities as any of my clients had been.

In my public presentations, I'd often bemoaned the fact that once we get married, all the space in the house is usually shared. If children arrive on the scene, they'll frequently be given their own rooms, yet their parents, who often have very different tastes from each other, are forever joined at the hip when it comes to space for living. What would happen, I asked, if we allowed ourselves the luxury of a small amount of space that we could make completely personal, for nurturing that part of ourselves that longs to express itself, perhaps through a hobby or through contemplation—a place of one's own? I hadn't realized that for all those years I'd been speaking about a space that I longed for.

As the design evolved, I found myself daring to consider this possibility. I felt almost embarrassed, not quite sure if this was really okay. I wanted a place to meditate and to write in, but I didn't want it to be officelike at all. It was to be my sacred space, my place in which to start expressing my vibrant inner world. This was my first foray into bringing it out into the open and into built form, and the further along we got in the design process, the more certain I was that it was important and should be included.

I finally located this space at the very top of the house, in a sort of garret accessed by a ship's ladder, with a window low to the floor so that I could sit on my meditation cushion and look out across the expanse of the Mississippi Valley. As a lover of things geometrical, I'd designed the room to be a perfect equilateral triangle, so it had steeply sloping walls and was very cozy—a place not for standing and striding but for curling up with a good book or listening to a favorite piece of music.

The day I stepped into that space for the first time and sat down on my cushion to meditate, a most amazing thing happened. I felt as though the person sitting there—supposedly me—had been sitting there for eternity and would continue to sit there forever. There was a timeless, placeless connection to my true Self—the more aware and thus higher aspect of myself—and all the occasions I could recall of my being completely engaged in the moment were right there too. It was a profound experience indeed, just as unexpected as that Olivetti moment from my childhood, and it had happened, in part at least, because I'd made a time and a place to be quiet and to listen to the wisdom of my own heart.

Over the next few months, with the Not So Big House prototype completed, the book of the same name started to take shape, and much of it was written in my attic space, my place of my own. What I discovered from the process of creating a place for my inner life is that when you make the time and the space for what you long to do, everything else shifts to accommodate it. In my experience it never works the other way around. If you wait until there's time to do what you want, you'll be waiting until your eighty-fifth birthday.

It never ceases to amaze me how insidious our conditioning is. I'm conditioned to be always too busy. For you it might be something else, something that seems equally real and equally frustrating. Just like the fish that doesn't realize it's surrounded by water because it's in it constantly, our conditioning is so much a part of our experience that we forget it's there and fall into the idea that the outer world is conspiring to keep us from doing what we want to do, when in fact our obstacles are self-generated.

Once you make the unequivocal internal commitment to do something—when you absolutely *know* this is the time and the place to act—the world around you will shift in all sorts of apparently miraculous ways to make it happen. But they're not really miracles. This is the fluid nature of both life and consciousness. When your intentions are clear, events move to support them and to expand the ripple effect of your efforts. I am devoting the time to write this book, and in a few short months you will be reading it, and the book will be influencing your life as it shifts mine.

Everything is always perfectly in balance when perceived from the perspective of the singular whole. And time, that elusive and enigmatic fourth dimension, isn't at all what

Isaac Newton's third law of motion isn't just about physics. It's about everything: For every action there is an equal and opposite reaction. An equally oft-quoted saying from ancient mysticism states the same principle in terms of the dynamics of consciousness in action: As above, so below.

we think it is. When we learn to engage it in a more conscious way, it can reveal an entirely new and vastly more amazing universe than we had realized is here, surrounding us in every moment of every day. We are, quite literally, fish in an ocean of time.

A Glimpse of Things to Come

We've been taught to believe since we were very small that the world is something that surrounds us and something that we engage in, but also something from which we are unquestionably separate. Every single one of us perceives our self to be the most important presence in the universe. The world appears to revolve around us. And though we may not think of ourselves as particularly extraordinary, brilliant, successful, or physically attractive, we'll go to the mat to defend our actions, our views, and our integrity. All of us have been conditioned by our parents, our schools, and our culture to become valued, contributing members of a society that depends on our willingness to play the game for its very survival. And we in turn oblige by going to work every day, bringing home a paycheck, providing for our families, and in the process purchasing an appropriate quantity of goods to support our consumer society. We rarely if ever stop and wonder if things are really the way they appear to be. Our conditioning tells us this is so, and we accept it. But could there be another way of perceiving things?

The only times we even think to ask such a question is when we're on vacation or when someone very close to us becomes seriously ill or passes away or when a national or global crisis occurs, such as the terrorist attacks of September 11, 2001, or Hurricane Katrina's devastation of New Orleans. Only then do we gain sufficient distance from our lives to recognize that what we do, what packs our calendars, is not who we are. Only then do we stop and wonder, "Is this what I really wanted?" "Is this what inspired me when I was younger?" "Is this how I imagined my life would be?"

The value of such moments is the first argument for slowing down. When we slow down, we have at least a chance of becoming present and of being able to hear the inner wisdom that's always available if we learn how to listen. Joseph Campbell, the author of *The Power of Myth*, said exactly this:

You must have a room or a certain hour or so a day where you don't know what is in the newspapers that morning. . . . A place where you can simply experience and bring forth what you are and what you might be. . . . At first you may find that nothing happens there. But if you have a sacred space and use it, something eventually will happen.

This isn't about hearing voices, and it's not about believing the admonitions, judgments, and justifications of the superego. The kind of insight that Joseph Campbell referred to, when you make both place and time, arises from what for now we'll call the higher self, or the Self with a capital S, the part of us that knows what's needed for our own growth and maturation. It's never petty, never judgmental, and never about someone else. It's a type of guidance that might be termed intuition, and it's perfectly attuned to the truth and completeness that you have the potential of becoming. Sadly, because we have no common language for this kind of knowing, we often discount it or assume it's something to avoid or fear.

In fact, it's exactly what so many people long for today—the path to a sense of meaning and fulfillment. But most of us are looking for this in the wrong place; that is, outside ourselves. As a culture we are engaging in more activities designed to help us find ourselves than ever before, but of course we're usually doing them on the run, squeezed into a lunch break or while the kids are at a swim meet or, better yet, at summer camp. Whether it's a class in yoga or creative writing, an eco-vacation, or a spiritual retreat of some kind, the underlying longing is for connection with the part of us that we know is more real, more authentic, and more in tune with the universe as a whole. Collectively we are reaching toward a new way of engaging in our lives. But without the language to share the desire and the vision and without an understanding of how to find the time to do it consistently, we're at a serious disadvantage.

Although the dimension of fulfillment itself isn't new—mystics and teachers have been describing it and pointing the way toward it for thousands of years—the ability to give people like you and me a glimpse into this dimension is new. The World Wide Web, our infant global brain, has allowed us to share our passions and enthusiasms much more rapidly and effectively over the past decade than was ever possible in the past, and it's become obvious that there are millions of people interested in topics that allow them to contemplate who they are and what life is really all about. Whereas in the past this was the territory of religions, governed and administered by a presiding clergy, today an increasing number of people are looking for their own direct experience of the moreness that they sense is possible. Seeing so many people like ourselves engaging in the same search on the Web, we have a new confidence in personal exploration.

The Desire to Understand Ourselves

When I was in my twenties, I would have lunch every week with two friends, both of them several years older than I. One was having a difficult time communicating with her husband and had been visiting a therapist on a regular basis for some time. I was fascinated by the way the process was allowing her to learn more about who she really was, and I wanted to gain the same kinds of insights into myself. I wanted my own taste of that kind of inspiration. I started to read books about psychology. Carl Jung, in particular, spoke to me. And true to form, I didn't want just a cursory intellectual understanding; I wanted to live it. I began journaling prolifically in an attempt to uncover the roots of my own idiosyncrasies and started to explore my dream life with a vengeance.

Not only did my dreams show up for documentation like obedient children each morning, but a number of people stepped into my life in almost miraculous ways to help me understand those pearls from the world of sleep, people with skills that I could not have imagined.

As my fascination with dreams developed, a book about dream interpretation entered my life, followed by a friend who, amazingly, had worked for a while with the author of that same dream book, and then by a radio program about actively engaging your dreamworld, and finally by a new architectural client whose primary specialty was the interpretation of dreams. None of these had I hunted down. They came into my life unbidden. All I had to do was pay attention and engage what was presented to me. If I were a skeptic, I would have chalked it up to coincidence and ignored the treasures being placed at my feet to help me understand myself better. It's so easy to look the other way or to believe we don't have time to fully engage whatever it is that intrigues us right now.

Your Turn

Look back over your life and see if you recall any situations where Providence moved to create the perfect conditions for your own exploration or pursuit of an interest or passion. Was there someone you met who changed your life, for example? Had you been looking for a job, perhaps, when someone halfway across the country offered you an opportunity to do something that was not quite what you'd been thinking of but ultimately much more beneficial? Make a list of the occasions you can think of, and over the next few days take note of any other associations or related events you recall. Often when you jog your memory or pay attention to what occurred in the past, you'll recall other details. If you don't remember any, don't worry. They'll begin to happen if you let them and if you stay aware.

The Power of Beauty

As I think back on how life ushered me into a career in architecture, I see that in large part what attracted me to residential design in particular was the realization that people really care about their homes and are inspired by them. They know that a house can be more than just a place to live in and a place in which to store their stuff. And many people are willing to immerse themselves in the making of a more expressive, more beautiful, and more functional dwelling place. Many of them know intuitively that this process of house making will help them realize more of the potential they sense lies just beneath the surface of their everyday existence. For the period of a home's creation—whether new or remodeled—the types of people I worked with would eat, sleep, and breathe our collective creation, making the process deeply gratifying for all of us.

But what I hadn't realized until recently is that it was their longing for something more that made them so attractive to me as clients. It wasn't just that they wanted a higher quality of living space. They also wanted a better quality of life, an increased sense of well-being, and somehow they knew that a beautiful and well-designed home could provide a more stable platform from which to seek this enhanced life. The very fact that they cared and that they were passionate about what they were pursuing made them automatically more thoroughly engaged in the creative process. I found that I was far more engaged myself when the people I worked for really wanted a wonderful result and enjoyed the process of getting there.

Although we normally associate the word "home" with a place that's built of bricks and mortar—or studs and siding, in today's version of building materials—in fact, home is much more than that. It is a feeling and a way of being in one's life rather than any specific place. As this realization began to dawn on me sometime during the early 1990s, I started to understand what my architectural colleagues and I are attempting to do when we design houses that are beautiful: We are creating a lens through which the inhabitants of the house can experience more of who they really are and who they are becoming. The beauty of the form provides places for moments of epiphany in the experiencing of everyday activities.

Just recently I found a quotation in a book by A. H. Almaas that perfectly describes this state of affairs:

> The fulfillment of our life is to see life objectively, to see what's really there. . . . Life is the expression and fulfillment and celebration of beauty. This is what we're here for. We're not here for anything else.

When your house supports the moreness that you are becoming, your activities transcend their normal boundaries. They're not just washing the dishes, helping the kids with their homework, and feeding the dog. They become mindful engagements in which the beauty of the surroundings gives you a foothold in a different level of awareness, a different state of being. Yes, you are still doing the same things, but you are in them differently because the stage on which they are performed inspires you. Perhaps there's a beautiful view to gaze at through the window above the kitchen sink. Perhaps there's a focused light falling on a vase of flowers on the table where your child is struggling with his first encounter with multiplication. Perhaps the cabinet where the dog food is stored has been crafted by a local cabinetmaker out of an oak tree that fell on your property after an ice storm a few years ago. Whether an object or a setting is beautiful or meaningful to anyone but you is irrelevant. It's what that thing or place is accomplishing in *your* life that counts.

When I was seven years old, I discovered the magic of falling in love with a beautiful object. The experience took me completely out of time, and I remember it today as though it had just happened. I was staying with my uncle and aunt in a quaint town in northern England, and as I walked to the town center, I felt excited because I'd just been given some money to spend while I was out—not a lot, but more than my regular allowance. There was a store that I'd passed many times that had always appealed to me, but I'd never had the chance to explore it. It wasn't a shop for kids, so the adults had whisked me along whenever I'd tried to slow down to look more carefully at the displays. Its window was filled with housewares of one stripe or another, but they weren't the run-of-the-mill variety. Each object was more like a work of art, some handmade and some manufactured, but all crafted with an elegance that made me want to gaze at them for a long time. This was the store I headed for.

Standing before the window, I felt exhilaration, an experience I still get today when I go to a good arts and crafts show. It's as though I could feel the creativity and care that had gone into the making of every one of these objects. My eyes moved slowly from one item to the next: a set of coffee mugs decorated with an unusual geometric design rendered in brilliant colors; a glass carafe, remarkably tall and sleek and perfectly tapered to a delicately folded lip; a dish towel imprinted with an intricate pattern composed of the overlapping skeletons of leaves.

And then I saw it—the object that captured my heart. It was a plate of plain white porcelain, very simple in form, with a design painted on its flat center that evoked memories of a wildflower garden. I can't tell you why it was this piece in particular that so captivated me, but in that extended moment of delight it didn't matter. I stared and stared, breathing deeply as I did so, completely unhitched from and unfettered by the world around me. I was totally intoxicated by the beauty of what I saw. I felt expanded far beyond the normal experience of my physical body, and it didn't occur to me to worry about what anyone might be thinking or how strange my behavior might appear to those around me. I was transported beyond time by the wonder and delight that this simple plate evoked in me.

Of course, after the moment passed and I remembered where I was and what I was there to do, this was what I spent my money on that day. It was a treasure I kept with me for many years. I remember the quizzical looks I got from my uncle and aunt and from my parents when I returned home with my prize. I'm sure they were wondering, "What kind of child would buy a plate with her pocket money?" But for me it was a souvenir of a profoundly moving experience, and every time I looked at it, it gave me goose bumps. I was able to retaste the timeless quality that had engulfed me on that first sighting. It was my most precious possession, and I put it to many uses over the ensuing decades, from exhibit to plant tray to, of all things, a dish for food. It became my reminder to pause and my excuse for a "beauty moment," an intentional breathing space in my day.

That experience was a pivotal "aha" moment in my life, the moment I recognized the power of beauty to transcend time and create the conditions for inspiration to take hold. It has become a tool for staying aware, and I use it still to help loosen the grip that time can have on me. All of us have experienced similar moments in our lives. As I began working on the proposal for this book and recounted the plate story to a friend, she told me of a similar technique she's developed for herself: In her bedroom, taped to the mirror above her dresser, is a topographical map of a place in Colorado where she often vacations. She told me that this is the only place she knows that can completely release her from her work and responsibilities. The majesty of the mountains and the dry crispness of the pine-scented air envelop her and allow her to experience herself as a creature of the universe and not just a worker bee in the city. By glancing at this map each day as she rises and each night as she heads to bed, she allows herself to remember what's important in life. It puts everything in perspective.

A more recent example of this phenomenon involves a tile that I purchased at a craft fair and that is now built into a sitting space in my newly remodeled office in my home in North Carolina.

I bought the tile more than a decade ago for clients who I thought might like the design motif for their kitchen backsplash. It was one of many very beautiful patterns made by an artisan, Nawal Motawi. I'd had a quick conversation with the artist and knew as I was speaking with her that there was great depth to her work, and that it embodied a very special quality of attention that she had come to understand. The care that she takes with her products can be imparted to those who appreciate them, just as the plate of my childhood had imparted its creator's state of being to me.

Although my clients had been unimpressed by the tile, I loved it, and I set it on my desk, where it provided endless inspiration for my architectural work. I had picked up the tile on many occasions, looking at the changing shadows cast by its relief pattern as I moved it in the light from the big window beside my desk. As my plate had earlier done for me and my friend's map has done for her, the tile held me in a sort of spirit dance, right in the middle of the day, unbeknownst to my colleagues who bustled around me. For a few moments, whenever I wanted, I could visit the font of vitality that beauty provides. I could breathe in the scent of the creative juice that the artist had poured into that tile and borrow its inspiration for the designs I was working on.

If we're struggling, thinking too hard, and worried about getting something done before our next meeting, our creativity is limited and derivative. But when we're attuned to the vitality of the moment, everything is informed by the creativity of that moment. It's not something we possess or master; it's something that we are. There's no separation between creativity and you. That's why the vibrancy of another person's creative act can inspire our own. It's the state in which the object was made that is contagious.

When I was finishing my office addition a year ago, I was riffling through a box of papers and office supplies from my Minnesota house when I found the tile, wrapped in bubble wrap, stuffed inside an old manila envelope. I was so pleased to have found it. The trim work was under way, and a spot beside the new skylight was presenting a challenge. At a point where the wall meets the sloped ceiling, I was looking for a graceful way for the trim to turn the corner, and I suddenly realized that this favorite tile might offer the perfect transition. By placing it between the upper band of maple trim and the lower one of cherry, I could make the change of direction look effortless, and the tile would have a place constantly in the light, where its relief would stand out and I'd be able to enjoy it every day.

The space it inhabits is at the entry to the addition, as well as in the transition zone between my inner office and my outer office—my writing

room and my communicate-with-the-world room. So every time I enter or exit the office and every time I move between inner and outer offices, I see the tile, and it prompts me to breathe. My heart skips a beat whenever I notice it. Each glance at this small point of beauty causes me to pause and to see with that other pair of glasses into the richness and meaningfulness of this moment.

That's what beauty can do. It's a doorway into the next dimension, the dimension that we normally think of as time but that really is beyond linear time, and in *real* time—in presence. Beauty, when you experience it fully, opens the door to being in the Now just as surely as any death-defying act, by stunning the senses equally as powerfully, though in a very different way.

Inspiration doesn't have to come just from the content of what you experience. In this instance it isn't the pattern or the shape of the tile that inspires me. It's the beauty that it exemplifies in my eyes and the quality of the attention I know went into its making, which in turn inspires me to pour the same kind of attention into my own creations. That attention can be brought to the creative process only when you are completely engaged, unencumbered by your to-do list, and unfettered by linear time. It can be brought to bear only when you are completely present in what you are doing.

Beauty can be a powerful tool in helping to transport us to that place beyond time. It is the coming through of a quality from a dimension beyond our normal experience. Though we can't adequately explain it, we can see and feel beauty, and when we open ourselves to it, it can in turn allow us to transcend linear time and breathe in the vitality of simply being. If you can surround yourself with objects of delight, they will feed you in ways you never imagined.

We Must Be the Change

All this sounds great, I know, but what do you actually *do* with it? How can you live your life differently so that it is constantly inspiring, so that time can be your friend rather than a tyrannical taskmaster? That's the subject of this book. I can't cover it in its entirety here at the beginning or in any single chapter, but perhaps I can give you a taste of the liberation that becomes possible when we look at things slightly differently.

Yesterday, as I was rereading this chapter, trying to determine how to convey this new perspective on time in an instantly graspable way, I received a phone call from a friend in California. Christi and I talk every couple of months, and we never know where our conversations will lead. Unlike the conversations I have with most of my business acquaintances, Christi and I have an unspoken agreement that when we talk we'll simply meet each other in the issues of the moment, which don't necessarily have anything to do with the other's life but which invariably provide us with exactly what we need to move forward in whatever we're doing currently. On this particular day I could tell right away that Christi wanted help seeing through the confusion she was in.

When I asked her how she was doing, she told me that she was completely overwhelmed. She and her colleagues had been working at least fourteen hours a day for several weeks, yet they couldn't keep up with everything they had to do. I asked her what they were working on, and she listed a series of projects, each one of significant scope and scale. But there was one in particular that was clearly eating away at her more than any of the others. She was trying to bring into being a new kind of green-building conference, one that focuses not only on the nuts and bolts of building sustainably and the geopolitical issues involved in natural-resource consumption, but also on the value of self-awareness and its relationship to the well-being of the planet as a whole. She wanted the conference to be perfect, and she was completely committed to bringing it into being, but she was finding it incredibly difficult to manage all the juggling required to make it happen.

She completed her account with these words: "I ask myself, and I ask my team, 'Who's slacking off here? Who's being inefficient? Why can't we seem to find the time to do all the things we have to do?'" I realized, as she spoke, that here was someone so busy battling with time that she couldn't see the problem even though she knew full well she was missing something obvious. She asked me if there was anything I could offer in the way of advice. Since I'd spent the past few months inquiring into, and writing about, my personal struggles with time, I described what I'd come to understand about my own confusion at such times. This is what I said:

Whenever we engage in a project, we perceive that project as being something out there in the world, something outside ourselves. But when our to-do list is running us instead of serving as a management aid, it's a flag that we've lost sight of the inspiration and vision behind what we're doing. Although it seems that the point lies in the successful completion of the project, in fact the only reason for doing it is to be fully engaged in the experience, so that we can learn more about who we truly are.

If we are trying to accomplish a project by frenetically racing around in a vain attempt to get everything done, the results will embody that frantic energy. But if we return to our original vision and hold that clearly in heart and mind as we engage each moment fully, the completed project will be an embodiment of this much more authentic expression of ourselves. This is the only way for something to be truly effective.

In other words, the point isn't the project itself. The point is to learn as much as we possibly can about ourselves, who we are now, and who we are becoming through the process of accomplishing the task at hand. As we engage in our project—our act of creation—there's an incredible kind of nutrition available in the experiencing of every moment as the results come into being. That's the only reason for doing anything. It's just that most of us don't realize that this is what's *really* going on, so we get sucked into the appearances of things—just like we get sucked into the plot of a movie.

Whatever the project—whether it's making a cake, fixing a car, or planning the next Olympics—the point is the same. In this case Christi was organizing a conference, but that was only a vehicle for her own self-discovery. Once you completely understand this, everything in your life will shift, and time won't appear to be beating you up all the time. If you can't get something done then, it wasn't supposed to happen. How can you know? Quite simply because it isn't happening. There may be people here or there who get frustrated because something you'd said you would do doesn't happen on schedule, but that frustration is *their* life experience, containing the nutrition they need for *their* growth. The dilemma is entirely in your head. It's not real.

From your perspective at this juncture, you may be saying to yourself, "That's all very well to say, but *my* boss wouldn't tolerate my being late with an assignment" or "That doesn't work for a job like mine, where everything depends upon my punctuality" or "I just don't have time for the luxury of engaging in self-discovery," but by the time we get to the end of this journey together, you'll be able to see things a little differently. You'll come to find out that it's only the meaning we attribute to our not getting something done that's a problem. The situation is the situation, and people deal with the consequences . . . maybe not always the way we would choose, but that's just more grist for the mill.

When we're in panic mode, it's almost impossible to remember that the only reason things seem so out of control is because we are making them so with our ideas about how things are *supposed* to go. For Christi, things were urgent only because of her attachment to a certain outcome: an idea that things should look a certain way. As soon as she remembered that the point was *not* the precise match between her imagined conference and what actually happened, all her troubles dissolved. By the time we hung up, she was almost giddy with a newfound sense of what it was she was doing.

So what happened to time in all of this? It was transformed from a bucket of limited size, into which Christi was trying to cram more activities, into an unfolding awareness of her direct experience of her own life. The metamorphosis was instant and total, and it happened because we were both completely there with each other and able to share one understanding of how things really are.

I've always loved Mahatma Gandhi's declaration that "we must be the change we wish to see in the world," which describes so beautifully what lay at the heart of Christi's revelation. I think it's worth exploring the context of Gandhi's observation, because it has so much to teach us about who and what we are. You may have heard his statement many times before, but there may be more to it than you've realized.

As the story goes, a woman came to Gandhi, imploring him to help her with her child, who was overweight and constantly eating pastries and candy. She wanted Gandhi to tell her son to stop eating anything containing sugar. Gandhi agreed to give it a try but told her to go away and return in a week. The woman was confused but did as she was bidden. On the appointed day she and the son returned, and Gandhi sternly and firmly told the child to cease and desist the ingestion of sugar-rich foods and treats. The woman asked, "Why did you tell us to go away for a week and then return? Why could you not have asked this of my son a week ago?" "Because, dear madam," replied Gandhi, "I did not know if I myself could accomplish that which you asked me to ask of your son. If I could not do it myself, how could I ask *him* to do it? We must *be* the change we wish to see in the world."

Gandhi's simple exercise in disciplining himself to abstain from sweets could then be passed on to the son. Discipline and knowledge can be communicated effectively only when the speaker is capable of them himself.

When I first fell in love with that quotation, a decade ago, I knew that I wanted to write more about how the world changes, but I knew also that I wasn't yet able to live what I knew intellectually. It's taken me a decade to put into practice in my own life what I knew was a better and much richer way to live. Now I'm ready. I'm living that life to the best of my ability, and so I can pass it on. I know with certainty that the *only* way to change the world is to change yourself. No amount of civic activism, protest, or erudite exposé can effect true change. Our confusion about what the quotation means lies in our believing that there is a world "out there" that needs to be fixed when in fact the only change we can effect is in ourselves. Change happens when the individual embodies what he or she knows and others see its truth and learn to do their version of the same in their own lives. Whether or not you put it into practice is up to you.

EXERCISE
identifying the significant
moments in your life

This exercise is designed to help you identify what really fulfills you. If you make a list of the most significant moments in your life—the ones that moved you to tears, filled you with awe, or made you feel that your heart was going to explode—you'll likely notice that most of them came about in completely unexpected ways. For me they've happened, more often than not, when I'm not in a rush and when I've given myself the time to engage in something fully—like the time I was sitting watching water rushing along a streambed and suddenly experiencing the flow as fluid energy, unbounded by time or space; or the time I rowed out into the middle of a lake in South Dakota late at night and saw the velvet black bowl of star-studded sky as I had never seen it before, an experience that filled me with wonder and gratitude for the great good fortune of being alive.

Had I been rushing to my next appointment or watching the evening news on television, these events simply wouldn't have occurred. It's the slowing down that allows the ineffable to seep in when we least expect it and that gives our lives meaning. For me these moments are often visual, but for you the dominant sense may be hearing, smell, taste, or touch. You may find significance through movement or through stillness. We're all different, but the experience of significance—that "ah" or "aha" feeling—is the key.

Before you read further, take your notebook and sit quietly for about ten or fifteen minutes in a place where you won't be interrupted. Settle your mind a bit, and let go of any worries that are currently concerning you. They can wait—nothing other than a physical emergency of some sort is so pressing that it can't be put off for a few minutes.

Now allow your mind to drift back to memories of events or occasions that had a profound effect on you. Breathe calmly, and don't expect too much. Nothing may come to mind right away, but if you maintain an openness and a receptivity to your own inner wisdom, experiences will arise from your past. Don't discount anything that comes up. Write it down even if it seems insignificant or idiosyncratic—you aren't trying to please anyone here. You're just using the lens of your inner wisdom to focus on experiences that fulfilled you deeply and which until now have most likely been outside your awareness. It's time to integrate them, time to appreciate their value so that you can recognize the conditions under which they arose.

If the well is dry today, put your notebook down and keep reading. But pay attention over the next few days to any memories that do arise, and see if they don't contain the seeds of significance. Sometimes we've clothed a memory in garb that makes its importance unrecognizable even when the experience itself was earth-shattering and powerful beyond words. Give yourself permission to observe these memories afresh and to remember them without the filter of past interpretations. If you find the memories overwhelming in either a positive or a negative sense, know that the next couple of chapters of this book will help you understand how to be with these recollections in an entirely new way.

These remembered moments of significance contain the quality of vibrancy that will allow you to unlock the door to your inner self. Though it won't be clear yet just how this can be so, the following pages will reveal the reason for these moments' significance and the quality they contain that opens you to the moreness you've been longing for.

PRINCIPLE
bigger isn't necessarily better

There's an assumption in our culture that if a little of something is good, then more of that same thing will certainly be better. We see this all the time with the designs of our homes, which have gotten so huge that they'll soon require battery-operated vehicles to negotiate their vast expanses. How much is enough? Apparently we're not there yet, but the proliferation of these supersized dwellings does make you wonder what could possibly be the reason for needing so *much* space. We share a collective longing for a sense of fulfillment, of feeling complete and whole, and we're taught that a bigger house is supposed to give us that feeling, so off we all go, dutifully building the bigger abode in the hope of assuaging that unscratchable itch.

But of course bigness isn't the solution. It's not quantity of space we need. It's quality. Instead of inhabiting a generic one-size-fits-all house with conventional features, conventional styling, and a conventional layout, what would it be like to live in a house that expresses something more about who you are? That's what a Not So Big House is all about—a house that is about you and about what makes you feel at home. Its scale isn't its most important characteristic. What makes it better than other houses is that it allows *you* to feel comfortable. If you like it, chances are your friends will too.

There's a perfect parallel between our attempts to find home by building bigger and our attempts to find satisfaction by buying stuff and staying busy. These obsessions have hidden from view what matters to us and what brings a sense of meaning to our lives. A bigger, busier, flashier life isn't necessarily a better life. But we're taught from an early age that that's what we should aspire to, and we rarely stop to wonder whether this is really the case. We can't, we tell ourselves—we don't have time!

Are bigger and busier really better? If not, what is all this supersizing and speeding about? In this chapter we take a look behind the curtain of all the rushing around and all the purchasing we do in search of answers.

THREE

Identifying
What Isn't Working

Not everything that counts can be counted,
and not everything that can be counted counts.
—ALBERT EINSTEIN

Our Love Affair with Stuff

The first step in implementing the blueprint for a Not So Big Life is to take a look at our lives to identify what stands in the way of living the way we'd like to be living. This isn't easy because it requires that we look objectively at many aspects of our daily life that we take entirely for granted.

But this is the same process you would undertake if you were considering remodeling a house. There are walls that you assume are structural and can't be moved, but a visit from an architect opens up all sorts of options you'd never considered before, and those walls may turn out to be expendable. Maybe they're not serving the purpose you thought they were, and by removing them, you'll be able to have an entirely new experience of your house. Without your having to add on or build a totally new house, it will feel a lot more spacious and give you more of the warm, homey feeling you've always longed for.

This is how we'll find some breathing room in our lives—by identifying the things we assume are very important but in fact are simply obscuring our view of what lies beyond them.

There are two major culprits responsible for our feeling overwhelmed. One is the accumulation of things we think we need; the other is the speed at which we race through our days. We barely recognize these agents of dissatisfaction because they are so much a part of the fabric of our existence, yet both factors significantly influence the way we live. In order to do something about them and to determine whether they are structural, we need to look at them more closely.

It's almost impossible for us to imagine a time when clocks didn't exist and the day unfolded on the basis of the sun's rising and setting. Before Thomas Edison invented the lightbulb, Americans averaged around ten hours of sleep a night. Today that number is closer to seven, though any parent or busy professional will tell you that seven is a lot! In the past, people's lives were filled with hard work, but the work ensured survival: keeping food on the table, a roof overhead, and clothing on one's back. It wasn't until the end of the nineteenth century that luxury and leisure became part of the working-class lifestyle. Remember Henry Ford's visionary notion of turning his Model T factory workers into his own customers? Even he would find unthinkable the kind of accumulation of wealth that's possible today.

One of my favorite books beautifully illustrates the limitations of our consumer approach to successful living. For *Material World: A Global Family Portrait*, the photographer Peter Menzel invited sixteen other photographers to travel to thirty countries, spend time with a statistically average family in each country, and photograph the family members in front of their homes, together with all their material possessions. Looking at the book's images, readers instantly understand that the Mali family, with only a few items for cooking and cleaning, has imbued those objects with deep meaning. On the other hand, the Kuwaiti family, with four cars and a forty-five-foot sofa, or the American family, with the contents of their home filling the better part of the cul-de-sac they live on, seem almost lost in all their stuff.

Although it's difficult to see our own lives so clearly, when we look, we can begin to make out the impact of material possessions and time on our lives and the ways they work together to sponge up most of our waking moments. Imagine a documentary film that recorded every moment of a day in your life. How much rushing around fills the day? Is that what best describes who you are and who you aspire to be? If not, what does it signify? And why is it that when we're not working our tails off, we're shopping till we drop?

There are thousands of reasons for wanting to own something, and some of them are eminently practical. But for most of us today the wanting is only that; it's not a need. We believe subliminally that the object of our heart's desire will somehow fill the sense of emptiness inside and make us feel more substantial, more significant both to ourselves and to others.

Your Turn

Bring to mind something that you recently set your heart on owning—something now in your possession or something you are still longing to have. Now turn the thing around in your mind's eye. What is it about this thing that so seduces you? Do you have the feeling that if you possess it, your life will somehow be happier or more satisfying? Do you believe that it will improve your image? Do you believe that people who own this type of thing are more respected? Do you believe that you need it in order to live in the manner to which you would like to become accustomed? Is it something you believe to be beautiful? Or is it something that will allow you to do something you currently are unable to do?

The sad reality is that no amount of stuff can fill the void created by our own absence. Stuff is no substitute for experiencing who and what we really are. If you stop now and recall one or two of the significant moments in your life that you recorded in the last chapter, would you trade any of them for the current desired object? No, of course not. Not even close. That's why so much spiritual literature points to the poverty of the wealthy and heralds the wealth of the poor. It's not that you have to be poor to live richly in your inner world, but the ability to purchase whatever you want—or the desire to—often becomes a huge obstacle to understanding what matters.

When we own stuff, we have to maintain it. We also have to earn enough money to procure it, house it, protect it, keep it clean, and insure it against theft or loss. So every purchase has strings attached. It will require a long-term commitment from you if you become its owner, and that in turn will keep you a little busier than you would otherwise have been. That extra busyness also makes it a little more challenging to show up in the rest of your life, to be truly present in whatever it is you are doing. Although when considered individually, each purchase seems fairly innocuous in its time requirements, taken collectively, the impact of all that stuff can be enormous. One new suit or sweater takes up minimal closet space, for example, but thirty new items of clothing may force a closet remodeling. That remodeling takes time, energy, and money, all of which can, if you are not paying attention, keep you from doing the things that have real meaning for you.

When I bought my first house after having lived in a small studio apartment, I was struck by how empty it felt when I first moved in. I had the same amount of stuff, but now it was spread over twelve hundred square feet instead of four hundred. It felt barren, to be honest. So I decided to go out and purchase some things to make it feel homier. I went through a period of acquisition, and when I could afford it, I'd buy the object that was currently on the top of my desired-stuff list. First it was a set of shelves for my stereo system. Then it was a couch and a love seat. Next, a coffee table. All of these things were useful, of course, but I started to become aware that I wasn't any happier than I had been when I lived in my apartment and had less stuff. I simply owned more things. My purchasing gave me the impression of getting somewhere, but I remember wondering, as I brought each new object into the house, what it was I was really creating. Was an improved nest truly giving me a greater quality of life, or was it more like an albatross? I didn't dwell on the question long enough to listen for the answer. At the time I was having way too much fun believing I was making it as a successful human.

There was a kind of longing that I often felt when I designed a new house or remodeled an existing one for clients. I saw what a beautiful setting I could create for their lives, and I wanted the ability to do the same for my own. It's clear to me now that I was trying to live up to the expectations of my clients. There seemed to be an almost universal expectation among them that I should be making enough money to afford to surround myself with a beautiful structure of my own creation. So pretty much on automatic, I went about trying to make this happen.

That's how most of our purchasing happens. There's a subtle pressure, one we are typically unaware of, to meet the expectations of our peers and colleagues and families by keeping up with, or exceeding, their purchasing. We have unconsciously created a huge game in present-day consensus reality that entails accumulating sufficient wealth to purchase our way into perceived respectability and so, we assume, into significance. But it's a hollow dream. There's no meaning in all those acquisitions and no meaning in keeping up with the Joneses, other than sharing with them the frustration of feeling overwhelmed by the magnitude of the task of keeping up.

What we are really looking for is a sense of the real and an experience of true significance, true meaning. That can come only from one source. Deep down inside, every human being hears the echo of the experience of unity and wants it back. So we live our whole lives with only a vague sense of what it is we want but with the absolute knowledge that we had it once and it's possible to have it again if we only knew how.

This is why falling in love is so powerful and why so many fairy tales speak so deeply to us, whether we're three or ninety-three. These stories encapsulate our longing for reunion with lost love. By falling in love, we lose our boundaries and our limited sense of self. For the period when we are intoxicated with love, we expand that sense of self to include the glorious other, and in this process everything else in our world becomes radiant as well. It's the closest experience most of us have to unity, and it's immensely freeing when it happens. It is also quite uncontrollable and so, to our logical, thinking mind, not a practical way to live. In fact, the thinking mind sees the heart as dangerous, precisely because it moves to its own drummer and dances a completely uninhibited dance.

So the thinking mind has been hard at work manufacturing counterfeit love objects that are unlikely to upset the apple cart but are still able to satisfy—at least temporarily—the yearning for union. Stuff can be desired, worked for, and won over without all the messy side effects of true love. Our love affair with stuff is a surrogate concocted by our heads to obscure the real longings of our hearts. But all of these inanimate objects of our desire are incapable of offering us the direct experience of greater vitality that true love can offer. They can't really feed our spirits. Our hearts experience the love they long for only when the boundaries that so rigidly define that sense of "me" from "you," self from other, are eroded.

No Risk, No Reward

Another variant of the search for significance is engaging in risky behavior. For many, taking risks appears to be a shortcut to living more fully in the present moment, and while it works temporarily, its benefits are short-lived, and, as we'll see, there are much less dangerous ways of becoming present.

I was watching an episode of the PBS series NOVA in which mountain climbers were being monitored to see how their bodies reacted to the extreme cold, extreme fatigue, and oxygen deprivation experienced at very high altitudes. One of the researchers observed that it is amazing that more climbers don't die under such conditions. They often push their bodies to the very threshold of death for the exhilaration of reaching the mountaintop. On a smaller scale, this is why roller-coaster rides are so popular. They give us a controlled version of riskiness, in which we know we won't be harmed. They don't have the transformative power of the real thing, but they give the rider a taste of living on the edge.

People who engage in the real thing—whether race car driving, mountain climbing, or any similarly dangerous endeavor—will tell you it's the risk of dying that makes their sport so alluring. They live for the exhilaration of that moment when they transcend the limits of their own small self and touch something universal, a heightened state of awareness that is inherently meaningful. It is, in the true sense of the word, awesome, and therefore worth risking their lives for over and over again.

However, it's perfectly possible in today's world to con yourself into believing you are a superb climber by purchasing all the gear necessary for climbing and even going to the mountains to climb, but never actually putting in the effort necessary to experience the aliveness. We do the equivalent when we buy a fancy sports car but drive it only in stop-and-go traffic on the freeway during rush hour. It's the dream of the speed that the car is capable of, the dream of the exhilaration and aliveness we'll experience that causes us to splurge, spending many thousands more dollars than is necessary for a car that gets us to and from work each day. In short, we're buying things that give us the image of aliveness rather than access to the real thing. We haven't understood that it's the real quality of aliveness we want and that the image of aliveness does nothing for us.

A few years ago, while reading Thomas Moore's The Care of the Soul, I was particularly struck by one of the author's anecdotes. He described the frustration of a man who believed he was a writer but had never written a word. He had bought all the accoutrements for the life he imagined a writer would lead; a fine desk, a beautiful fountain pen, an ink blotter. But the act of writing something, even the experience of having something to say, eluded him. He was living a dream, not reality. Writers don't start with accoutrements. They start with a burning desire to express something. I'm guessing that few writers need any of the props this man had assumed were necessary for writing, and most would carry on somehow whether they possessed them or not. When you are passionate about writing, you will write anywhere.

The story appealed to me because it so perfectly encapsulates a pattern of behavior that I see played out constantly in today's world. We're buying stuff that fits our image of who we'd like to be rather than tools to help us become who we actually are. This is why so many McMansions, or starter castles, as I call them, include top-of-the-line kitchens with all the best and most expensive appliances, cabinets, and countertops even though their owners go out to eat nine nights out of ten. The ideal of domestic bliss includes gourmet food, when often the skill of cooking has not yet been mastered. Fancy equipment can't make someone a good cook. Learning to cook takes time, effort, and practice. And *those* are what have the power to make you feel more alive—not the accoutrements.

The Case for Slowing Down

In many ways we have gradually lost touch with why we do what we do. We've come to believe that the more things we accumulate and the more we accomplish, the more we have lived and the more meaning our life must have. Yet when we stop to reflect for a moment, we realize that the things that make us feel most alive and most whole have little to do with our working lives, our acquisitions, and our accomplishments.

A few years ago I designed a new house for a couple who had decided to retire early, after one of their closest friends died without warning from a heart attack. He was fifty-eight years old and still working hard to save for his retirement years. It had never occurred to him, of course, that there might not be any retirement for him. But his sudden death brought that possibility into sharp relief for my clients, who were already older than their departed friend but still working long days with the same objective in mind: a comfortable retirement. What their friend's death did was allow them to see that spending any more time trying to secure something for a future that might not come to pass was patently absurd. A few thousand dollars more in their retirement nest egg wasn't going to make the ensuing years any different. But by putting off the time when they could start enjoying life, they were gambling in a game they might not win. The time to start living their lives was right now—and in fact had been so all along.

It wasn't so much that they wanted to retire from working but that they wanted to retire from doing things that had no meaning or joy in them anymore. They'd been involved in their respective careers—he as an investment banker and she as an attorney—for thirty-five years or so. That's a long time to do anything, and though they were both highly accomplished and respected in their fields, the acclaim no longer meant anything to them. They wanted something else, something that would make them feel more creative and more alive, so they determined to start doing on a more regular basis what they loved, something that inspired both of them: buying and selling antiques.

What they realized over the next few years was that they could have shifted to antiquing as the focus of their lives many years before. They'd always made money at it even without trying, but it hadn't occurred to either of them that they could do what they loved and make it their livelihood as well. In the belief system they'd been raised with, the process of buying and selling antiques didn't constitute a career; it was a hobby. So, in deference to those beliefs, it had to wait—until they'd paid their dues in the "real" working world.

To some of you who are reading this, their blindness to the possibility of an alternative career may seem ridiculous, but we all have blind spots. They are so much a part of the fabric of our lives that we don't even know they are there. It's only when something shakes us up or forces us to stop and take stock that we catch a glimpse of them before they're subsumed again by the busyness of daily life.

This is in large part why September 11 was such a wake-up call for so many people. Like the death of my clients' friend, all those lives lost so suddenly brought home to each of us the ephemeral nature of our own existence. We were also instantly made aware of our collective belief that to be a good person, you need to be a hard worker and go off to an office for most of your waking life. I can't tell you how many people called or wrote to me after that fateful day to tell me that they were making some changes in their lives. They were rethinking their priorities and were now going to be spending more time with their loved ones, more time at home, more time doing the things they really cared about. It didn't last more than a few months in most cases, but it *did* bring about a period of recognition that the live-to-work, work-to-live mentality of present-day existence isn't all it's cracked up to be and isn't serving our longings for meaning, connection, and significance.

The Race to Succeed

We've become incredibly productive in recent decades, and our successes are measured by income and by acquisitions. But in terms of fulfillment, what do these things offer us in return? A bigger house, a more expensive car, the recognition of our peers, perhaps, but what about how they make us *feel*? Although there's nothing wrong with success, if pursuing it occupies most of our waking life, it's no wonder something feels out of balance. And for many millions of people today, this is indeed the case.

People are working longer and longer hours, and those who put in the longest days are often the ones perceived by upper management to be the most devoted and the most productive. But are they really? I watched a story recently on CNN in which a somewhat horrified and unbelieving reporter was describing the thirty-five-hour workweek and seven weeks of vacation that are the basic right of every worker in France. Although the story was ostensibly about increased productivity and worker satisfaction, the underlying slant was that we in America are superior because we certainly don't need such cushy conditions in which to do our best work. There's a machismo that develops in those who overwork. It's similar to the disdain for even the suggestion of flab among those who train their bodies to look like those of comic-book superheroes. Collectively we've learned to see less than a fifty- or sixty-hour workweek as wimpy.

Add to this all the gadgets, gizmos, and time-saving devices that allow us to do more in a shorter period of time, and you have the makings of a peculiar type of hell right here in the heart of the empire of freedom and prosperity. Let's take a closer look at the situation for a moment, without the absolving mantle of the overwork machismo.

If you were in the workforce before the mid-1980s, consider how much the tools of your work life have changed. Remember when the fax machine arrived in the office and you were suddenly able to send a drawing or memo across the country instantly, without having to wait the three or so days needed for the U.S. Postal Service to deliver it? It felt like an amazing moment in history, yet it would soon be dwarfed by the popularization of the personal computer.

I recall vividly the architectural office where I worked in the late 1970s and the hours of repetitive, mindless work required of our support staff every time we made a change to a set of specifications for a building project. Our specifications books were often one hundred pages long or longer. Just imagine: each time a change required the addition of a line or two in the text, the entire manuscript—or at least the chapter or section in which the change was made—had to be retyped. There was no way to save in memory what had already been typed. The only place the document existed was on paper.

Even as I'm typing this, I'm asking myself, "Can that be right? Did they really have to retype *everything* in order to make a small change and keep the pagination correct?" The answer is yes. That is how it was until just a few decades ago. The laboriousness of that task seems overwhelming today, but thanks to the various and remarkable shifts in the ways information can now be manipulated and shared, our lives seem much simpler.

But is that in fact the case? The day I sent my first fax, it was to a building site in Hawaii where a house I had designed was under construction. Without the fax machine there would have been no way for me to work on the project. Every day the builder had one or two questions, and instead of trying to explain in words what he needed to know, I was able to fax a sketch and then discuss it—a vastly superior form of communication when it comes to something three-dimensional.

Prior to the advent of the fax machine, all my jobs had been local, and without the ability to send faxes, I would have passed up the project. So although I could communicate much more quickly and effectively with this new tool, without it the project would not have been a part of my life. The efficiency was actually a complication in disguise. It simply added another project to my workload. Now, don't get me wrong— I loved being involved in a project in Hawaii, and I wouldn't have traded the experience for anything. But any belief that the new tool—the fax machine—was saving me time was an illusion.

Now fast-forward to today, multiply the number of new tools by a factor of at least ten, and you can instantly see why we all feel like chickens running around with our heads cut off. In fact this is an excellent metaphor. There are so many communications waiting for responses in our lives that there's often not enough time to engage our heads. With all the instant messaging, e-mailing, and cellphoning going on, often simultaneously, there's not nearly enough thought or discernment involved in any of it. We're engaged in a race against time, but the race itself is entirely fabricated and of our own making. And we're rarely present in our interactions at all.

This hyperactivity isn't restricted to those in the workforce. A few years ago I was working with a young family to remodel their house to include space for home-schooling their three children, ranging in age from three to seven. As I got to know them better, I began to notice that it was nearly impossible to find a time when the mother could squeeze in a meeting longer than a half hour. I asked her to write down a typical week's schedule. No problem there; she printed it out for me on the spot. This was a woman who was ostensibly a stay-at-home mom, but with all the extracurricular activities in this household, staying at home was unusual. Even the three-year-old was taking violin lessons, and her older sisters were almost as solidly scheduled as their mother. Whatever happened to childhood and learning the fine art of creative play in an almost entirely time-free zone of life? What would be the long-term effects, I wondered, of this kind of scheduling on such young lives?

In probing the question of why there were so many classes, sports events, and tutors in these children's lives, I learned that the woman and her husband had determined from the start that they wanted to give their kids the advantage of early training that both of them felt they'd missed in their own childhoods. They believed that given the right stimulus, any child can and will unleash an innate creative genius. Given the value of the goal, in this couple's worldview the cost—no free time for Mom—was well worth it. But it is interesting that the underlying belief—that a worthwhile life comes about through personal achievement and the recognition of brilliance—was never questioned. What is genius anyway? Does it really find its expression through early training? And why was the idea of genius so important to this couple in the first place? By constructing their everyday reality so that they never had time to think of these questions, they never doubted that they were engaged in something important.

But in fact the speed at which the entire family was moving was a veil concealing their real motivations. Once again, apparent efficiency was in fact an avoidance mechanism to ensure that there was never enough time to experience deficiency and inadequacy or for the *parents* to experience their own inability to live up to *their* potential. It wasn't about the children at all but about the parents themselves. Had they slowed down, they might have become aware of what was driving them. But without a moment to breathe, this insight was guaranteed never to occur. Theirs was a race that generated stress, not genius. And a lifestyle that, from an outsider's perspective, might be assumed to be quiet and unhurried was in fact just as rushed as that of anyone working in corporate America.

I have a friend who was in financial straits, partly by choice—if you can call it a choice—because she was doing so much volunteer work at a hospice that she didn't have time to look after her own needs. This was a case of putting the cart before the horse if ever there was one, but it's not all that unusual. My friend was brought up to believe that the only virtuous way to be in the world is to give generously of yourself. There's nothing wrong with that, but if you are suffering severely because of all the giving, you can't truly give of yourself. You have to be in balance, or what you are giving is your own imbalance, which of course is no gift at all.

With the help of several friends, teachers, and therapists, she's begun to see the dysfunction in her ways and has learned to give priority to her own financial needs before engaging in volunteer work. This in turn is allowing her to take care of herself as well as those in her care. Her hidden belief was this: Not only was she supposed to give generously of herself, according to her family's mores, she was also supposed to ignore herself completely. Any thought given to her own well-being was considered selfish and therefore clearly not "good." To avoid feeling the pain of her own neglect, since this, too, would have been a selfish act in her worldview, she simply pushed harder, taking on more volunteer work and driving herself to exhaustion. There is a parallel to the life of the "stay-at-home" mom: Just because you aren't getting paid doesn't mean you're impervious to the overcommitted and overstressed lifestyle that's in vogue.

Adrenaline: Our Drug of Choice

I was visiting my chiropractor, Dr. Alan Celeste, a few weeks ago, and while he worked on adjusting the muscle in my shoulder that always knots up when I've been doing too much leaning over my drawing board, I told him about my plans for this book. I also asked him if he had any insights for me. He did. He told me that almost all the problems he sees each day are related to stress, which brings with it a flood of adrenaline. He even refers to stresses as adrenaline stimulators. Whereas in the lives of our ancestors, adrenaline was critical for self-preservation, providing the surge of physical and mental acuity necessary to determine whether fight or flight was the best course of action, today we've become addicted to the rush that adrenaline brings, without experiencing the life-threatening circumstances that warrant its release.

He pointed out that in the twenty minutes it took me to drive from my house to his office, I'd probably pumped more adrenaline than most of our ancestors would have generated in a year. Although we take the risks and challenges of driving for granted and become accustomed to its stresses, it still engages the fight-or-flight response every time we go through an intersection or pass another car. This is just the nature of the game, one more hazard of living in this era.

Even when we're looking for ways to relax, we'll often select adrenaline stimulators. Consider the fact that most prime-time television these days focuses on crimes and disasters, natural and otherwise. The stuff we call news isn't considered newsworthy unless it presses the adrenaline release button in our guts at least a few dozen times over the course of thirty minutes. Things that make us feel good about ourselves, or safe or comfortable, just don't hold our attention anymore. Even programs about something as innocuous as remodeling a home have to include the component of rushing. In *Extreme Makeover: Home Edition*, for example, the entire remodeling process is conducted in an absurdly short period of time, during which we, the viewers, get to watch the team of designers and builders functioning in a state of extreme stress and sleep deprivation as they attempt to get the featured house completed in time for the vacationing homeowners' return. By the end of the project, the designers and builders are so strung out that a large part of the "entertainment" is watching the participants lose their tempers with one another. We've got to be on the edge of our seats and biting our nails at all times in order to feel alive.

How has it come to this? How did we get so addicted to something that can do so much damage to our physical bodies as well as to our emotional, psychological, and spiritual well-being? It doesn't have to be this way. Balance is tricky, it's true. It requires understanding rather than effort. It requires some observation of what's driving us to do so much, and that observation can happen only when we slow things down so that we can engage first our minds, then our hearts, and then gradually the inner wisdom that will arise when we give it a chance to help us see what's really going on behind the scenes of the self-generated movie we call reality. There's a big difference between efficiency and effectiveness, and right now most of us have lost that distinction. We can't even find time to assess whether the tools we're using to be so productive and so efficient are in alignment with our longings for meaning and fulfillment. It's time to slow down a bit and consider some alternative ways in which to engage in our lives.

The Real Addiction: Nut Accumulation

Every morning as I sit on my porch with my husband and drink that first cup of coffee, I watch the squirrels who live in the big oak tree right outside the door, as they busily gather acorns. They seem to have an insatiable appetite for these nuts, which they clearly find tasty. They stash them away in the fall and dig them out in the spring, and in what seems to be an endless process there are always more to be found, more to be buried, more to be excavated and, once in a while, even eaten. Acorn management is the name of the game for these little guys, and they provide us with endless entertainment as they go about their busyness. We often wonder out loud, "What are they up to now?" Whatever it is, it's never over, and it's never done slowly. Even nut consumption—a ritual of cracking, turning, nibbling, munching, and discarding—is performed in a blur of activity.

As you look at the content of your days, perhaps you've started to see your own version of acorn collecting. Your nut of choice may be the adrenaline jolt that comes from coffee. It may be the endorphin release that comes with working out in the gym. It may be the surge of pride that comes with the acquisition of a desired object. Or it may be the hit of feel-good juice that comes with receiving the latest text message on your cell phone: You've made the deal; you've landed the new project; your child has made the honor roll. All these things are human versions of acorns, and they're constantly fascinating to us because of the tiny hormone rush they give us. Nut accumulation is our game, too, yet most of us have never even considered that, with the specifics peeled away, it is what we're doing in lieu of actually being here.

The question is, what would happen if we stopped to consider the possibilities inherent in the word "enough"? It's a word that we hear all too rarely in our daily lives and in our own thinking. "I have enough"— how does that sound to you? Your car may not be a BMW, your television may not have a flat screen or high resolution, your house or apartment may be a bit smaller than you'd like, the kitchen appliances may not have been made in Europe, and your clothes may not impress your friends who place an emphasis on designer brands, but if you can provide the basics for yourself and your family, you do in fact have enough.

The opposite of enough is too much. And many of us today are at the point where we have too much already and don't need more. We don't need more adrenaline. We don't need more muscle tone. We don't need more goods to fill our houses. We don't need more text messages to make us feel alive. We can keep playing this game until the end, but it's just not satisfying anymore. Life is not dependent on any of these things. And so we have this vague—and sometimes not so vague—feeling that we are missing out on something huge. There's a giant hollowness that we experience occasionally when we stop for a moment. And we're afraid that if we stop for too long, that hollowness will swallow us whole.

But the truth is that that fear of stopping is separating us from real meaningfulness—the objective of our misguided accumulation behavior. We know deep down that there truly is more somewhere. We just don't know where to find it. And the last place we're likely to look for it is in the place we most fear—underneath the feeling of hollowness itself. If we don't let ourselves slow down and stop the accumulation behavior for a while, we will never see what is hidden below, obscured from view by the all-consuming nut management game.

This is why we need a life remodeling—because, as is the case with the remodeling of a home, the real problems are not the ones we can name and therefore do something about with relative ease but the ones that are hidden from view. So what does it mean to make your life Not So Big? It means to be free from the driven, automatic behaviors that keep you asleep at the wheel, while propelling you willy-nilly through your daily routine. All the addictive time consumers I've described are capable of giving you only surrogate experiences. The ability to remain objective as you engage in any of them—that is, the ability to keep from getting sucked into the story—is possible only when you are present in the moment. For that to begin to occur, you need to slow down and let go of— or at least loosen—the habits you are addicted to. The point is not the amount of time that's reclaimed in the process but rather the engagement in whatever you are doing in a more conscious way. This is where you'll find the real aliveness and meaning that you seek.

EXERCISE
understanding
your relationship to time

It's time now for you to take a good, hard look at yourself and at your own relationship to time. Keep in mind that for things to change, you must start from the place that you are right now in your life. It requires no other preparation. The important step is simply to begin.

First, try to understand the way your life is organized at the present time: how you live day to day and how you orient yourself with respect to time. For this you need some data, and the best way to get it is to ask yourself the questions contained in the following Time Orientation Questionnaire. If other questions occur to you as you answer these, feel free to expand on the list and tailor it to your own life circumstances. You'll find a downloadable version of the questionnaire on the Not So Big Life website, which you can print out and include in your notebook if you like.

By undertaking this exercise, you will be assembling the raw material with which to evaluate your life's relative balance. Don't be too shocked when you discover discrepancies between the way you thought you were living and the way you wish you were living. For those who don't normally look at their lives in this way, the difference between what they think is happening and what is actually happening can be overwhelming. But don't worry—simply performing the exercise is the first step toward reconfiguring your life, but it won't come all at once, and you won't be personally responsible for its implementation. When you start to see imbalances in the system, and when you recognize the desire for a more integrated, balanced, and meaningful existence, things will automatically begin to shift. When you perceive the possibility for change, Providence moves to support that perception. Watch as things shift over the next few months, and you'll discover that the results provide you with your own window into the dynamics of consciousness in action.

You may want to designate an hour or two some evening or weekend during which you can devote yourself to this exercise without interruption. If at any point you find yourself getting bogged down, skip ahead and come back to the troublesome question or questions later. This exercise is a valuable tool only if it helps you see yourself. If it causes consternation, it's not serving its purpose.

Time Orientation Questionnaire

YOUR GENERAL RELATIONSHIP TO TIME

- How much time clutter fills your day? Make a list of the things you do that seem superfluous or unnecessary.
- Would you characterize your pace as fast, slow, or somewhere in between?
- How do you prioritize your daily activities?
- Are you a list keeper? If so, how do you relate to your lists? Are they tools that help you organize your day, or have they become burdens?
- Do you do the things you enjoy the most first, last, or somewhere in between?
- Is your general approach to the activities you engage in efficient, inefficient, or somewhere in between? What makes it so? Is your general approach to the things you engage effective, ineffective, or somewhere in between? What makes it so?
- Do you feel awkward when you find yourself with time to spare?
- What do you do when you *do* have time to spare? (If you never have spare time, conjecture about what you would do if you did.)

SLEEPING

- How much sleep do you typically get?
- Does your weekend sleep schedule differ dramatically from your weekday schedule?
- What are your attitudes and beliefs about sleep?

- Are you aware of how much sleep your body really needs in order to feel fresh and rested in the morning?
- How does this compare with the amount of sleep you are typically getting?
- Have there been periods of your life when you have had difficulty sleeping?
- What did you learn from those periods?
- Do you often remember your dreams?
- Do you wish you had more time to sleep?
- Do you think you sleep too little or too much?
- Are you a "morning" person, an "evening" person, or somewhere in between?
- How does this orientation affect your sleeping pattern?
- Have you ever intentionally changed the time you go to bed and the time you rise? If so, what did you learn?
- Do you look forward to going to bed? If so, do you know why?
- Do you look forward to getting up in the morning? If so, do you know why?

ADRENAL STIMULANTS

- What are your favorite "nut" generators?
- Do you consume significant quantities of caffeine each day? If so, in what form or forms?
- Do you consume significant quantities of sugar each day? If so, in what forms?
- Are there any other drugs or stimulants that you depend on to keep you alert during the day? If so, what are they?
- Are there any other drugs or intoxicants that you depend on to help you calm down after an overstimulated day? If so, what are they?
- Do you consume any of the above in quantities that suggest addiction? If so, what would be a more appropriate quantity?
- What do these adrenaline producers or suppressors do for you?
- Have you ever tried shifting your behavior patterns related to them?
- If so, what did you notice about the quality of your day?

PHYSICAL EXERCISE

- Do you regularly engage in physical exercise?
- If so, what type, how often, and for how long?
- How much difference is there between your plans for exercising and what you actually do?
- Why do you exercise? Is it an obligation, a way to discharge physical or emotional tension, or a way to make yourself more alert?
- Do you enjoy the form of exercise that you do, or do you do it only because it is supposed to be good for you?
- Does it give you an opportunity to get outside?
- Does it give you a chance to engage in a team activity?
- Does it provide an opportunity for social interaction, or is it a time to be alone?
- What are your beliefs about exercise?
- Do you struggle with exercise in any way? If so, how?
- Do you overexercise? If so, why? What would be a more appropriate amount of exercise?

RELAXATION

- What do you do to relax?
- When do you relax?
- Do you have unscheduled time with your spouse or a significant other (including your pets)?
- If so, when does that time usually occur, and what are some of the things you tend to do?
- If you have children, do you have unscheduled time with them?
- If so, when does that time usually occur, and what are some of the things you tend to do?
- How often do you take a vacation?
- How long are the vacations you typically take?
- Do you take vacations alone or with others?
- Do you find vacations relaxing or taxing, exciting or frustrating, or none of these things?
- What are your goals for the vacations you typically take, and do they meet those expectations?

- Are there any observations you have made about your daily life upon returning from a vacation?
- Are there any changes you have made in the past based on those observations?

TELEVISION AND INTERNET USE

- What do you watch on television?
- How much television do you watch, and when do you watch it?
- Do you turn on the television for background noise when you aren't watching it?
- Do other members of your household use the television differently from you?
- Do you watch television together or separately? If together, do the television habits of others influence your own? If so, how?
- If you were left to your own devices, how would your television habits change?
- Do you have a television on while you eat?
- Do you get the munchies when you watch television?
- Respond to the preceding six questions for each member of your household.
- Respond to those six questions with respect to the computers and Internet usage in your home.
- What would your life be like if you turned off the television and/or the computer?
- What else might you do with the time you now spend watching television or using a computer?

WORK

- Is success preoccupying you?
- Do you like your job? Do you dislike it?
- Do you like your immediate supervisor? Do you dislike him or her?
- Do you enjoy the company of the people you work with?
- Do you work at home?
- If so, are there any problems associated with this arrangement?
- Do you prefer to work at home or at a place away from home?

- How far is your place of work from your home?
- How long is your commute each day?
- Do you drive or take a form of public transportation?
- Do you engage in any other activities during your commute? If so, what are they?
- Do you put in more hours than your co-workers? If so, why?
- How many hours a week are you at work?
- Is your job particularly stressful? If so, what makes it so?
- How many people do you interact with on a typical day at work?
- What supposedly time-saving gadgets and gizmos do you use?
- What have you discovered about them?
- Do you find any of them running you rather than serving as a helpful tool?
- How many phone calls do you receive in a day? How many do you answer?
- How many e-mails do you receive in a day? How many do you answer?
- How many spam e-mails do you receive in a day? How long does it take to delete them?
- How many meetings do you attend in a typical day?
- How much time do you have available to accomplish the primary functions that you are hired to perform? For example, for an architect—how much time is spent designing? For an editor—how much time is spent editing? Or for a teacher—how much time is spent teaching?
- Do you bring work home to do in the evening or on weekends? If so, why?
- Do you go to the office to work on weekends, even when this is not required?
- Do you consider yourself a workaholic?
- Have others implied or explicitly stated that you are a workaholic, even if you don't perceive yourself that way?
- Do you consider yourself lazy?
- Do you consider yourself a procrastinator?
- What is a typical week's schedule? Write it down.
- What are the underlying beliefs behind your schedule?

OTHER ACTIVITIES
- Do you engage in any regular evening and weekend activities?
- Do you ever have friends or business associates over for dinner?
- If so, do these occasions make you tense, or do they relax you?
- If so, do you have any objectives in organizing these events, other than to have fun?
- Are you involved in any extracurricular activities associated with your children, such as attending sports events or driving the children from place to place?
- If so, how much time per week do you devote to these activities and when?
- Do you have any passions that you regularly pursue outside your job?
- If so, how much time do you devote to them?
- If not, are there things you'd like to be doing but have never made time for?
- Do you engage in any hobbies, or are you a collector of some kind?
- If so, how much time do you devote to these activities and when?
- Are there other activities in your life that haven't been covered by any of the above topics?
- If so, identify when you engage in them, how much time you devote to them, and what purpose they fill in your life.
- Do you engage in any activity excessively? If so, what would be a more appropriate way of engaging in it?

ASPIRATIONS
- Does the way you live now resemble the life you aspired to when you were younger?
- How would you change that picture to depict your longings more accurately?
- What makes you feel most alive?
- Does this have any relationship to the things you do each day?
- Would you like to retire from doing things that have lost their meaning for you?
- Do you have something you love to do that you are putting off until you retire or until you've accomplished some other goal?

- Do you plan to retire?
- If not, what are your reasons? Do you love what you do? Do you have trouble imagining what you would do if you weren't working? Is there some other reason?
- If you plan to retire, at what age do you plan to do so? How many years is that from now?
- Is the way you are living in alignment with your longings for meaning and significance?
- What are you not fully engaging in right now that you wish you had time for?

    With your answers to all these questions, you have the raw material with which to evaluate your life's relative balance. As you continue to observe your behavior related to time, your primary objective is to be on the lookout for patterns of time usage that necessitate multitasking and rushing or that result in procrastination and resistance. You'll be able to use the results of this exercise to inform your approach to the subject of the next chapter, which takes a look at your conditioned patterns of behavior and how they shape your life experiences.

PRINCIPLE
openability

In order to move from place to place in a house, we typically connect rooms with doors that we open or close according to how much privacy we want. The problem is that most doors are rather narrow and greatly limit the view from room to room. When a door is closed, you can end up feeling isolated.

There are less confining ways of creating connection without using the standard swinging door. You can use a sliding door, which takes up no floor space because it is housed in a wall pocket. You can create a wider doorway that's opened or closed with double doors, an accordion door, or drapes. You can even make an entire wall out of a series of screens that slide sideways along a heavy-duty track, providing a wide, unobstructed connection between the spaces to either side.

When such openable surfaces are included in the design of a house, the experience of the affected rooms changes dramatically. With a sliding door or screen closed, the rooms on either side seem contained and secluded, but with the sliding door or screen open, the same rooms seem spacious and flowing.

Our lives could benefit from this kind of flexibility, but most of us have only standard-size swinging doors between the various compartments of our lives, giving us a limited sense of flow. Because our ideas about what we can and can't do and what we like and don't like seem absolute, we take for granted that these things will never change, and so we feel trapped in our lives and by the things that frustrate us.

We don't realize that by widening the openings between the rooms, or aspects, of our lives, we can change our experience considerably. Because of the restricted views that we take for granted, our impression of ourselves is limited to the particular activity we are engaged in at any moment. By widening the connections between our various aspects, we can see more clearly why we are the way we are and allow ourselves to see that the things we thought were fixed walls of our inner structuring are in fact movable. With an unobstructed view between rooms, we get an increased sense of space, and we begin to understand what has made us feel cramped and limited in the past.

This chapter looks at some of the ways to add wider openings and doorways to our lives so that we don't feel so limited or even trapped. It's time to build in some new connections and create some breathing room.

FOUR

Removing the Clutter

Do not keep anything in your home that you do not know
to be useful or believe to be beautiful.
—WILLIAM MORRIS

Finding Time

In the remodeling of a house, it is important to throw out the things that are no longer useful before you start designing anything new. These things may include old furnishings that served an important function years ago but now give the structure an outdated appearance and restrict movement; old patterns of behavior that remain only because of the existing layout of the house; old piles of junk—stuff that should have been thrown out along the way but wasn't; and finally, all those things we have kept for their sentimental value, which we now barely remember, things that now just clutter up the house, making it difficult to move freely or bring in anything new.

Our lives have lots of leftover piles and patterns as well, and in order to implement the blueprint for your own Not So Big Life these must also be identified and dispatched. There's an amazing amount of wasted space and time in our lives, which, when cleaned out, reveals a lot more room to work with for our life remodeling. You can think of the process as the psychological equivalent of a spring cleaning. The difficulty is that we've come to see our homes—and our lives—as fixed entities; unless we stop to think, we accept that the stuff we have in them and the way we feel when we're in them are givens.

If you consider an average day in your life, you may be starting to realize that there is time available to do whatever it is that you would like to have time for, but right now it's invisible because of the way you engage the events and obligations that define it. The art of finding time has primarily to do with seeing how we obscure our desires by filling the day with not very important stuff that we think is impossible to avoid. That impossibility is an illusion. It's a filter covering what's really here, like a filter you put over a camera lens to block out a certain part of the light spectrum. We could have all the time in the world, but if we continue to experience our lives through the same old filters of conditioned behaviors and thinking, nothing will ever change.

So the first step in finding the space and time in your life to do what you'd really like to be doing is to become aware of your habitual patterns, all of which are based on hidden beliefs; these constitute your own particular filter over reality.

My friend and assistant Marie, for example, has a set of conditioned patterns that are almost polar opposites of my own. Whereas I try to pack too many things into a day and then feel frustrated that I haven't gotten everything done, she gets totally immersed (or "lost," as she puts it) in one project at the expense of everything else. In this way she maintains the illusion of controlling her environment by refusing to rush. According to this description, you might think that Marie feels much less stressed than someone like me. But that's not the case, as she always has more to do than she can handle, and she has no overall sense of her priorities. So the net result is similar. I overcommit, while she undercommits, but neither of us leaves time for what we really care about, at least not if we allow our conditioning, our habitual patterns, to run us.

Both approaches to time also ensure that we are never present in what we're doing, by which I mean that we are never fully engaged in the moment. I'm too busy juggling to be present, while Marie is too absorbed. Both of us have had to recognize our conditioning and the beliefs that underlie them and to enact some countermeasures in order to shift the ways in which we engage, both in our work and in our everyday lives.

I have learned some disciplines that certainly don't come naturally but make a huge difference to the amount of busyness I experience and are key to the remodeling of my life. For example, my best creative time is early in the day, before I've engaged the communications deluge that waits in my in-box and voice-mail message box. So I've put into practice a strategy that allows me to protect that time of day. I simply don't look at or listen to outside stimuli until after noon. I don't check e-mail or answer the phone. This way I can write and think with genuine clarity. I know I have to be present to engage this material, and, as we've established, task juggling and presence rarely coexist.

I find that even one phone conversation or a quick glance at my e-mail convinces me that there's something that needs attending to right away. Before I know it, a couple of hours have evaporated, and the creative potential of the morning has disappeared along with the time. The trick is to recognize your conditioning and work around it. If I'm aware of an urgent issue, I tend to deal with it right away. The allure of ball juggling is irresistible. But if I don't know about the apparent urgency, it turns out the matter will always wait until I do know about it. And I have the power to determine when I learn about something, through the simple discipline of not looking or listening until I'm ready to attend to it.

In addressing this issue, I've also uncovered one of my underlying beliefs. I've been conditioned to believe, since childhood, that an effective person takes care of problems *as soon as they arise*. That doesn't sound like a bad thing. But it does have unintended consequences, the most obvious of which is that if you're always attending to problems that arise, you get around to what really matters to you only after you've taken care of everything else.

Until I recognized this pattern in myself, I never understood why the part of being an architect that I enjoyed the most—the design part, where you sit down and develop the shape and character of the house or addition you are working on—would always be the last thing I'd get around to during my day. In fact, I'd often take the design work home with me and do it late at night, when there was nothing to interrupt me. What I see now is that there was always something more urgent and always someone needing something from me during the day while I was at work. In order to do the things I enjoyed doing, I needed to be alone.

If I allowed my personality or self-image—the collection of all my conditioned patterns—to construct my reality, I would rarely engage in anything that was meaningful to me. This is my version of self-imposed hell. For the most part that's what most of us are doing, each in our own unique and perfectly frustrating way.

Marie's countermeasures to her conditioned pattern of zoning out are almost exactly the opposite of mine. Instead of placing limitations on interruptions as I do, she actually plans them, building times into her daily schedule to remind herself to check on what else needs her attention. She sets her computer's calendar to remind her to do various things each day that she might well otherwise be oblivious to once she gets caught up in a project. The bell that sounds with each reminder is enough of an interruption to break her concentration on her one activity and remind her to look for other obligations and priorities.

The hidden belief behind Marie's zoning out is that it's good to go with the flow. Planning and making decisions might limit what happens next, so it's better to make as few choices as possible. With no decision making, however, comes no sense of direction and no sense of relative importance. Her personality's vision of a perfect reality is to be afloat in a sea of unscheduled time with no interruptions and no commitments; it ensures nonengagement and a lack of anything meaningful in her life. Although hers is the reverse of my own unsatisfactory existence, it's just as miserable, and escaping from it requires just as much attention and effort.

Working with habitual patterns in this way may sound a bit like training Pavlov's dog, but habits are insidious things. Anyone who has tried to quit a behavior they'd rather not have knows how challenging this can be. And sometimes, to quit a behavior, we must take measures that elicit the desired response. Implementing these measures is no different from what we do when we train a child, except that now we are our own students. We recognize the need for a change, and we devise a plan that will have the desired effect.

Your Turn

In reading through this discussion of hidden beliefs and the habitual patterns they've helped generate, what has come to mind about your own relationship to time? Are your patterns similar to the ones described above, or are they entirely different? Can you identify the underlying beliefs related to the way you engage time? And can you identify some countermeasures that might help you do things differently? Take a few minutes to write down in your notebook any thoughts and ideas about your relationship to time. There may be more habitual patterns that come to mind as you read the next few pages as well, so keep your notebook handy.

Play It Again, Sam

Our conditionings and habitual patterns of behavior are similar to recordings on an audiotape or CD. You can play them over and over, and every time they come out the same way. We've all known elderly people who never seem to tire of telling the same story from their youth over and over again, until their friends and family can't resist saying, "Yes, Grandma, we know. You've told us before." It's as though something in that person's psyche has hit the replay button and there is no off switch. It plays through to the end no matter what anyone says.

Our conditioning is very similar. Just like Grandma's retelling of her favorite story, a conditioned pattern is a set of actions and responses that you've set to replay on automatic because it worked for you once a long time ago—the first time a particular circumstance or stimulus presented itself—and you've continued to replay the pattern every time the same conditions arise ever since. So a conditioned pattern is essentially a one-time learning that sets a behavior in stone, even though it is not necessarily applicable to every similar situation.

Some conditioned patterns are useful, of course. They allow us to function as civilized human beings. Others were useful when we were children but should have been retired from duty long ago. Yet others have never been useful, filtering our experience of reality in a way that shuts us off from our full potential. Imagine what our reality might be like if we were unencumbered by the outmoded and no longer useful patterns. Things would, without question, look very different.

One of my greatest trepidations while growing up was encounters with anger. Somewhere in early childhood I must have experienced anger and decided that this was something to be avoided at all costs. So I learned to stay well away from confrontation by being a very good kid. I was always helpful, always anticipating others' needs and fulfilling them before being asked. As I got older, this behavior turned into a pattern of constantly responding to urgency, which meant attempting to provide anything that anyone might need that I could help with, preferably before a request was even made. My underlying fear of confrontation created a habitual pattern of need anticipation and fulfillment, which as a child was richly rewarded with praise and gratitude from my parents. But when I became an adult, the consequences of the pattern were different.

No one praised me anymore, and my seeking and responding to urgencies made me perpetually too busy. This pattern continued unabated until I was able to observe myself more objectively and see through the smoke screen of appearances to what was really going on, including what was creating my particular filter.

Once you can see the dynamic, although it's still likely to replay itself for years to come, you don't have to buy into it anymore. You can see it sufficiently to be able to say to yourself, "Ah, yes. This is where I start juggling too many balls," or whatever your particular habitual pattern is. And over time you can get enough distance from the pattern that you can recognize it for what it is—just a pattern, a recording that plays itself on automatic until you find the off button. When the conditioned pattern stops playing, your experience of time will change because you will no longer be struggling with your imaginary boogeymen, those old conditioned responses that are no longer serving you.

The above description sounds very nice and tidy and very obvious in many ways, especially to someone with a pattern significantly different from those I've described. It's easy to see the conditioned patterns of others precisely because they are wired differently. It's the contrast with our own perceptual filters that makes them so apparent. I think of the young architect who worked for me for a number of years who would always, with clockwork predictability, underestimate the time a task would take him by a factor of three. He never seemed to see his own failing, even when it was pointed out to him. He simply couldn't believe that something—anything—would take as long as it actually did. His underlying belief was that speed was of the essence and that, given willingness on his part to work hard, anything could be done in record time.

I also recall a builder, an excellent craftsman, who would never bring up with his customers the costs associated with the changes on a project until the very end of the construction process, a pattern that of course inevitably caused an enormous amount of turmoil. He couldn't understand why his customers became irate. He was, after all, only presenting them with the bill for the work they had requested. Withholding information until the eleventh hour didn't seem unreasonable to him. In his mind he just hadn't gotten around to talking about it earlier because he'd been too busy getting the job done. Everyone around him, including the three carpenters who worked for him, could see the problem clearly. But as much as we all tried to help him understand why his behavior upset his customers, he didn't get it. Whatever the root of this pattern, every one of his projects became a living nightmare for him at the very end. Finally I stopped recommending him to my clients despite the proficiency of his craftsmanship.

These are just a couple of examples of how outdated behavior patterns shape our reality, but as the proud owner of one of these conditioned patterns, I know its resolution doesn't present itself so readily. It's taken me years of watching, learning, and inner listening to be able to recognize and write about my own patterns. Why should something so simple be so difficult to see? Because these conditioned ways of responding to the world form the very foundations of our internal universe, of who we understand ourselves to be. The exercise at the end of this chapter will help you identify some of the conditioned patterns that have created the foundations of your world.

Kaleidoscope Worlds

Think about a kaleidoscope for a moment. When you look through its lens, you see colored patterns created by the refraction of light from internal mirrors. Usually there is some sort of disk at the end opposite the lens that contains small translucent colored sprinkles, petals, or the like that in combination create dazzling geometries. If you remove just one or two of the sprinkles, the patterns that result are quite different. That's how it is with our personal filters on the world: They can and do change the way we experience what's happening, and not just a little bit but dramatically.

As you are undoubtedly beginning to recognize, our ideas of ourselves construct the reality we experience. Although whatever is happening seems ever so real at any particular moment, we know from experience that two people rarely remember the same event the same way. Think of siblings growing up in the same house with the same parents: They recall childhoods that to the outside observer might seem completely unrelated to one another.

Our experience is almost entirely based on our conditioned patterns and the filters they put into place. Imagine, for example, the situation if the builder I described had been able to remove his filter so that he no longer put off the discussions about money that made him feel uncomfortable. By discussing the costs associated with each change as it was requested during the construction process, he would no longer have been subjected to the wrath of customers who felt victimized by his lack of communication about the price increases that had silently been accumulating along the way. He'd have felt completely different about the success or failure of his performance, and he'd have been receiving the accolades that his craftsmanship deserved rather than feeling the effects of his customers' fury as they responded to their shattered budgets. His entire life experience would have shifted, just by removing one relatively simple conditioned pattern.

Or consider the young architect whose time estimates were so far off base. Because he committed himself to accomplishing things in vastly less time than he needed, he was constantly working late into the night, constantly racing frantically to complete the task in front of him so that he could get to the next one in line. Without this one pattern, his life would have been significantly calmer; he'd have had time to sleep and eat properly, and he'd have been able to take greater pride in his work. He'd almost certainly have gotten a lot more out of every task he undertook because he'd have been able to enjoy doing it rather than rushing through it in sprint mode.

Years ago, when I was responsible for managing an architectural firm in Minneapolis, I worked with an office manager who didn't believe that we, the staff with architectural training, cared about her needs. She felt like an outsider—a common problem in companies where most of the employees are engaged in a professional discipline with a shared vision of what's important. To our way of thinking, we were creating works of art for our clients to live in, and like many artists we ignored a lot of administrative details. The office manager brought this pattern to our attention, and we made a concerted effort to be mindful of her concerns.

The biggest and most volatile issue involved time cards and their being turned in on time. One latecomer could throw off the entire payroll process and make the office manager's life more difficult and more stressful. So we devised a way to avoid being late: We were all to get our time cards in by 9:00 a.m. on the day before they were due. This should have been the end of the issue, but it wasn't.

The first month with the new procedure in place everything went without a hitch, and everyone, the office manager included, seemed content. But at the beginning of the second month, I arrived in the office at 8:45 a.m. on the day designated for turning in time cards and watched in amazement as the office manager became upset because one time card was missing. At 8:57 a.m., the offending party sauntered up to the front desk and proceeded to talk with the receptionist, time card in hand, until one minute past the hour, when he nonchalantly placed the missing time card on the office manager's desk before returning to his work area.

It took about three seconds for the office manager to arrive at my desk, her face flushed with indignation. "See?" she seethed. "They don't care! They just don't care! What's the point of all the work we put into the new system?"

So what had happened? One person was one minute late with his time card. Perhaps his behavior was intentional (and if so, it had everything to do with his conditioning and hidden beliefs). But the office manager chose to see one "late" time card as confirmation of her worst fear: that people were unwilling to comply with her wishes, which, according to her underlying belief, meant that people didn't care about her at all.

Without this filter of her own conditioning, she might have been delighted that all the time cards were in her possession twenty-four hours earlier than they had been in the past. She might have interpreted the one tardy individual's behavior as a great improvement over previous occasions and thanked him for his willingness to work with her, which might have predisposed him to do better the next time. But instead she chose—or, rather, her conditioned pattern chose—to read into the circumstances evidence that *nobody* cared about her needs.

I use this example because the pattern is so clear. In psychological terms this kind of pattern is often referred to as a "hole" because no matter how hard one might try, it can't be filled; it can't be satisfied. You may think as you read this that you don't have that problem, but all of us have holes. And just as the office manager couldn't see her own conditioning, until you've done some inner work to identify your own patterns, you won't see yours either—I guarantee it. They'll just seem eminently reasonable to you. But they're not. They are holdovers from your past. They're no longer useful, and unbeknownst to you they are wreaking havoc with the peace and joy that otherwise could be your everyday experience. You may recall that in chapter 2 I spoke of the predicament of the fish, unable to perceive the water it swims in because it is such a constant. The same is true of our conditioning. It's only when we are very still, or when we intentionally shift the way we do things, that we have any hope of seeing it. I've described just a couple of patterns, but in fact the way we experience our world is constructed of hundreds, even thousands, of such patterns, which may seem more than a little overwhelming, especially if you were hoping to get to the bottom of all this in a hurry.

The art of engaging any of this material is to appreciate from the start that a Not So Big Life is not, as the saying goes, a destination. It's a journey, one that lasts a lifetime and allows you to come to see and understand more and more of yourself. If you focus on goals and objectives and if you try to force things to happen, doors will remain firmly locked. You can do this work only by being as open as you can to what life presents you. Absolutely everything in your life contributes to your growth when you learn how to see things differently, and recognizing your primary conditionings is a huge step in that direction.

EXERCISE
revealing the underpinnings
of your personality

Collectively, all our conditionings define the thing we call our personality. Although in colloquial contexts, we tend to think of personality as a "good" thing, as can be seen with such statements as "He's got a great personality" and "She's bubbling with personality," the reality is that the personality is not really our friend. It evolves to protect and defend our self-image—the idea of ourselves that we call "me"—from everyone else. The problem is that in the process it also cuts off our connection to our true Self—the one that would be present if there were no filters obscuring our lens on reality. So the personality is simply a collection of conditioned patterns, many of them founded on inadequacies and insecurities from early childhood and all of them filtering the full experience of what's really here.

In order to uncover more of your true potential, it's necessary to become familiar with the primary conditionings that shaped your personality and who you've come to believe you are. In order to do this exercise, you need to be very honest with yourself. Some of what you are about to look at may seem insignificant or, worse, embarrassing. You'll tell yourself that some things are common to everyone and therefore aren't worth writing down, and others you may feel so deeply ashamed of that you simply *can't* acknowledge them. But if you are to come to know and understand your personality structure, it's important to look at all your conditionings and especially at those that make you the most uncomfortable.

As you go through this exercise, it's critical that you remember that these ways of behaving aren't "you." Conditioned patterns are like recordings, and listening to those recordings over and over again has shaped your experience of who you are. In fact, you've gone so far as to believe that those recordings are who you really are. But it just isn't so. The recordings are what get in the way of your experiencing your full potential. You are the equivalent of the tape or CD upon which the recordings have been made, but you are not the recordings themselves.

When practiced over time, this exercise will allow you to find the off buttons for each of your conditioned patterns. It will take years to see some of them, and there may well be ones you'll never spot, so be gentle with yourself. This process isn't helped by pushing and forcing or by self-judgment. It requires an attitude of allowing in order for the unfolding to take place. If you develop your inner ear—if you listen for the inner wisdom that's inherent in all of us—the patterns will gradually present themselves, and you'll learn more and more about how you came to experience things in the way that you do.

Here's what you need to do to work through this exercise:

1. Write down all the things you can think of that make you frustrated, unhappy, or discontented. Write each item on a new line. You can use the following questions to get started, but there's no need to restrict yourself to these.

   Are there particular words that cause a negative reaction in you? Are there particular people who drive you crazy? Are there places that you dislike intensely? Are there objects, animate or inanimate, that always irritate you? Are there particular events or circumstances that cause you discomfort? Is there anything else along these lines that come to mind? Write them all down.

2. On the next page of your notebook, following the same procedure, make a list of all the things that make you feel happy, joyful, or delighted. Here are some questions—just the reverse of the ones above—to help you get started:

   Are there particular words that evoke positive feelings in you? Are there particular people whom you are always happy to see? Are there places where you feel particularly comfortable and contented? Are there objects, animate or inanimate, that always delight you? Are there particular events or circumstances that always make you feel particularly joyful?

3. This step is the key. Next to each item in the two lists, or on a separate page if you like, see if you can remember the event or situation that first catalyzed your response. Don't restrict the flow of what comes to mind. Use as many pages as you need in order to elaborate fully. Sometimes an exercise like this will bring to mind situations that you'd entirely forgotten until now, and writing them down allows you to look at the dynamic underlying the situation more carefully than you could if you kept your ideas in your head.

   For example, if you always have a negative response to roses, can you recall why? Was there perhaps a mean old man in your neighborhood when you were a child who shouted at you once when you stepped into his garden to take a look at a rose that caught your eye? That, in turn, may have made you think, "Well, I hate roses anyway!" If you can recall it, you will be identifying the root of a conditioned pattern that has been affecting how you experience roses ever since. The recognition of where the aversion came from can open a door to a new way of experiencing roses, allowing you to see them without the filter of the old memory. But if you never identify the conditioning for what it is, it will continue to filter your perceptions and deprive you of the delight that a rose can offer.

   If you indeed had that experience as a child, chances are you'd think to yourself, "No loss there. I don't want to experience roses anyway." Recognize that this is the personality speaking. It's the tape playing back what it learned the day that old man shouted at you. Although this example might seem an odd one, our conditionings are often equally as absurd. Many of them are defenses, and they cause us to react in ways that to others may seem ridiculous. But make no mistake, that recording is depriving you of something wonderful, and the only person it's hurting is *you*.

4. If you can't remember the first time a conditioned pattern was set in motion—and that may well be the case for most of the items on your list—you can use the following process of making associations to access at least some of the original stimuli that created the pattern. In the center of a page, write a word or phrase describing the issue. Now, in a flower of associations surrounding that center, write down all the words that come to mind. Don't edit. It's best if you can write down

your thoughts as quickly as possible so that you don't have time to an-alyze what's coming up. Even if the associations seem way off base or completely unassociated with one another, let them come. Evaluation can come later. Here's an example of what a flower of association looks like:

No knowledge of any thing   Don't know who I am
No hope   Desperate Lonely So alone
Miserable Frightened Powerless Shallow
Suffocated Challenged Small Helpless Wisdom
Lost Loss (When someone gets angry) Lost Missing
Worried Hurt Fear Wanting Fear No love
Shattered Painful love Horror
No center Where am I? Who am I? Loss

Every iteration of the exercise will bring forth different fruits, but in my example, I am able to see that whatever the source of the condi-tioning, it almost certainly happened when I was very small, when I was still obtaining at least some of my sense of who I was from my caregiver. It's not important who that was. It could have been a babysitter, a parent, or a sibling. That's just the story line of the con-ditioning event—it's the surface clothing, and not the dynamic be-neath. What matters here is seeing that I have a hidden fear that when someone gets angry, I may disappear or lose my sense of who I am. Checking this out with my experiences as an adult, I recognize that this explanation correlates with what I feel.

Having lived for a couple of years now with some understanding of the pattern's roots, when I encounter this kind of situation, though I still feel the fright, I no longer lose the sense of myself or my cen-teredness. This revelation has dramatically changed my experience of everyday life, as I now understand that confrontation and anger are not life-threatening. Though I knew this intellectually, my condi-tioned pattern was telling me otherwise, and my personality attempted to arrange my life so that I never came into contact with anger. I was in effect tuning out a large segment of reality because of my fear.

In these last two steps I've used examples taken from the list you made in Step 1 because they tend to be the conditioned patterns that affect your life experience in an adverse way, but you can use precisely the same techniques for the items on the list from Step 2 as well. These conditioned patterns appear to have a more positive effect, but they are still part of your personality and are shaping your experience just as much as those from Step 1.

You can continue to play with this exercise your whole life. Once you get the hang of it, you'll find yourself doing it almost automatically. Simply bringing awareness to a pattern and being able to say "Aha, this is a replay of such and such conditioned pattern" gradually drains it of energy; once you see your conditionings for what they are, it's hard to buy into them anymore. Over time your personality will relinquish the reins, and there will be less and less filtering of the world you experience—and that process will allow you to experience ever more of what's here.

PRINCIPLE
interior views

One of the most important principles in house design has to do with *interior views*—designing the vistas offered by the home's interior. Although we're usually pretty good at thinking about what we will see of the world outside when we look through the windows, we often forget that most of our time inside is spent looking from one interior place to another. These interior views can be every bit as engaging and inspiring as dramatic panoramas of the great outdoors. And when a house offers such nourishment for the spirit, we tend to feel much more at home because the house is conversing with us, in a way. Through visual dialogue it provides a delightful and constantly stimulating backdrop against which to live our lives.

There's a perfect parallel between these interior views in a home and the views available in the world of introspection and dreams. When we remove the obstacles to self-observation, and when we add to this what we can learn from dreams—both sleeping and waking—our views of that inner world become even more inspiring and much, much richer. Until you realize you can use your everyday experiences to learn more about your inner nature, the only thing you tend to be concerned with is how the outside world looks—and how it treats you. This is the equivalent of considering only what you can see from your home's exterior windows.

Imagine how dramatic and exciting life will become after you start crafting all the interior views in a house. The effect on your senses will be vastly magnified. You will become aware of a sense of spaciousness, of the constantly changing quality of light, of the comfort and relaxation to be found in the home's natural order and inherent beauty. A similar effect is in store for you when you explore the interior experience of your own life. That's what this chapter is about—how to look inside and find some completely new and unexpected views.

FIVE

Listening to Your Dreams

When you eventually see through the veils to how things really are,
you will keep saying again and again,
"This is certainly not like we thought it was!"
—RUMI

The Search for Meaning

One of the most important parts of any remodeling project is paying attention to what you really want your house to do for you. Deep down we all have big dreams for our homes, but because most of us believe we can't afford to implement them, we never give them much consideration. They stay in the "someday it would be nice, but" category . . . indefinitely relegated to the back burner.

But what if you were to start listening to those dreams? What would they tell you? The only way to find out is to try it and see. The trouble is that we have been taught to discount our dreams; they're not practical. In much the same way that our focus on size has caused us to lose track of the important qualities of a house, we've been trained to focus on cold, hard facts and not the dreams. But dreams can teach us an enormous amount; if we constantly tune them out, it's as if we were putting blinders on. Certainly a dream is far less definitive than a fact, but that's its very nature—and its gift. It is there to help orient us, not to give us all the directions for making something specific happen.

So this is the next step in the remodeling of your life: tuning in to your dreams and understanding what they are conveying to you. If you learn how to use them, they can provide you with one of the most useful tools in establishing a Not So Big Life because they facilitate the communication between the part of you that you are already familiar with—your personality—and your as-yet-unexplored inner nature. Dreams contain a kind of meaning that we're not used to paying attention to in this era of material mastery, but unless you learn to listen to them, your remodeling may be functional but uninspiring. A Not So Big Life contains both qualities—function and inspiration—in equal measure.

I remember vividly the day in my sophomore high school English class when we were introduced to the idea that authors of fictional works might have a message for the reader that underlies the story itself. We were reading J.R.R. Tolkien's *The Hobbit*, and our teacher told us that although Tolkien himself had denied that his tales held hidden meaning, in fact there was much to explore beyond the book's entertainment value. Mr. Molchan asked us to write a book report identifying the larger messages of the book.

I went home that afternoon filled with excitement. I was an explorer preparing to delve deep into a jungle thick with imagery and characters, to root out the golden thread that gave the story universal substance. And my teacher's simple observation inspired me to see everything I read from then on in a new light. I felt as though I'd been given an extraordinary new tool through which to perceive meaning that reached beyond the characters and into my own life. It was utterly thrilling, and I began to read voraciously, everything from Camus to Dostoyevski, from Heinlein to Ionesco, from Steinbeck to Twain. Stories in and of themselves had never seemed worthwhile to me; I didn't enjoy entertainment for entertainment's sake. But hidden meaning—well, that was something else entirely.

It is possible to relate to the content of our lives just as we do the story line of a novel, the plot consisting not only of settings, characters, and events but also of themes, patterns, and hidden meanings. And we can do so while still engaging in our everyday lives just as we've always done, but with new awareness.

If you've seen the movie *The Matrix*, you'll know that the protagonist, Neo, gradually learns to see that the world is not at all as it appears to the naked eye. It is instead a huge and complex computer program regulated and controlled by software that can take whatever form it needs in order to accomplish its objective of keeping humans unaware of the true nature of the dream world they inhabit. Neo is one of a handful of people who can see through the dream to the data stream beneath the surface. Once he no longer believes in the absoluteness of appearances—of what he sees, feels, and otherwise senses—he can escape the clutches of the program. Could it be that what is really happening in our own world is dramatically different from what we believe to be the case?

After reading this chapter, it will be well worth your time to watch a movie like The Matrix, The Truman Show, *or any other movie that encourages you to think outside the box of consensus reality. It will help to give you another way of thinking about perceived reality—not necessarily how it actually is, but differently from the way we normally think of things. Another favorite of mine is* Waking Life, *a cleverly animated film that requires some intellect to follow but forces viewers to inquire into their beliefs about reality. There's a list of movies on the Not So Big Life website if you need additional suggestions. After watching the movie you choose, ask yourself, "How do I know that things are the way I've been taught to believe they are?" and "What would convince me otherwise?"*

Imagine for a moment that you were born fifteen hundred years ago. Everyone in your world knows that the world is flat, so the world is flat. Now fast-forward just a century or two, and there's general agreement, based on the work of Pythagoras, Aristotle, and Euclid, that the earth is spherical and the center of the universe. Fast-forward again, and, thanks to the work of Nicolaus Copernicus in the sixteenth century, the earth is understood to rotate around the sun and not the other way around. Consensus reality keeps changing. It will never be correct from the perspective of future humanity.

If we look at what consensus reality tells us today about human existence, it might look something like this:

We are born into a world in which the challenge is to learn enough in our formative years to become productive and financially self-supporting citizens. Marriage and procreation are strongly encouraged though not required. We spend most of our adult lives working, usually for someone else, to earn a paycheck with which to purchase the basic necessities: food, shelter, clothing, transportation, and so on. Once these are adequately covered, we purchase upgrades that make life a little easier, such as better-quality food; a better form of shelter with time-saving appliances like a built-in heating and cooling apparatus, a dishwasher, and a television with access to dozens, even hundreds, of channels; better clothing purchased new; better health care coverage, including dental care; and a privately owned form of transportation, usually an automobile. Once relative comfort on the home front has been acquired, we might add an annual travel vacation, regular entertainment, and an occasional restaurant meal.

After we've taken care of all the purchases necessary to ensure the comfort of our household, we upgrade to increasingly bigger, better, and more prestigious versions of everything related to food, shelter, clothing, health care, transportation, and entertainment: regular dining at the finest restaurants; an ever-bigger house with larger rooms to accommodate our expanding collection of possessions, high-end finishes, and all the latest top-of-the-line gizmos; designer-label and tailor-made clothing; regular visits to a massage therapist, chiropractor, and psychotherapist; a bigger and more expensive car of the latest model; and vacations in second homes we now own.

While accomplishing all of the above, we put away in a safe place the money we save for our retirement years, an idyllic period after the age of sixty-five when we won't work and are given permission to enjoy ourselves. And we are taught to expect to spend the remaining years of our lives primarily in the entertainment and vacationing mode, until our bodies run out of steam. At this point we are placed in the care of either a planned retirement community or our aging children—assuming we have children—who will help keep us busy with not-too-challenging forms of entertainment, such as card playing and television watching, until we "pass away"—a euphemism for dying.

That's the game—the consensus reality—as it's presented to most middle-class North Americans. This is how it will look for the lucky few who "win," who don't fall prey to the sand traps of credit-card debt, noncovered medical costs, and an inadequate retirement income. If the game sounds a bit stark, that's because nothing personal is included. It's the bare-bones structure of what we're taught to aspire to, minus any of the experiences that make it either painful or fulfilling. We orient our entire adulthood toward the means by which we procure our paycheck, an activity most of us select when we are in our teens or early twenties and engage in for more than a third of our waking hours as adults. Even if we succeed in acquiring all the features of a "successful" life, we continue to pursue our career path long after we have life's essentials covered and long after we've secured our physical comfort for the foreseeable future. But if you were to ask most people why they do what they do, they'd probably look at you in confusion and ask, "What else is there?"

This is a description of a system that was originally designed to secure our physical well-being, but it doesn't offer any vision of what should be done once that physical well-being has been adequately accommodated. When we see our lives in this light, it's pretty clear that we're living by the dictum that if a little physical well-being is good, more must be better. But the questions we need to ask ourselves today are "When do we know we have enough?" and "What could we do with our lives if we weren't so focused on acquiring more?" It is time for consensus reality to offer a new vision of why we're here, or at least some new options.

Learning to Read the New Blueprint

Now that I've loosened up your belief in the edicts of consensus reality just a little and painted an unembellished image of what we are taught to aim for, let's imagine some ways to rethink what's going on in life. Let's dream a little. Throughout the centuries, people have posed the questions "What am I doing here?" and "What is the meaning of life?" These are, of course, *big* and almost impossibly profound questions that usually lead us nowhere. But the older we get, the more urgent they seem to become.

There's a wonderful teaching by Jelaluddin Rumi, the thirteenth-century Sufi poet, which can help us see what we're missing:

There is one thing in this world you must never forget to do. Human beings come into this world to do particular work. That work is their purpose, and each is specific to the person. If you forget everything else and not this, there's nothing to worry about. If you remember everything else and forget your true work, then you will have done nothing with your life.

Rumi goes on to explain that the raw material we are given through birth is an incredibly precious material that can be formed into anything at all. "It's a golden bowl," he says, "which is being used to cook turnips, when one filing from the bowl could buy a hundred suitable pots." We're using what we've been given for a far lesser function than its true capacity. We think we are being good, productive citizens because we are cooking up a storm with our bowl, but we're not seeing what the bowl really is and what food that bowl could provide us if we knew how to look at it differently.

So there is one thing in the world, according to Rumi's teaching, that must not be forgotten. Although that one thing isn't articulated, when we engage in these conversations about the big questions, we feel it, and we implicitly understand its enormous value. But once the conversation is done, we tend to forget it and go back to life as usual. There are other moments too when we sense that our bowl could do more than cook turnips. When we experience moments of epiphany or insight and when we notice our heart's desire for something we're passionate about, we recognize the possibility that there might be more to life than we know. But we ignore these clues to what really matters because they're not acknowledged by consensus reality as of value.

That one thing Rumi refers to is the point of existence, the point of our being here, which our conditioning almost completely obscures. Because we can't name it and can't pin it down, it's very easy to reject the promptings of our inner wisdom to pursue our longing to understand. We simply carry on as though nothing were more important in life than the next paycheck or the next automobile or the next house or the next grandchild.

It's not that any of these things can't bring us pleasure or satisfaction, but they are only the contents of our waking lives. They're not the meaning. To find that, we need to learn to read our lives in a different way. And this is why we need a new blueprint. The plans given us by consensus reality provide only directions for a life that's defined by both cultural and personal filters. They don't describe the other dimensions of living that are possible when these filters are removed.

As I describe this new way of living, I sometimes think about what it must have been like before most people knew how to read. Imagine how miraculous it must have seemed when someone trained in reading could look at the markings on a clay tablet or a sheet of papyrus and derive from them a consistent meaning.

I believe that in the not-too-distant future the skills needed to access the treasures of our inner world, the ones you'll be learning in the pages that follow, will be as commonplace as those you're using to read this book today. Everyone will learn them as part of a well-rounded education. And when that happens, our priorities will change. In the same way that literacy expands our horizons, the skills that will allow us to read our lives more completely will markedly affect the choices we make. We'll be able to discern much more readily what will allow us to grow and flourish and what will not; and we'll be able to avoid dead ends that keep us stuck in the story line of our everyday lives, where we're unable to discern any greater meaning or opportunity for fulfillment. As these new skills become commonplace, our collective efforts will reflect the newfound value we place on meaningfulness rather than on the content alone. The implications of this change in orientation are inconceivable to us right now, but they will be just as dramatic as those that widespread literacy has brought about.

Another special language is the one that an architect uses to communicate with a builder to describe a home's design and construction. On a series of drawings that we call blueprints, the various lines and markings tell the builder what goes where and how everything is to be assembled. But for someone not trained in reading these drawings, they're impenetrable. This is another metaphor for the remodeling of our lives that we're working toward.

So what is this new dimension that the blueprint for our life remodel delineates? And what does it mean to learn to read our lives? We don't usually realize that there are many more layers to who we are than are visible on the surface. By learning to see through these layers, many more interior views are revealed that allow us to understand ourselves more completely once we become proficient in recognizing them. In order to see them, to interpret them, and to extract meaning from them, we have to learn how to read a new set of symbols, just as we did when we learned to understand written language.

In each case we understand that the extraction of meaning is not a linear process and what we come to understand is not a rigid, fixed thing. The reason that learning to look for hidden messages in a novel is satisfying is that it gives us insight into human nature and into ourselves. The new blueprint allows the same kind of extraction of meaning from a story line and from symbols, but now the story you are observing is the one you call your life. Once again, the real fun and satisfaction come from looking beneath the content, beneath the story line, to the real meaning below.

The Nature of Dreams

When you know how to look at them, dreams can provide a launching pad for the exploration of your inner life, as well as offer guidance and insight into some of the hidden layers of yourself. They also give you a porthole through which to see your daily life in a new way. So this next section is important for two reasons—it gives you a map to follow for looking at the content of your dreams, and it gives you a model for how to apply the same techniques to your waking life. We know our nighttime dreams aren't real—that we wake up from them—but we generally don't believe this is possible with the story line of our daily existence. By probing our ephemeral nighttime realities, we're going to learn how to interpret our daytime reality in a more flexible and creative way.

Gradually, consensus reality is opening to the possibility that our dreams are more than just recycled fragments of the previous day, and that they can hold up a mirror to aspects of ourselves that we don't yet understand. Over the past hundred years, since the groundbreaking work of Sigmund Freud and Carl Jung, there has been significant interest in probing the potential meanings in those enigmatic universes that arise in our sleep. But because of our culture's preference for known quantities and scientifically provable results, many people have discounted the possibility that their dreamworld can offer them anything of value. So when they awake with a memory of a dreamworld thick with imagery and stories, they don't explore it. But when you search for hidden meaning, you open up the possibility of insight—which is a type of epiphany—a thrilling experience, and one that makes you feel more alive.

If you have never paid attention to your dreams because you believe they are meaningless, I ask you to open the door just a crack to let in the possibility that there might be something more to them—not rigid and definable meanings, but meaningful*ness* that comes from the exploration process itself rather than from any specific interpretation.

Even if you are the kind of person who can't remember any of your dreams, it's still important to read this section. It's the dynamic of the exploration process that matters. Whether or not you begin to remember your dreams, the skills you'll learn here are fundamental to living Not So Big because they show you the way to see what's hidden beneath the surface appearances.

Living the Questions

Ever since I was small, I've been intrigued by dreams. When I started, as an adult, to read more about interpreting their imagery, I was fascinated to discover that every character in your dreamworld can be understood as a representation of an aspect of yourself. If there is a character in your dream whom you can't abide, ask yourself, "What aspect of myself—an aspect that acts something like this character—am I rejecting?" If you have an accident in your dream, you might ask yourself, "Am I avoiding looking at something that is going to cause problems if I don't start paying attention?" By being open to the answers, you may be able to uncover motivations, fears, and internal processes that would otherwise be invisible to you.

Dreams are rarely if ever literal. I remember years ago reading Anne Tyler's wonderful book *Breathing Lessons*. One of its stories is about an old man, Mr. Otis, who is deeply frustrated by the verbal abuse of his wife, Duluth, a believer in the truth of her dreams. After she dreams about her husband being mean to her, she takes revenge the next day for what he did to her in *her* dream. We can laugh at this, yet it's amazing how difficult it is for us to accept that anything and everything in our dreams is *not* about that other person but about ourselves. Each player in our dreams is selected by our subconscious to depict most accurately an aspect of our self.

Perhaps you have a dream in which an aggressive and domineering man attacks you while you are building a sand castle, for example. This doesn't mean you are going to be attacked by such a person in real life, but it *does* point out an aspect of your own personality that is aggressively attacking another part that is being constructive. Your associations with sand castles can give the dream very different meanings. If your associations are positive, perhaps dating back to when you and your father built a sand castle together when you were five years old and he encouraged you to make something wonderful with your own hands, the dream's symbolism is constructive. But if the first thing that springs to your mind is "building castles in the air," which to you suggests a pipe dream, the meaning is quite different. In this case, the aspect of you that is being attacked is in all likelihood the unrealistic dreamer.

Dream interpretations are completely dependent on *your* associations and attributed meanings. No one can tell you what your dream imagery means to you, although someone may be able to help you identify those associations. And there's no right answer. It's only by being open to your dreams that insights and understandings come. If you're too demanding or too literal, you'll just become frustrated. Dreams only point toward meanings; they are not absolutes.

A wonderful piece of advice given by the twentieth-century poet Rainer Maria Rilke in a letter to an aspiring young poet beautifully describes the attitude necessary for working with dreams—and in fact for exploring anything that's not clear to you:

> Be patient with all that is unsolved in your heart and try to love the questions themselves like locked rooms and like books written in a very foreign tongue. Do not now seek the answers which cannot be given you because you would not be able to live them. And the point is to live everything. Live the questions now. Perhaps you will then, gradually, without noticing it, live along some distant day into the answer.

Once you learn how to use them, dreams can be incredibly evocative and dynamic tools by which to see more of your own inner workings. By engaging your dreams with an inquisitive mind, you will be living the questions, as Rilke puts it, and in the process shedding light on many dynamics of your personality and your potential that are normally invisible. The exercise at the end of this chapter will help you with the exploration of your own dreams.

The Nature of Our Waking Experience

Our next step in learning to read the new blueprint for our life remodel is to transpose what we've learned about the dreams that occur while we sleep into the interpretation of our waking experiences. How often have you awoken from sleep to discover with great relief that what you were experiencing was only a dream? And how often have you wished your waking life were something you could wake up from? Well, you can, but perhaps not in the way you might imagine.

I've been wondering just how I might describe this alternative way in which things can be experienced, and this morning I woke up with the answer. It came to me, perhaps not surprisingly, in a dream, so I'm going to share it with you here as a way of exploring both how to be receptive to what your dreams and experiences can reveal based on the questions you are currently living, as well as how to see through the surface of things in your waking life to another level that surrounds us at all times—the new dimension that the blueprint reveals. The hidden benefit of seeing in this new way is that when you learn to see through the content of your life to its essence, your experience of everyday reality will shift dramatically. It will be imbued with a much more meaningful quality while the actual content of your surroundings stays the same.

Here's the dream.

I am in Los Angeles, though the topography is more like that of San Francisco, and I'm in a car with my sister and my brother. My sister is driving. As we crest a very high hill (a lot like the top of Lombard Street in San Francisco), we are looking almost directly down onto the ocean below. I immediately see something incredible beneath the surface of the water. It's an enormous whale, and I mean *enormous*, perhaps three hundred yards long. "Look, look!" I exclaim. "Do you see that enormous whale swimming right there, close to the beach?" My sister gasps. Now we both see it. But I can tell that my brother, who takes this road a lot and has seen many dolphins and other smaller sea creatures here before, hasn't really looked. He starts talking about how sea creatures are often visible from this spot, but he doesn't bother to really look.

The whale seems prehistoric or, perhaps more accurately, timeless. The markings on its back are like continents seen from outer space, irregular patches of green and sandy gray-brown on its long body. Moving through the water from left to right, it nears land, raises its body slightly out of the water, and enters a wide, low opening in the rock that must be its lair. Another whale of similar size is following close behind, and this one, too, moves toward the underwater sanctuary. The feeling in the dream is totally exhilarating.

The following process of working with the symbols in the dream and the associations I have with each one is an example of what I describe in the dream exercise at the end of this chapter. It is intended to assist you as you engage your own dreams, as well as to explore what my whale dream might mean when examined through my particular set of filters.

The whale: To me, whales are extraordinary creatures, highly conscious and aware. When I've been close to whales, I've felt vital and alive, as if all my senses were heightened.

The steeply sloping road: The experience of cresting Lombard Street in San Francisco is one that I've had only vicariously, when visiting Disneyland's Circle-Vision 360° Theatre in 1971, shortly after moving to this country. A scene in the movie, which completely surrounds the viewer, gave me a breathtaking view from the basket of a fire truck barreling down Lombard Street's steep hill. So my associations are of experiencing things from an entirely new perspective and with being in a new country that offers an abundance of previously unimagined and completely encompassing experiences.

Brother and sister: I do in fact have a brother and a sister, and they do live in Los Angeles. My sense is that they represent traveling companions through this life. In this dream I don't know if they can see what I see, but I really want to share it with them. Since the dream occurred in response to my question about how to explain this new way of seeing to you, the reader, they also represent you—the part of me that doesn't yet see what the more awake aspect sees.

The feminine aspect of me—my sister, who in the dream is driving—is able to see the whale after I point it out to her. I associate the feminine with intuition, with receptivity, and with openness to new perspectives.

The masculine aspect of me—my brother in the dream, who's been down this "road" before—thinks he knows what I'm pointing out, and so doesn't bother to look. I associate the masculine with action, with getting things done, with intellect, and with acquisition.

The ocean: It has always seemed both mysterious and wonderful. I love its color, and I think of it as the primary identifying feature of this planet. Without water there would be no life. I've also come to associate the ocean with the sea of consciousness, which I now understand to be the fabric of everything, and the surface of the ocean with the membrane that separates what we see in our waking world—our waking dream—from the reality of what's actually here. The surface can, if we let our eye's gaze stop there, keep what's below from entering our awareness.

My challenge, which the dream illuminates, is to convince you that what we see with our eyes and what we interpret as solid, fixed, and un-equivocal is in fact only one way of seeing, a partial view at best. Fortu-nately, I have supporting evidence provided by science. Particle physics tells us that what we see is limited dramatically by our senses; if we were able to zoom in closer and closer to our skin's surface, for example, with ever-increasing magnification, we'd find that the solid boundary we can see so clearly with our eyes isn't solid at all.

There's a wonderful video called *Powers of Ten*, which you can view on the Not So Big Life website. Zooming in through decreasing orders of magnitude, it takes us on a journey from the Milky Way, which is around ten million light years from Earth, to the electrons contained in a leaf on an oak tree in Tallahassee, Florida. It's a remarkable ride from one end of the spectrum to the other, and it leaves you with the very clear under-standing that what appears to have substance becomes merely a void when seen from the next level of magnitude.

That's not to say that what we're seeing every day is wrong. But it is incomplete. We have learned very effectively to keep our eyes trained on what's outside us—all the people, places, and things that constitute our world. So the world is considered by most of us to be "out there." It af-fects us, and we in turn react to it. There's a split between the subject, "me," and the object, "it," or the world out there, while in fact our sense of ourselves as inherently independent is an illusion. Seen from outer space, we are each of us as much a part of the Earth's surface as a cell on the surface of the leaf on the oak tree in Tallahassee, and every time sci-entists think we've reached the outermost or innermost boundary of the universe, we find there's more, like fractal patterns that continue to un-fold as the viewer moves toward any point.

Now back to my dream. You can probably begin to see why it pro-vides such a good metaphor for my dilemma. I want my brother and sis-ter to be able to see through the surface of the ocean below. Translation:

I want my traveling companions, who include you, the reader, as well as the masculine and feminine aspects of myself, to be able to see through the surface of things to the magnitude of what lies there right in front of us. The whale is a metaphor for greater consciousness and intensified vitality. It's huge, and it's moving from left to right, just as our eyes move when we read. Translation: We gain greater awareness of how we fit into the entirety of existence by seeing through appearances, and as we learn to "read" our lives as integrally interconnected parts of this magnitude, everything takes on intensified vitality.

What's more, we're cresting a hill, and we're about to zoom down toward this new vision of reality at a disorienting though exhilarating speed. We're moving fast, but not all of us can see through the surface of things. The dream suggests that those who think they know what's there beneath the surface may remain unaware of newly visible wonder and vitality, whereas those who are receptive to alternative views of what lies below surface appearances may see something profoundly life-changing. These observations refer to aspects of myself, obviously, but they also point directly to the new dimension that the new blueprint has the ability to reveal. This is how dreams provide insight. My asking the question of how to describe the dimension was all that was required.

Seeing Through the Veils

Once in a while, you may have a dream that distinguishes itself from the others by a feeling of profundity. If you work closely with these dreams, they can become almost like living things, helping to shape the course of the next few months and years. If you have such a dream, you'll know it. It's as though your inner wisdom is speaking directly to you through its imagery, and it will seem often especially luminous or brilliant. You can't will such a dream into existence, but if and when one does come, pay attention to it, and it will bring gifts into your life that you couldn't possibly have imagined.

One of the most profound dreams I've had occurred shortly after I began to document and explore my dreams and as I began to ponder some of the big questions. The dream made me aware that the worlds we visit when we sleep and the world we inhabit during our waking hours are far more linked and interconnected than I'd previously imagined. The dream contained an image that was so powerful that I simply *had* to draw it afterward. In the dream I was walking along a road with a number of other people toward an enormous moon, perhaps a third of whose surface was covered by shadow. Beside us were steeply sloping woodlands that separated the road from the primordial river below. A number of different paths led down to it. There was a lot of discussion between my fellow travelers about which would be the best path to take, but I knew—and I mean here *Knew* with a capital K—that it didn't matter which one we took; all that was important was that we stay with that *one* until we reached the river. The feeling conveyed by that moon, so huge and serene, was extraordinarily powerful. Unlike a typical bright white moon, it was almost pink, with a pearl-like luster.

Although I was able to explore my associations to the dream's images using the process I describe in the exercise at the end of the chapter, I still felt there was something more, something I needed to remember. It was at this point, three or four days after the dream occurred, that I committed the image to paper. In my mind's eye I could see every fissure in the rock's

face and the exact locations of every branch on each tree. With the drawing complete, something inside me was satisfied, and I was able to put the dream aside. Though I didn't completely understand it yet, I had the sense that this dream would take a while to reveal itself and that this wasn't the time to push too hard to extract more meaning. I felt the beginning of its almost living presence in my life, though, and I had a feeling this wouldn't be the end of it.

A few weeks went by, and my brother called to tell me that he was moving to a new home in a place he knew I loved—Topanga Canyon near Los Angeles—and asked if I'd like to visit for Thanksgiving. I took him up on the offer, and two weeks later, there I was, enjoying the natural beauty of the area. The morning I arrived, we decided to go for a walk, and as we did so, my brother told me that there would be a total eclipse of the moon that night, which would be easily visible from the place we were coming to ahead.

Just as he said this, we rounded a corner of the one-lane road, and I stopped dead in my tracks as we stepped into the set of my moon dream from a month earlier, complete with trees, ravine, and rock face. I was stunned. Nothing like this had ever happened to me before, yet it was unequivocal. I knew that I had no way of understanding what was happening but that it was happening nonetheless. It's the kind of thing that you can't believe until it happens to you. But once it does, you have to admit that you really don't understand how the universe works. I remember thinking to myself, "Okay, you've got my attention. I'm listening. Now what?"

Suddenly the image of the moon from my dream sprang to mind, and I could now see an association I hadn't had at the time I'd had the dream: The shadow partially obscuring the moon's face alluded to the impending eclipse. My brother and I resolved to return to this spot to watch the celestial event that night, which we did. We found a comfortable perch for ourselves on one of the rock outcrops and watched the proceeding from start to finish. I'd never seen a total eclipse of the moon before, and it wasn't until the moon was entirely in shadow that I saw the last allusion of my dream. When the moon is completely covered by the shadow of the earth, it doesn't disappear, as one might expect: it turns into a spectacularly beautiful pink pearl. The quality of the light from my dream moon was perfectly replicated by the real moon in eclipse.

I was in awe. It was as though something magical were being revealed to me, and it happened through the linking of my night dream with my waking reality, pointing out in no uncertain terms that I had much still to learn about the mysterious workings of the universe that surrounds us. It also indicated through its intensity that these images— the moon, the primordial river, and the journey between—contained more meaning than I could at that time perceive. In the ensuing years, by paying attention to references to these three images in my waking life, I've learned a great deal about the process of waking up to what's really here.

Today, as I use this dream to illustrate how sleeping and waking dreams are part of one journey, it reveals an additional meaning that's for all of us who are traveling this road together. I associate the moon with the various cycles of the heavens, our planet, and our bodies, all of which govern our existence though we don't begin to understand their workings. I associate the primordial river with the source of the wisdom that informs our journey through life, as well as the original fluid from which we emanate—the truth of who we are. The journey between I associate with our individual and collective adventure to find the truth of who and what we are, which was, in fact, one of those *big* questions that precipitated the dream. The answer to that, so the dream explained, is that we are of both Heaven (moon) and Earth (primordial river). And as the dream so clearly stated, it doesn't matter which path you take, only that you stick with it. The journey to understand ourselves is one path, defined by our life's story line, but the path is there to be explored as something sacred and profound, not just plodded along without awareness.

By constantly listening to your dreams and treating every event and appearance as a clue to the questions you are most interested in, the things you want to understand will be revealed, just as this dream has done and continues to do for me. Although your own wake-up call will likely be very different from the one I describe here, your willingness to look, listen, and live the questions is what's key. The point is to remain alert to the possibility that, as Rumi puts it in the verse that introduces this chapter, "This is certainly not like we thought it was!"

EXERCISE
exploring
your dreamworld

There are many ways of doing dream work, and none is right or wrong. The magic of the process is that once you start, it will guide you to the materials and approaches most suitable for you. We often get so hung up on finding just the right tool and trying to find the "best" option that we never actually begin. So let's start simply. Just keep some paper and a pen by your bed, and tell yourself before you go to sleep that you want to remember your dreams. In the morning, lie quietly when you awake and see—without trying to force it—if they come back to you.

Don't discount anything. Write it all down, and don't edit. Things that seem insignificant when you first wake up can gain value later as you look at them. Make sure to include not just the images and the story line, if there is one, but also the feelings and qualities that accompanied the dream. Were you frightened, excited, enthralled, or lost? Did you feel completely engaged, or were you dispassionate, more like an observer than a participant? Were there any colors, sounds, or light qualities that you recall?

I find that it's usually best not to try right away to interpret the dreams you've recorded. The process takes time and consideration, and when you've just woken up and have the obligations of your day to consider, you may be inclined to rush, which isn't likely to breed meaningful insights. The process I implemented was to set aside time in the evening, after I returned home from work, for exploring a dream from the night before that was particularly powerful.

The next step is to expand on the imagery in the dream. First, take the dream and reread it. Underline or highlight the major characteristics, such as people, places, events, objects, feelings, and qualities.

Then, take each underlined word or phrase in succession, and identify your associations with it. For example, if your friend Penelope shows up as a character in a dream, write down all the associations with Penelope you can think of. What does she represent for you? How would you describe her personality? Is she always helpful to others—perhaps to a fault, in your estimation? If so, make a note of that, because this is a characteristic that your dream is using to help you understand something about yourself. If the dream took place in your high school gym, look at the associations you have with that place. Did something exciting happen there, perhaps? Did your high school graduation occur there, or did you win lots of basketball games there? Or do your associations have more to do with not being particularly good at athletics and feeling humiliated because you couldn't perform as well as you thought you should?

Once all your associations have been identified, it's time to piece them together to uncover the dream's potential insights and meanings. For example, if your friend Penelope was trying to help you perform better on the balance beam by offering her hand to support you and you were feeling frustrated by her assistance, wishing she'd leave you alone, the dream might be pointing to your rejection of the inner support that would allow you to maintain balance. In this example, it would be valuable to look at whether you are rejecting assistance with something in your everyday life and, if so, why.

As we've seen, the meanings you gather from dreams are not hard and fast. There is no right answer. There are always layers of meaning, and insights often continue to unfold days or weeks after you've worked with a dream. Although this may sound frustrating, if you can live the questions rather than insist upon answers, you'll get much further with the engagement of your inner world. The very act of expanding a dream, as described here, will inspire further dreams to clarify the dynamic you've identified—often through new images that point to more precise understandings of what you are dealing with in your life at that moment.

reflecting surfaces

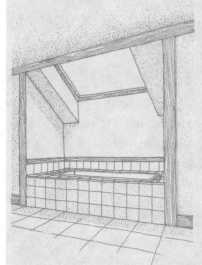

There is a way of letting light into a space through a window or a skylight so that it bounces off adjacent surfaces and bathes a room in reflected daylight. Not only does this make the room feel cheerier, but it also makes far more use of the light that enters.

On the other hand, if you place a window in the center of a wall or a skylight in the center of a ceiling, you get a shaft of light but little reflected light, so the room seems dark by contrast. Given the stark difference between light and dark areas, it's not easy to see well when you are any distance from the light source.

The life parallel is that every experience in your life is a window capable of reflecting light on your inner world. All the events of our lives are like the walls and ceilings of a house, and our experiencing of those events can, when we know how to use them, allow us to see ourselves better. But in order for this to happen, we have to have the right orientation and relationship to what we are experiencing. We need to recognize the reflectivity inherent in our experience of anything and to learn how to position ourselves—just as we do a window or a skylight—to let in as much of that life experience as possible.

A mirror is the ultimate reflecting surface. According to the basic principle of reflection, the cleaner and more perfect the mirror, the more capable it is of reflecting what is in front of it. This chapter will allow you first to recognize the potential reflecting surfaces in your life and then to clean and polish them to make them highly effective in revealing your inner landscape.

SIX

Learning to See
Through the Obstacles

We are the mirror as well as the face in it.
We are tasting the taste this minute
of eternity. We are pain
and what cures pain. We are
the sweet, cold water and the jar that pours.
—RUMI

Everything's a Reflection

A house is often described as both a reflection and an expression of the people who live in it. Often when people are planning a remodeling, their primary motivation is based on their inability, despite their best efforts, to get their house to reflect who they are and the way they feel. The remodeling, they hope, will bring their house into alignment with who they perceive themselves to be, as well as with their functional and aesthetic desires.

As we proceed with implementation of the plans for a Not So Big Life, this next step is vital. You have to be able to see through the apparent problems and obstacles preventing you from making the changes you want to make, or your efforts will not result in the remodeling you long for. It's not enough to move the furniture around; if you are like most people, you've already tried that. To bring your life into harmony with who you are inside, you have to see where the obstructions to that aim reside. Much as reading a floor plan provides you with an abstracted view of a higher dimension, reading your life reveals a new dimension of who you are, one that can make remodeling your life considerably more exciting, as well as easier to implement.

The key is this: to take what you've learned about dreams and apply it to your waking existence. Viewing every part of a dream as an aspect of yourself proves very revealing, and the same holds true when you analyze the contents of your everyday life in a similar way. But merely sighting the whale—the greater consciousness and vitality beneath surface appearances—is not enough. Now you must integrate into your waking hours the experience of being close to the whale so that you can become more awake in your life. This doesn't require that you change anything in your outer world. You simply have to be in it differently. You have to become both a participant and an observer.

Our lives are a lot like a personal movie in which we play the starring role, and our perspective on the world is the focal point through which we experience reality—much like the lens of a movie camera. If you think about an event in your life—a scene in your movie—it will be very different when seen in someone else's movie through *their* lens, even though the event itself is exactly the same. That's because every scene of your life is colored by all those conditioned patterns, both cultural and personal, that have led to the creation of the person you believe yourself to be.

In an ideal world, most of us would shape our personal movie to give us the best experience possible—not the life most jammed with stuff or stressed for time, but the one that's most rewarding and meaningful. But how can you do that? There is in fact a way. By cleaning the lens of our camera, our movie will change, and many of the old and frustrating repeats in the story line will shift and gradually disappear. As we continue to polish the lens over time, everything will appear more vibrant and alive simply because it's reflecting more of what's there in front of it. This sounds good, I know, and you may have the urge to leap up and start cleaning and polishing right away so that you can make yourself a new movie. But before this can happen, we must learn the basics of moviemaking.

The very essence of making a believable movie is fully engaging the audience in the plight of the celluloid characters. When we watch a movie, we are willing to suspend disbelief and take the story in as though it were really happening. But if directors allowed themselves to fall under the spell of their own movies, they would become so caught up in them that they would completely lose their ability to craft the story line.

That's the problem with our participation in our own movies, our waking dreams. We believe them completely, and therefore we have no way of stepping outside the story line to craft their direction. To do this, we must learn how to be objective and how to see what's really there, not just what our filters and conditioned patterns tell us.

You may have wondered sometimes why the story line of your life always seems to stay essentially the same, no matter what you do. The reason is that you can't move beyond your conditioned patterning until you've really understood it, metabolized the food that it offers, and integrated it into your life. If you do this, the good news is that things do change. What most of us don't recognize is that consciousness—the sum total of our collective waking dreams—is far more fluid and malleable than we've been led to believe. Let me give you an example of what I mean.

For many years the story line of a former client of mine had perplexed me. Lucy was almost constantly in turmoil, confronted by obstacles that would make your head spin. She often seemed contented one day and overcome by mayhem the next. And I could never quite determine what was making the difference. A couple of years ago she decided to leave everything in her home state of South Dakota and come to North Carolina. Her move was precipitated by a desire to leave behind all her troubles: her difficult boss, her aging condo, and the battle with winter that she had been fighting for fifteen years. North Carolina looked like paradise by comparison, she thought.

Until she got here. The troubles she encountered weren't exactly the same, but they sure seemed similar. The job she'd been promised evaporated before it began, and her hunt for something else produced no results. The place Lucy moved into temporarily while she looked for a house to buy became permanent as her financial resources dwindled. Unfortunately, it had a nasty cockroach problem, as well as a plumbing system that regularly malfunctioned, filling the house with a most unpleasant odor.

Finally she located a suitable position in her field, but with a schedule that would have been her last choice had she been offered one: working nights and weekends. She took the job anyway. At least she was working and earning an income. But the schedule turned out to be the least of her troubles. Things about the job she'd thought she could count on kept shifting. She was asked to work more hours. Her boss got promoted and was replaced by an ogre. You get the picture. Life was definitely not all peaches and cream, and many of the same frustrations she'd experienced in the Midwest came back full force in the South. This new movie looked a lot like the old one. But why—Lucy had started over, hadn't she? Surely things should have changed. Yet they didn't, because she hadn't understood the root cause of the chaos in her life.

As it turns out, I stumbled over that root while talking with her one day about her latest calamity. I'd heard her occasionally refer to getting only four or five hours' sleep, and I'd assumed this was a rare event. But one day something about the way she described her sleep schedule made me ask how often she experienced such sleep deprivation. Her response astounded me. "What do you mean by sleep deprivation? I've been living on four or five hours of sleep a night for most of my adult life. Doesn't everybody?" Aha! We'd struck pay dirt.

It took a little while, but Lucy finally came to appreciate that surviving on so little sleep was a recipe for chaos. Without sufficient sleep, the body is in constant distress, and the world you experience is seriously out of kilter. I know this firsthand, having gone through a period of insomnia several years ago. It's a difficult experience to describe to someone who's never had the problem, but the more sleep-deprived I became, the less I recognized myself. I became overly emotional on a regular basis. I couldn't work effectively because my brain wouldn't function properly. And I was scared a lot of the time, afraid that I'd never regain the energy and balance I'd always counted on so that I could make my way in the world. Most disturbing of all was that time simply wasn't behaving the way it did when I was healthy and replenished each night by sleep. It left me feeling constantly disoriented, unable to discern what was important or how to make decisions. It is, in short, an awful state to be in.

This, I realized, was Lucy's normal condition. She'd been sleep-deprived for so long she'd forgotten what it was like to feel balanced. Her hidden belief, which we were able to uncover with a tool that I'll share with you shortly, is that sleep is a luxury, something that no good, hard-working person should indulge in more than absolutely necessary. She'd learned this from her mother, whom she idolized but who had died when she was quite young. So her mother, who had lived in a state of significant chaos herself, represented everything good in life. Now, thanks to a lack of sleep, Lucy was experiencing the same chaos.

Lucy's belief that sleep was an indulgence had given rise to a conditioned pattern that tuned out her body's natural urges to rest, so she lived largely in panic mode, with her survival systems worn down to the nub. The degeneration of both her house and her job was a metaphor for the state of her life. Until she learned to question the legitimacy of her belief about sleep and to implement countermeasures to refute it, I knew that her personal movie would continue to provide variations on the same theme because the story line is a perfect reflection of the spiritual, mental, and physical state of the moviemaker.

I'm glad to report that with a little encouragement and some dedicated inner work, Lucy has learned to discipline herself to go to bed at an appropriate hour each night and to stay in bed until the appointed time, even when her old conditioned pattern protests. In this way she has been able to condition herself to adopt sleep habits that give her life a natural rhythm and order. Things are no longer falling apart all the time: She now has a stable job, a boss who appreciates her, and a financial situation that is gradually improving. But it wasn't until she recognized that her hidden beliefs were the real problem that things began to improve.

Your movie will change only as you change because it's just a reflection of your inner world. So to change your movie, you must learn to recognize and call into question all the hidden beliefs, patterns, and conditionings that are making you act and react the way you do. It's not that moviemaking itself is a problem. It's inevitable, in fact. But by believing the story as though it is the full extent of who you are, you'll always be like a celluloid character, your emotions keeping you identified with the part you are playing.

Remember, it's the perfectly polished lens that reflects objectively as a director sees, so your aim must be to constantly clean your lens so you become less and less identified with the story line of your movie. If you learn how to look and listen, your everyday experiences are perfectly crafted to wake you up by giving you the clues needed for that process. All the signs are there, but you won't recognize them if you maintain your belief in the outside world as completely separate from yourself.

The World Is in You

There's a dictum that Eastern sages use, and if you learn to live by it, it can change your life absolutely:

> The world is not out there; the world is in you.

Translation: Although it may appear that the forces of the world act upon you, without regard to your wishes, in fact, as we've discovered, the world is just reflecting *you* back to you. And our most debilitating beliefs, the ones that make the world appear to act in the ways that are most painful, are usually completely invisible to us. So without some guidance from sources outside ourselves, it's difficult, if not impossible, to make the changes needed to reestablish balance, as we don't even know those beliefs are there.

Remember the movie *Field of Dreams* and its unforgettable line "If you build it, they will come"? In order to apply that line to our waking dream, we can change it slightly to say "If you believe it, so it will be." That's how it works—believe something, and your movie shifts to reflect that belief. It's one of the most astounding attributes of consciousness, although we have a hard time accepting that something so simple can be true. Yet once you start observing both your own life and the lives of your friends, you'll start to see it everywhere.

I was startled to discover an example of the way the world is in me and not the other way around just a few years ago, when I became aware of the existence of one of my own hidden beliefs. I had gotten caught up in a situation at work with one of my colleagues that seemed both irresolvable and deeply distressing. Julia had been a close friend of mine for many years. I admired her creative abilities tremendously and wanted to support her in whatever way I could. We had worked on a number of projects together, and the results always seemed richer when we collaborated than when we worked alone.

But gradually our relationship started to shift. Julia began criticizing me for not giving recognition to others for their contributions to projects on which I was the lead designer. Then she started to believe that I was claiming for myself the recognition she rightly deserved for her projects. This upset me deeply because our company prided itself on giving credit where it was due. The partners encouraged the architects to cite themselves first and the company second whenever they were describing a project; in the field of architecture, this was nothing short of revolutionary. These values were something that my partners and I held dear. We believed that if people are allowed to be creative and if their creativity is recognized, they will be happy, productive, and fulfilled. That sounds all well and good, doesn't it? But for me at least, there was a hidden belief beneath this one that I didn't become aware of until much later. That belief has to do with *keeping* everybody happy and fulfilled all the time.

I'm going to go into this story in some depth so that you can see first-hand how hidden beliefs play out and how they provide the perfect conditions for allowing us to see ourselves. My fear of confrontation, which dated back to my childhood, meant that it was tremendously important, in my life, to create an environment in which people were unlikely to get angry, most especially with me. If I was always supportive and always trying to ensure a fulfilling environment for my co-workers, how could they ever fault me? On the surface the plan looked fail-safe, but that didn't take into account Julia's conditioned pattern, which was to be on the lookout for inequity and for ulterior motives. So every time she perceived me doing something self-sacrificing or altruistic, she grew wary. She was sure I had a hidden agenda. This was true, in fact, but not in the way she imagined. I was trying to guarantee peace and harmony to protect myself, not with a subversive agenda. The result was a combination of conditioned patterns perfectly devised to reveal me to me.

But it took me a long, painful time to get it. All I could see for at least a year, maybe longer, was that Julia misunderstood me. I tried everything I knew to prove to her that I was trustworthy. I was painstakingly considerate in anything related to her or her work. I solicited her opinion on things that I would normally have taken care of myself. And I was fastidious in giving her the recognition she deserved, hoping this would make everything better. But of course Julia, through the filter of her conditioned pattern, interpreted my care and attention as evidence that I was hiding something. With my every attempt to be solicitous, things seemed to get worse, and I couldn't understand why.

Then a friend who worked as a management consultant offered to moderate a meeting between Julia and me in the hope of resolving the issue. Julia and I agreed. At this point I was in a lot of pain, and I simply wanted the trouble to stop. I knew I was a good and kind person. I was sure that if Julia and I could talk reasonably, we could leave all this silliness behind and get on with our work and our lives. Surely she would quickly come to see that I was trustworthy.

Notice that, at the time, all of this was the "other" person's problem. "Julia just doesn't understand me," I thought. But remember that this was my movie, my waking dream. Though at the time I believed the problem was Julia's and I just happened to be an innocent bystander, in fact this is never, ever the case. If you are emotionally involved, if you are having a reaction to someone or something in your life, it is the world reflecting you back to you. This "scene" is appearing in your movie to allow you to understand yourself better. It has nothing whatsoever to do with the reactions *others* are having to you; that's *their* movie. That's for them to deal with, if and when they choose to do so. But that's not your business. Your business is to understand why this scene is taking place in *your* movie.

At our meeting the consultant asked Julia to tell me what she thought of me and why she distrusted my intentions. I don't recall Julia's words at all. All I remember is a growing sense of doom as I realized just how strongly she felt. "How can I ever bridge this gulf?" I wondered. When the consultant asked me if I would like to respond, I shook my head. I was speechless. I was afraid that I might make matters worse, so I just sat there mute, longing for Julia to understand how much I cared about her.

All this was perfectly normal behavior for me when someone in my presence was angry. I *knew* that when someone was angry, you should remain silent until they calmed down and it was safe to speak. That was one of my most deeply hidden beliefs. If your conditioned patterns are different from mine, at this point you are thinking, "That's crazy! How can you ever resolve any dispute if you don't speak?" But I was blind to this at the time. There was one absolute in my universe: If someone is angry, don't speak. To express your own thoughts and feelings in such a situation is dangerous.

After the meeting ended, the consultant asked me why I hadn't spoken up for myself. She asked me if I realized that my silence had in all likelihood confirmed Julia's belief that I was conniving and untrustworthy. But at that point I couldn't think or feel much of anything. I was in a state of very deep distress. I still didn't understand that the problem wasn't Julia's. To expect the solution to come through a revelation on Julia's part is like expecting a character in your nighttime dream to get the meaning of your dream for you. The point was not for me to help her solve *her* problems but for me to identify the blocks in *my own* engagements with the world. And those have very little to do with the specific content of the situation, which is simply there to reveal the underlying dynamics of your conditioned patterning.

In other words, it's all your stuff. The world is not out there; the world is in you, just as your nighttime dreams are in you. It's not that there aren't real people and places and objects surrounding the object you call your body, but all the meanings you attribute to everything that happens out there are in your waking dream alone. To shift the story line, you have to begin by seeing the dynamics at work below the content.

For that to occur, you have to be willing and able to look at that content objectively, without defensiveness and without self-righteousness. It's no small task. All our lives we're taught to protect and defend our thoughts, feelings, and experiences and to believe without question that they are who and what we are. But it's not until we can look at these things as dispassionate observers that we can start to digest the fragments of conditioned patterns that are getting in the way of our seeing clearly what's really happening. Once you do see, and once you engage in those dynamics differently, everything will change without your having to do anything at all, because your waking dream will be reflecting the new you, absent the old filter.

Once I came to see the hidden belief behind the way I'd acted with Julia, the experience of my waking dream shifted dramatically. It turned out that it wasn't only with Julia that I was not speaking up for myself. There were several situations in my life at that moment in which I wasn't saying what I needed to say because I thought that doing so would make the other person more angry. No wonder I'd been feeling blocked up. My life had a severe case of constipation.

At the time all this was happening, I was beginning to work with a spiritual teacher, Al, who quickly recognized the nature of the distress I was experiencing with Julia and with others. In order to evoke the fear of speaking up when in the presence of an angry other, he enacted the role of a fierce and irate combatant. He instructed me to hold on tight to one end of a rolled-up towel while he held on to the other. He began tugging hard at the towel, so that I had to clutch it to my solar plexus in order not to lose it. While continuing our tug-of-war, he started to taunt me and aggravate me in such an amazing variety of fearsome ways that by the end of twenty minutes I was shaking with fright. But still I hadn't spoken. It hadn't occurred to me to speak. I was too afraid, and my conditioned pattern was still firmly in place, telling me in no uncertain terms that it wasn't safe to do so.

Whereas in everyday life the antagonism usually subsides, he didn't stop. He jeered at my refusal to respond verbally. He pushed me to stand my ground, to argue, to say what was going through my mind. I knew what I had to do, but still I couldn't do it. It felt too dangerous, even though I knew my current predicament was just a scenario intended to evoke this very fear. He kept at me for forty-five minutes, until finally I cracked. I felt a surge of indignation, a rush of fierceness that had been held down by the fear, and then the liberating exhilaration of saying what I needed so desperately to say. A string of expletives erupted from my mouth, and I nearly yanked my teacher off his feet with a strength I didn't know I had. He had me repeat my primary and most wrathful declaration (a much less hygienic version of "I'm mad as hell and I'm not gonna take it anymore!") again and again, so that I could feel completely the fury that I'd kept bottled up inside for so long. It was, in a word, *great*. He had just administered an amazing psychological enema, and I suddenly understood how to engage the energy of speech under fire.

I was no longer mute. I was suddenly able to speak the words I needed to clear up each of the blockages in my life, not by contriving or planning but simply by saying what came to mind in the moment, unfiltered and unobstructed by the conditioned pattern that used to tell me it was too dangerous to do so.

That may sound too easy, but it really happened that way. Speaking up simply wasn't an issue anymore and no longer evoked a reaction in me. It didn't even come out as anger. I just did it. That's how you can tell that the hidden belief that created a conditioned pattern has been fully understood, not just intellectually, but through and through. No more reactivity.

In all likelihood, what was making Julia distrustful was the very fact that I was making an effort to fix things, to make them better for her. This act was by its very nature not *real*. Instead of telling her what was really going on inside my mind—my frustration at being misunderstood and my fears about the potential volatility of the situation—I was instead pretending that everything between us was fine. So I wasn't really acting out of concern for her but in large part to protect myself from confrontation. It was a contrivance, and Julia was sensitive enough to pick that up. But what she read into that contrivance arose from *her* hidden beliefs and *her* conditioned patterns. That issue was part of her waking dream and not for me to concern myself with. It's not my job to change her. In fact, it is completely impossible for me to do so. The only thing I can change is my-self, and when I do, the rest of the world shifts simply because it now re-flects the new version of me rather than the old one.

Your Turn

As you read through my description of working with and changing my patterns, you may be wondering how to create the same kinds of circumstances in your own life. Here's how to create the condi-tions that can lead to understanding, and so to change.

1. Observe yourself carefully as you engage in a situation in which fear or anger normally arises.
2. As you are experiencing it, see if you can identify the hidden be-lief behind the fear or anger. It's often quite obvious at such times.
3. In naming the belief, allow yourself to feel completely whatever arises mentally, emotionally, and physically, while staying aware that the response is simply the product of a conditioned pattern and not reality.

In this way you are simultaneously experiencing your normal response and maintaining objectivity, which makes it possible for you to move through the block that created the hidden belief in the first place. If you engage in this approach, the circumstances to help you refute the belief will present themselves, and you'll be able to grow beyond the limitations of the unwanted conditioned pattern.

It looks and sounds so straightforward when put this way, and it is al-ways easier to see the patterns at work in other people's stories than your own—to see how and why they cause imbalance. But as the story about Julia so clearly illustrates, it's not much use just to see and understand someone else's conditioned patterns. Of course you'll understand them because they're not your issues, your hot buttons. But if you want to lib-erate yourself from your same old story, what matters is seeing and un-derstanding your own hidden beliefs. And that's the only way, short of a lightning bolt of grace from above, to change the quality and character of your waking dream.

All There Is, Is You

I've described this particular situation so fully because it was, for me, the moment when I understood the phrase "All there is, is you," which is one of my teacher's favorites. In your waking dream, you play every role. Your life is experienced entirely by you and serves to reveal the real you to yourself. Simultaneously, all human beings have their own points of experiencing—all engaged in their own versions of the projection we call the world.

Whenever I contemplate this notion, I often envision the human race as the compound eye of an insect. Arthropod eyes are made up of thousands of individual lenses, all bringing separate views of the surrounding reality to the brain. Each one of us is something like one of these lenses, each a separate point that's focused on the experiencing of its surroundings. We're all immersed in the same reality, yet each of us has a unique perspective on it that creates a completely different life experience, a different waking dream. No one perspective is more valid than another. The perspectives are separate but equal, and collectively they form the totality of what it is possible to experience in human form. And however wondrous and honorable, horrific and despicable we might consider some of those lens views to be, the whole would not be complete without all of them.

This idea is very difficult for us to accept because from our earliest days we're taught to differentiate right from wrong, good from bad. So our world is quickly divided into polar opposites, which we then internalize. Most of us like to identify with the forces of light—all those positive attributes that we are told are the ingredients of a good and civilized world. But as long as we live in this universe of duality, there will also and always be the dark "other."

To see with objectivity, we must be able to look at both sides of any polarity without instantly judging what's right and wrong. As difficult as this may seem, in order to find the resolution to our own pain and suffering, as well as that of the world that surrounds us, we must be willing to remain open to the possibility that we are not seeing clearly and that there are some firmly placed filters that are obscuring what's really here.

When we learn to see reality with true objectivity, we begin to appreciate that everything that happens, whether good, bad, or neutral, is simply the movement of our collective dreaming. It's just the dynamics of consciousness, and it's all happening in order that our small, individual subjective selves can start to experience more of the totality and more of the unfiltered reality that surrounds us. The point is not to develop preferences for one way of being over another or one type of experience over another but simply to engage in every experience and event in your life, good or bad, happy or sad, as an opportunity for learning more about yourself.

It's in the process of the experiencing itself that real living happens. All the rest is memory and conjecture. To fully experience life, all you need to remember is that all there is, is *you*, looking through *your* lens, your point of experiencing life, and learning to see with objectivity the unfiltered truth of existence. This is true *reality*, and when you experience it firsthand, you'll know unequivocally its vibrancy, aliveness, and meaningfulness.

Doing Double Duty

But how do you get to this point? Where can you learn the skills to stay objective in the midst of all the challenges that life throws at you? The solution lies in developing an internal observer, or "watcher," who simply takes note of your personal reactions to the events of your everyday life, much as a lab technician might watch the behavior of a chimpanzee in her care. The lab tech might write down on her clipboard, for example, the following notes while observing one of her charges:

> An hour after feeding, Rosie (2-year-old female) moves to upper-right-hand corner of loft, where she naps for 35 minutes. When startled awake by sibling, Randall (3-year-old male), she exhibits first fear, by huddling close to the corner of the cage, and then irritation, indicated by shrill chattering and boisterous shaking of head.

Notice that the observations make no assumptions about why anything happened, who was in the right and who in the wrong, whether Rosie had good reason to be afraid, or what caused the change in her behavior from fear to irritation. Notes are simply a record of what happens. That's the kind of technique we need in order to see our own behavior more accurately.

There are no judgments being made, only a record of behavior. As soon as you make judgments and determinations, you are functioning from a subjective perspective that is bound to be colored by your conditioned patterns and associated hidden beliefs. If you don't take this to heart and understand the absolute importance of impartiality, you'll find that your personality, depending upon its conditioning, will either use the data collected to beat you up internally, make you out to be some sort of higher life-form, or both. Never underestimate the personality. It's a wily opponent of objectivity.

The exercise at the end of this chapter is meant to help you develop your own watcher. When you use the technique to observe yourself, you'll be doing double duty. On the one hand, you'll be going through your routine, doing the things that you need to get done, and having your usual responses to the events that color your days. On the other hand, you'll be watching and observing *how* you are engaged and what occurs as you engage. This is one of the most valuable features of the new blueprint. It allows you to see from two perspectives simultaneously.

Once you've been observing yourself for a week or two, you'll start to notice patterns you weren't aware of before. I'll give you an example of something I observed by developing my own watcher—paper shuffling when I'm on the phone and feeling impatient. Nowadays when I find myself starting to shuffle paper instead of engaging fully in a phone conversation, I'm able to discipline myself to stop and give the conversation my undivided attention. But because I've come to know, through observation, that my paper-shuffling behavior is a signal that there are things outside my awareness that need attention, once the phone call is over, I look at my to-do list to see if there's anything I've let slide.

Now I know to look for them actively rather than let them sneak up on me and elicit my usual sense of impatience, which makes me less effective at everything I do that day, from then on. In this way I am *present* in the phone conversation and am much more likely to be present in whatever happens thereafter as well. The observing has allowed me to preempt the reflexive response of my conditioned pattern at having too many things to do.

What You Believe, That Just Ain't So

If you learn to be truly dispassionate in your observing, you may find—perhaps for the first time—some behaviors that directly contradict who you thought yourself to be. Let me give you an example. Josephine, a woman I've known since college, had always appeared mousy and tentative. In this way she conveyed her belief that she was incompetent and unreliable. She'd say things like "I probably can't do it" or "I'm not sure I'll be able to get it done in time. Perhaps you could find someone who works a little faster." Yet when she was given responsibility, she did a really good job; contrary to what she said about herself, she was both efficient and dependable.

When Josephine engaged in the watcher exercise, she wrote down events but neglected to record her reaction to them. (Keep in mind that noting and recording one's reactions is different from judging them.) She told me once that her reactions felt too big and too ugly. She recorded the external events of her day, but she'd leave out the responses, the barrage of internal dialog that colored her inner world. (This would be like the lab technician writing down all the chimp's actions but omitting a record of the many sounds the chimp made over the course of the day.) Until Josephine wrote down the thoughts she was having, very little could be revealed about her hidden beliefs. It was only once she allowed her watcher to see and record her internal self-deprecation that she was able to see a pattern that had debilitated her for decades.

In one of her early notes, she wrote, "Went to grocery store and accidentally bumped into another woman's cart. Much self-judgment ensued. Also felt judged by the woman for being such a klutz." This was a start at least, but it doesn't tell much—just that there's some internal tongue-lashing going on and she believes she's being judged by people around her. Later she began writing down more of the self-judgment. She wrote, "Took my daughter to school and watched myself as I started to feel guilty. The principal was walking around outside, apparently looking for someone. This was the sequence of my thoughts: 'Have I done something wrong?' 'Am I late?' 'I screwed up, didn't I?' 'She's judging me for being a poor excuse for a mother.' 'I'm a hopeless mother. How could I be late?' and 'Now I'm really in trouble, aren't I?' Noticed after the principal went back inside that no one said anything about my lateness. Still felt convinced that she was judging me and that I'd hear about it later. Many other children, mothers in tow, were still arriving as I hugged my daughter good-bye and left rapidly to avoid being caught and reprimanded. Had the thought 'They deserve to be reprimanded too! But the principal didn't see them, so I'll get all the blame.' "

After a while, Josephine was able to both experience the fear that arose in such situations and simultaneously observe herself having the fearful reaction. She was able to stay on the lookout for the hidden beliefs that caused the fear, and she was able to see that her assertions about her ineptitude were entirely of her own making. Thanks to the development of a watcher, she was able to see, for example, that the principal's behavior had nothing whatsoever to do with her. The judgments Josephine believed others were making about her actions were imagined. The guilty feelings arising in her had absolutely no basis in the outside world, although they seemed unequivocal in her experiencing of her waking dream. Over time the exercise of observing her behavior broke things open for her and she got some breathing room from her internal judge. She grew more able to understand that her thoughts were not her—that she was something much more capable, much more whole, and much more profound than the caricature her personality had created for her.

Breathing Space

When I talk about house design, I discuss the need for breathing space there too. It might seem that the Not So Big House wouldn't have one square foot of unused space. But this isn't the case. We need places from which to look into the more active areas of the house—observing places, if you will. Those breathing spaces—such as a landing at the top of a staircase or the area just inside the family entrance to the house—give you some perspective on the rooms you are about to enter and let you breathe and get your bearings before you proceed. If such a space is small and cramped or gives you no room to stop for a moment to look around, it feels claustrophobic, like Josephine's life before she became practiced with the watcher.

In Josephine's case, the hidden belief in her ineptitude was derived from childhood, from an overly demanding parent for whom nothing was ever good enough, fast enough, or proficient enough. So by the time Josephine was four or five years old, she had developed an internal parental voice that beat her up ahead of time in response to everything she attempted and that, unbeknownst to her, also projected these imagined forces of judgment onto others around her as well. Until she used the watcher, she'd assumed everyone lived as she did—that everyone carried on this kind of incessant internal self-criticism. Although she is not yet completely free of its presence, most of the time now she is able to remember that this voice of judgment is a self-imposed filter over reality and not what's really there.

Josephine has also learned that the louder and more insistent the self-judgment gets, the more crucial it is for her to take time to rebalance. If she sits quietly for a few minutes to shift her state or if she goes for a walk when she's feeling distraught, things will calm down. This is the effect that the breathing space makes possible.

Here's another way to look at it. If you've ever been to SeaWorld, you know that when you go to see the performance of the killer whales (a spectacular display of leaping majesty), the lower down in the amphitheater you sit—the closer to the so-called soaker seats—the more likely it is you'll get wet. When you sit in the upper part of the amphitheater, you have an entirely different perspective on the proceedings. You aren't directly involved, and you can see the whale beneath the surface before it launches itself miraculously into the air. You can see the moment when the body of this enormous creature floats for a split second in the air before the laws of gravity return it to its natural habitat. And you can watch the disturbance in the crowd below as soaked humans shriek, leap up, grimace, and shake themselves off. It is possible from the upper levels to observe the full dynamic of the process—and not get the least bit wet. This is what the watcher allows, too. You observe, and you understand what's happening, but you don't get lost in the emotional reaction.

When you engage the watcher, it's as though you are split into two characters. The part of you that's seated in the soaker section—we'll call him Hey!—is getting totally drenched by the whale as it hits the water. Hey! is experiencing the shock, the fear, the frustration, and the discomfort of the soaking, but he is also not doing what he would normally do: jumping up out of his seat and yelling at the top of his lungs. Meanwhile, the other part of you, whom we'll call Be, is seated high up in the amphitheater, looking down and watching the soaking as it happens. Both parts are communicating with each other throughout the proceedings. From time to time Be is asking Hey!, "What are you experiencing right now?" and Hey! is giving reports to Be of all the thoughts and feelings that arise as he sits there in tension, overriding his reflexive impulse to leap and shout. As the water settles back down, Hey! discovers that he is unscathed but for the wetness. With the assistance of Be, he has put in place new conditioning that contradicts the belief that to sit still and not react as usual might be life-threatening. The old belief is thus drained of its power.

So when you find yourself in life's soaker seats, allow your watcher to head for higher ground and take a look at things from that position for a while. It will allow you to see the more complete picture. The wetness—those emotional reactions—you are experiencing is only the result of one of your inner killer whales—your conditioned patterns—rising above the surface and making a splash in the middle of your life.

This is where it is absolutely crucial to remember that the world isn't doing all this stuff to you. It's *your* show, taking place in *your* amphitheater. And so when you shift your state—when you calm down, slow down, and head for higher ground—so does your waking dream because it always perfectly reflects your inner state. This doesn't mean your life is completely uneventful. There can still be lots of stuff happening, but you aren't upset by it because you are able to look down on it rather than getting soaked all the time.

I found a wonderful quotation recently, author unknown, emblazoned in large letters on a greeting card:

Peace. It does not mean to be in a place where there is no noise, trouble or hard work. It means to be in the midst of those things and still be calm in your heart.

It's so simple but so elusive until we understand how to shift states and become more present in everything we do.

EXERCISE
developing a watcher

This exercise is designed to help you see yourself more objectively, without all the conditioned patterns obscuring what's going on in your life.

Earlier in the chapter, I asked you to imagine watching the actions of a chimpanzee in its interactions with its sibling. Now it is your turn to try the technique on yourself. To begin, select a routine activity from your day and simply observe what happens. Without evaluating them, make a mental note of the thoughts that go through your head. Be aware of how your body feels and whether there are any places in the routine where you speed up or slow down. Observe your emotional state of being. Anything that comes up is there to be observed by your watcher. Choose something basic—cooking dinner, getting ready for work, driving home from a friend's house.

After you have finished the activity, write down what occurred, including all the thought streams you can remember. Don't judge or analyze—just record.

Now you are ready to explore the data you've collected to see what it reveals about your conditioned patterns and your hidden beliefs.

Question 1: Did you have few thoughts or many? Did you observe a common theme in the thoughts you had? Did you notice any pattern in where thought streams began and where they ended? How did each thought stream make you feel?

Question 2: What observations did you make about how your body felt while you were doing this activity? Did you feel tense or relaxed, tired or invigorated? Did you have any aches or pains? If so, are those common complaints, or do you experience them only when you are engaged in this activity? Did you have any other physical responses?

Question 3: What emotions, if any, did you feel while you were doing the activity? Were you angry or joyful, bored or excited? Did you find yourself wishing that you were doing something else or that the task would go more rapidly? Did you notice any internal turbulence, self-judgment, or self-congratulation in response to how you were performing the task?

Once you have practiced using your watcher on routine activities that don't have a lot of emotional charge for you, try using the technique in a more difficult situation, such as when you are upset or when things are chaotic. Maybe you have to make a big presentation at the office, and you dislike public speaking. Maybe you have to have dinner with your mother-in-law, whom you don't get along with very well. You can use the same set of questions, but now you'll find there's more to report.

You don't have to do anything more than this for now—it's the observing that is important. After you've been doing it for a while, things begin to shift all by themselves. What you will start to see is that from the higher vantage point of a more objective observer, you can automatically build in some space between yourself and your normal response to a situation, allowing you to recognize that your response is not *you*. You'll be able to step back from your reaction and note, "Hey, I'm really getting upset. I always react this way when such and such happens." It sounds like a small thing, but it is amazingly liberating. Over time you'll notice everyday nervous habits, like my paper shuffling, and bigger, less frequent reactions, such as angry outbursts or sudden tears. Both types of behavior are flags to tell you that there's a hidden belief behind the scenes and a conditioned pattern at play.

It is through this process of observation that the patterns that have been running you without your awareness will become more obvious. Once you can see them, you can train yourself to build in some breathing space and pause before you overreact, you can try alternative responses, and you can start to explore their roots.

In everything I present from here on out, it's important to understand that our personalities are easily threatened by perceived challenges to their control, and they will surreptitiously use anything and everything at their disposal to undermine our efforts to see ourselves more clearly. This may seem surprising, but, as we discussed in chapter 4, the personality, for all its charm, is in fact the obstacle to understanding, and not the savior it believes itself to be. For the personality to maintain its existence, it has to keep you convinced of the validity of your hidden beliefs, so it's going to start squawking any time now. But if you keep observing rather than evaluating, the personality runs out of material and falls silent.

It's in this stillness that something new—a Not So Big Life—can emerge, but it won't be you who makes it happen; your life circumstances change as you learn to get out of the way. Developing objectivity is a big part of that process. The watcher is your partner in seeing through the obstacles to the calmer, more contented you that you've always known was there.

PRINCIPLE
light to walk toward

Whenever I need to give a brief example of one of the design principles I describe in *Home by Design*, which is essentially a visual dictionary of all the terms used in the *Not So Big House* series, I use the principle I call "Light to Walk Toward" because it's so simple to grasp, yet so profound in its effect. You may have heard people describe near-death experiences this way. But you might not know that it also describes a conditioned response that's hardwired into our physiology and is thus just as applicable when we are very much alive. We are in fact biologically programmed to move toward light, so it's an extremely useful tool in making any room or hallway feel more inviting. Simply place a window or a lighted painting at the far end of any walkway or vista, and its brightness attracts you like a magnet. It animates the space and makes it seem significantly more vital.

The same is true with being present in your life. When you start to experience moments of presence, the result is very similar to the response to a bright window at the end of an otherwise unremarkable hallway. You'll suddenly feel more alive, and you'll want to move toward those engagements that give you the opportunity to experience presence. As you become more proficient at opening the door to *real* time and to being completely engaged in whatever it is you are doing, you'll realize that you can be present while doing anything at all.

As you start to become aware of the attractive quality of presence, take a look at the places in the buildings and houses you visit each day that make you feel most vital, and in all likelihood you'll see the principle of Light to Walk Toward at play. As you grow to understand what presence is, it will have this same power to affect your experience, and, like the brilliance pouring in through the window, it will give you an entirely new feeling about your life.

SEVEN

Improving the Quality
of What You Have

Today I recognized that that jewel-like beauty is the presence.
—RUMI

So Much to Do, So Little Time

A very important and frequently overlooked step in remodeling a house is upgrading what is already there—not the areas where walls will be removed and windows and openings inserted but the parts of the house that are in constant heavy use and aren't slated for any structural work. We all know the benefit of a new coat of paint, but there's more that can be done to spruce up the place and make it a delight without having to do a lot of work. A couple of new light fixtures, some artwork, a little splash of color here and there, and the house feels entirely different and much closer to the vision of home in your mind's eye. Big changes don't always require a big investment.

The same thing is true in our lives. Although there are certainly things that need structural work to open them up, the life equivalent of a fresh coat of paint and better lighting can have a huge impact on your daily experience. The trick here is to make what you already have more enjoyable to engage in, and, as we'll see, the delight comes primarily from changing the *way* you are involved in what you do rather than from *what* you do. It is quite a revelation to discover that a fresh perspective, like a fresh coat of paint, makes life look entirely different and feel vastly more enjoyable.

Here's where we find ourselves face-to-face with the illusion of time. When we most need the time to restore our balance, our waking dream tells us there's just not time to do so. The more we put it off, though, the more out of balance we become. Although many of us have this experience individually, this is also a dilemma we face collectively, with the world moving at such an incredible pace that we seem unable to slow things down enough to tend to even the most basic physical necessities. All we can do is attend to the needs and dictates of the dream we're so convinced is real.

It's time now to take what we've seen about the nature of our waking dream and learn how to participate in it differently. This will require a new way of engaging time, a way that expands our experience of it to give us all the time we need without our ever feeling rushed. This may sound like a pipe dream, but it's not. It's entirely possible and entirely within your reach, just as it's entirely possible to make a house feel more spacious without adding any square footage to it.

The problem we have in accepting this is our belief that time is linear, divided into increments, or containers, into which we place our engagements and activities. A football game on television requires at least a two-and-a-half-hour container of time, for example, while a game of solitaire might take only a three-minute container. We might reasonably assume, then, that if we were to play twenty games of solitaire per hour for two and a half hours, our experience of time would be the same as that of watching a football game. But that isn't the way time works. Whereas a half hour of solitaire can be calming, two and a half hours would make most of us a little crazed.

That same container of time, though, passes much more rapidly when you are engaged in something you really enjoy. So for a football enthusiast the time spent watching a football game might pass rapidly, while for someone who is bored by the sport, the time might crawl by. And for someone engaged as a participant in the game, time might well disappear altogether. Being completely at one with the game means that the particular moment being engaged in is the only thing there is, just like that Olivetti moment from my childhood; time is no longer part of a linear progression but one continuously unfolding moment. For that player, now is all there is. By being completely present, he is outside of time in the way we normally think of it, and for him the question of too little time or too much doesn't even come up. When you are completely present, time is simply not an issue because in a very real sense you have at your disposal all the time in the world.

Think back to the days when you were in elementary school or junior high. Remember how summers used to stretch out endlessly? When I think back on the summers of my childhood, I recall them as never-ending, at least until the week before school started again. Every day seemed like an endless expanse of time waiting to be filled with whatever my siblings and I could dream up to do—playing with friends, riding our bicycles, painting and coloring, watching television. Although we were pretty good at entertaining ourselves, there were times when we didn't know what to do next. Then it felt as if we had too much time—a far cry from the experience of my adulthood.

Searching for a Sense of Home

So our primary problem with engaging time in the conventional way is that we're thinking of it as a container of a specific size—a 24/7 size, as we are fond of saying today—when in fact our experiencing of time has almost nothing to do with the size of the container. If you are familiar with my books about architecture and house design, you may hear a resonance in these words. When I speak about today's houses and why they are getting bigger and bigger, I often say this:

We are all looking for home, but we're looking with the wrong tool. We are trying to find home through more square footage, when in fact the quality of home has almost nothing to do with size. Instead, it's to be found in the *qualities* of space rather than the *quantities*. And when you build space that's beautifully tailored to your lifestyle rather than filled with all the latest rooms and gizmos, there's a kind of moreness, and that's what really makes you feel at home.

I believe we all want to feel at home in our lives as well, but once again we're using the wrong tool. We are trying to find more minutes and hours in each day to do the things we value when in fact the way to feel at home in our lives has almost nothing to do with duration. It's to be found in the qualities of time rather than the quantities. And when you engage time by being completely involved in whatever it is you are doing rather than trying to cram everything into it, you experience a moreness that makes you feel at home in your life.

But how can you let go and just be in the moment when you've got a to-do list that's a mile and a half long and everything on it has reached a crisis point? Think back to Josephine. She learned that what seemed to be the very worst moment to sit quietly for a few minutes or go for a short walk was the very time when such an activity was most needed. At such moments everything inside you will scream, "That's crazy! I'm making a huge mess of this as it is. All hell will break loose if I step away now!" But in fact the opposite is true. If you *don't* take time now, all hell *will* break loose, because the world is not out there, the world is in you. You are generating the frenetic pace, as well as the feeling of being limited by time. If you are calmer, things won't look the same way. All the chaos and panic and pressure will be unrecognizable when you are present, when you are completely at one with what you are doing.

Back before I understood this myself, I used to try to rush through my to-do list so that I'd have time to be present afterward. I was still buying into the time-is-a-container mentality, believing that the to-do list required a certain quantity of time and if I speeded up a bit, I could carve out some minutes or hours within the time container that I could then use to be present in.

But presence is not something you decide to experience when you have time. Presence *is*. Presence is *now*, and now is eternal, without boundary. You have to show up, however, to really be here, to experience it. Whether you are the kind of person who obsessively overschedules or the kind who resists the very idea of a schedule, the same principle holds true. If you can engage each item on your to-do list by being completely at one with what you are doing, you will discover there's plenty of time.

When you are fully engaged in what you are doing, there's no planning going on in your head about what you are going to do next and no thinking about how well you did what you did last; there's no procrastinating or worrying about all the things still to be done—in other words, there's no past or future. The result is that you'll feel totally at home in your life because there is now no separation between you and what you are doing. You can be relaxed and present in everything you do.

I know what you're thinking: "She can't be serious. How can I be at one with what I'm doing when I've got _____ to do?" (Fill in the blank with the items on your impossibly long list.) Or "She doesn't know my situation. It's different. I'm a _____." But I *am* serious. And in fact this is the only way you will ever get out of your time bind and lower the stress level in your life. So even though it seems impossible to accept right now and even though part of you probably doesn't even want to believe it, remember that this is just the conditioned pattern your personality has developed as a survival mechanism. Keep reading, and I'll show you how this can work, even for you.

Going with the Flow

Think of leaves on the surface of a stream. They're floating along, carried by the current. Some drift from one side to the other as the stream flows along, whereas others appear to be floating more or less down the central channel. If you follow one particular leaf with your eyes, however, you'll discover that a leaf that's moving fast at one minute will be aimlessly sidelined a few minutes later, and a leaf that is slow-moving at this minute will become speedy the next. Every leaf has its natural passage downstream, but if you were to try to write a script for each leaf and coordinate it with the scripts for all the other leaves, you would have a monumental task on your hands. If, in addition, you thought you were responsible for getting each leaf to its proper destination and if you believed that your not doing so would result in all the leaves bumping into one another and blocking their collective progress downstream, you'd be thinking like a typical micromanager, a "time obsesser." If, on the other hand, you believed that no leaf should be forced to flow if it didn't want to and that it was up to you to hold back the flow so that each leaf could exercise its free will, you'd be thinking like a "time resister." Neither approach is tenable. The river and the leaves will move and flow just the same, and all you'd be doing by obsessing or resisting would be burning yourself out.

At my Minneapolis architectural firm we developed a personnel and project-management system that was based more on the dynamics of unrestricted leaf flow than on time management. Although we were often met with raised eyebrows from colleagues in other companies when we described the system, it worked beautifully and continues to do so to this day. In most firms, the task of scheduling personnel typically falls on a single individual—usually one of the partners. With larger projects, where a number of people work on a single assignment for months at a time, this works well, but for a firm like ours, with many projects with unpredictable ebbs and flows, the normal management model for architectural firms was highly inefficient.

So ours was a system invented out of necessity. As the staff grew from two to five to ten and up to around forty-five by 1999, when I left, it became clear that if all of us—principals included—wanted to continue to engage in the activity we loved most—designing—we'd have to develop a system that allowed for individuals to communicate easily and regularly with one another about their workloads, personnel needs, and time commitments. Because most of our projects were small, each project architect had multiple projects going simultaneously. Trying to track and orchestrate personnel requirements for all the projects we had going at any one time would have been more than a full-time job, and not one that any of us would have relished.

By the time we were about ten people strong, the typical approach to scheduling wasn't working well, so we decided to implement a weekly lunch meeting for all employees, at which we would share our current work needs and obligations. The beauty of the system was that it allowed all of us to identify our needs from our particular perspective and permitted the firm as a whole to respond. So a draftsman was able to let all of us know that in two weeks he'd be available to work on a new project because his current work was coming to an end. A project architect was able to indicate that she needed an architecture student with good model-making and drawing skills to help with two remodeling projects. Another project architect could let us know that one of his biggest projects had been put on hold and that he needed more work ASAP.

As each person spoke, others around the table could indicate their availability or their ability to provide work for someone else. And without any apparent effort, matters always seemed to work out. The meetings allowed us to see into the near future without making complex charts, and they kept us from attempting to fix and make concrete a flow that was constantly moving and changing. As the firm grew, we kept the system in place but birthed new "branches" of the office, keeping each branch to twenty-five people, the maximum number with which the system could retain its agility and effectiveness. When I left, the firm had two branches. Now it has three. The identities of the branches are both collective and separate, with work flow needs shared among the branches just as they are among the individuals in each branch.

What most of us don't fully understand but this system acknowledged, more or less by accident, is that when things are allowed to flow, they get resolved. They resolve themselves in the moment and not through planning or trying to take control of the process. When leaves are allowed to move freely, as our workload lunch meetings proved time after time, they find their way downstream almost effortlessly. In so doing, for purposes of this metaphor, they are perfectly present in their activity of floating. They are doing what's in front of them to do—moving with the current—and in the process, as a by-product of their engagement, they're moving downstream. The objective of each leaf is not movement downstream but engagement with the current, which results in the experience of floating.

It's when we try to make a script to follow exactly or when we ignore the passage of time entirely that we get into trouble, just as the leaves would if they tried to get to the right place at the right moment or if they struggled to stay put rather than where the current was taking them. We assume that what's important is the movement downstream—the destination—when in fact it's the involvements with ourselves and with one another in each new moment that really matter, that bring satisfaction and meaning into our lives. And that involvement, of course, is the journey—the process of engaging fully in every experience that comes your way. That is what creates the natural flow and constant unfolding of a Not So Big Life.

It's not that preplanning is either good or bad, but you have to use discernment to determine what requires some planning and what can be allowed to unfold. For the time-obsessed, it's the contrivance of preplanning every interaction, the "efforting" involved in the implementation of that plan, and the lack of unscripted time in which to do what *really* needs to be done in the moment that cause problems. For the time-resistant, it's the determination to stay free of time's limiting characteristics, the absence of any planning whatsoever, and the resulting lack of awareness of what *really* needs to be done in the moment that cause frustration. Either approach keeps you out of the natural flow, separated from the knowledge that everything is moving exactly as it needs to; in truth, there's not a leaf out of place.

Being in Your Doing

With the leaf example in mind and its lessons more or less understood, we can now look at how we might be present in our everyday activities.

But first, I can almost hear you resisting this idea. If I were in your shoes, reading this notion for the first time, I might be saying this to myself:

She can't be serious. How can I be at one with what I'm doing when I've got a book to write in six months? In the meantime, I have to travel all over the county to promote my last book; I have to design and coordinate with a group of colleagues the production of a show house for the International Builders' Show in January; I have to conduct dozens of interviews for radio, television, magazines, and newspapers, explaining everything from how to redesign a bathroom to how the house of the future will be made differently. And just to make things a little more challenging, soon I'm going to travel to India for two weeks. *She doesn't know my situation. It's different.*

I won't go on, but yesterday I had to deal with all these things as well as a lot of other minor management items so that everyone involved could keep doing what needed to be done and the various deadlines involved could be met. If I were to try to orchestrate my time with a fixed script, I would feel overwhelmed almost instantly. But that's not the way I engage it. I have interviews scheduled, and I have my writing time designated and treated as sacrosanct, but all the other bits and pieces I stay aware of and complete as opportunities arise. It's almost as though they are floating around my mind like balloons but I'm actively thinking about only the one I'm involved with at the moment. When I don't try to push or force things to happen, everything miraculously gets done. And sometimes things that appeared to be important items on my to-do list evaporate altogether as the result of a change or shift behind the scenes or at someone else's workplace.

I'll give you an example of the minimiracles that occur when you let go of trying to control the process of executing your to-do list. I didn't, in fact, end up starting the perspective drawing yesterday that I'd been planning to work on for the showhouse at the International Builders' Show because I found out that by waiting a few more days I would be able to get a computer-drawn model from the company producing the blueprints, which would save me several hours of drawing time. This was well worth waiting for. Had I plowed ahead in a more rigidly determined way with this seemingly high-priority item on my to-do list, I wouldn't have discovered that the computer-drawn model was available because I wouldn't have had time to respond to an e-mail, the response to which provided me with this piece of information.

By opening up the time when I'd assumed I'd be drawing, I then became available to take a phone call and find out that a change in the plans for the showhouse would allow us to provide a better display area for a favorite participant in previous showhouse projects. This participant, a sponsor, had told us that he couldn't participate this year because there wasn't sufficient space for his display. I'd been disappointed, but at the time there was nothing I could do to remedy the situation. Now I had time to call him and discuss the new opportunity. He signed on and then told me about a sister company that would like to work with us in another area of the house, the kitchen, where for some reason we'd been having a hard time finding an appliance sponsor. Suddenly, in a matter of a half hour, by simply going with the flow of the day, we now had two new sponsors on board for the showhouse, and a major difficulty—no appliance sponsor—had been resolved.

This is *real* effectiveness, and, as you can see, it has almost nothing to do with the container vision of time. A certain chunk of time opened up because I was relaxed enough to let things shift, and then the mini-miracles started happening. No amount of planning or scheduling could have made these things happen. It was one of those moments when you might say, "I was just in the right place at the right time." But that isn't really accurate. A better way of saying it is that "I was simply being in my doing." When you are present and receptive in what you are doing, things move effortlessly to resolve areas of tension, just as the flow of the current loosens a leaf from an obstacle, and you find that what you need is provided for you in ways that you couldn't possibly have imagined.

Following the Synchronicities

A woman named Dr. Jan Adams—the first person I ever asked to be my teacher in the art of living more consciously—gave me a valuable piece of advice a few years ago. She told me, "Follow the synchronicities." She explained that when you start to see synchronous events in your waking dream, it's a pretty good clue that you are "in tune" with the flow of the moment. So, for example, when I heard a radio program about famous gardens around the country and the story referred to a chapel designed by one of my favorite architects, E. Fay Jones, at the Powell Gardens just outside Kansas City, Missouri, I made a mental note. Two weeks later, I was invited by some clients to visit them in Kansas City, and the synchronicity of the radio program and the invitation led me to accept the offer. I made a point of visiting the gardens and the chapel, where I noticed a construction detail in the roof design that perfectly solved a design problem I'd been struggling with.

The more synchronicities you see, the more in-tune-ness that particular path will offer. This may sound like magical thinking, but in fact it's fundamental to how things work. Consider the principles of musical harmony for a moment. We know that when the strings of a violin or guitar are in tune, the music the instrument produces is much more harmonious than it would be if they were out of tune. In the same way, when you are in tune with the world around you, the movements of your waking dream are harmonious. By following the synchronicities, you are simply receiving clues from your waking dream that show you the paths to greater harmony.

And when things seem seriously out of tune and nothing seems to be cooperating, it's worth looking to see what, if anything, you are resisting. What is being asked of you that you are refusing to do on principle? What is the hidden belief behind that refusal? Pause, take a deep breath, and see if there isn't a way to be in what you are doing differently, in a way that isn't either micromanaging the flow or hanging on to your preconceived ideas of how things should be.

Just because you are in tune and following the synchronicities, however, doesn't mean there won't be bumps in the road, as well as major hills and valleys. Those are part of the harmony of the unfolding, just as crescendos and diminuendos are parts of a piece of music. Synchronicities can and do abound amid periods of strife and angst as well. Just because things don't feel good or don't coincide with your vision of harmony doesn't mean they're not providing just what you need in order to learn more about yourself. We often mistake the meanings of harmony and peace. It's the stillness and calm in your heart in the midst of whatever is happening that matter—how you *are* in your various activities, your doings. This is where presence resides, in the place where you and what you are doing are one and the same.

The moment you wonder, "Am I present?" you're not. That's why it's so tricky initially, because when you are present, you aren't thinking about yourself at all. You are simply and completely engaged in what you are doing. You are, in those moments, in the *now,* and time, paradoxically, is both nonexistent and infinite.

If right now this all seems impossible or frustrating and beyond your capability, relax. It'll come. Just like any other skill you learn, it takes—what else?—time. When you learn a musical instrument, the first few weeks or months can be a challenge because you've only barely learned to read music and are still fumbling to find the correct position for your fingers on the keys or the frets. But over time you don't even need to look for the notes anymore. It is your practicing while staying relaxed and open to what is being learned that allows the music making to become effortless.

The art of presence is very much the same. Stay relaxed—no obsessing or resisting required—and in short order you'll be experiencing the flow for yourself.

Burnout

Before I learned about presence, my life, like that of so many people today, was anything but effortless. There was a period in my life, maybe a dozen or so years ago, when I thought I was going to go insane, given what I had on my plate every day. The architectural firm that a partner and I had founded was flourishing. We were receiving lots of press for our work, and that in turn was generating a host of inquiries about our services. We had to develop a process for managing all the interest, and every architect in the firm was stretched to the limit, trying to keep up with the needs of existing clients as well as the influx of new ones.

During one week in particular, I attended six or seven meetings with potential clients. Because all of the potential jobs were remodeling projects, I went to the clients' houses rather than having them come to our offices. Everything was going along more or less okay—although I was way too busy and feeling pretty stressed—until it came time for a follow-up meeting with one of the prospective new clients, who called to say yes, she had decided to hire me. As the new customer rattled on enthusiastically about the things she wanted to do with her home, I realized, with a sinking feeling in the pit of my stomach, that I couldn't remember which of the houses I'd seen was hers. I'd conducted so many meetings with potential clients that week that all the faces and houses had merged in my mind. I fumbled through my notes, attempting to figure out who this person was, but I couldn't remember. And the more I worried, the more confused I got.

All my life I'd prided myself on being organized, on top of things, capable of juggling many projects simultaneously. Had I reached my limit? After getting off the phone, having successfully veiled the fact that I couldn't remember who the client was, I looked up her address in my notes, got into my car, and drove past the house. As I turned the corner onto her street, all the specifics of the meeting I'd had with her flooded back, jolted into memory by the visual characteristics of the house and the street. Breathing a sigh of relief, I returned to the office and launched the project—the addition of a family room and a kitchen redo—in a more composed frame of mind. But the experience taught me an important lesson: When you try to squeeze into your workday and workweek more than they can readily accommodate, you lose track of what you are doing, and you can't do any of it well.

One of the most difficult skills to develop is the ability to say no when you know that's what the situation requires. Because we place such a high value on a can-do attitude, we lose sight of what's actually possible. We give one another accolades for doing more than is humanly possible in less time than is feasible and assume that the results are good. But they're not. They're not good for the people performing the superhuman feats. They're not good for the people receiving the services performed by the overtaxed workers. And they're not good for future generations, who will inherit the results of work performed by individuals functioning at the precarious edge of their capabilities.

A co-worker at one of the first architectural firms I worked for used to put in twelve to sixteen hours a day on a regular basis. I found him sleeping under his desk a couple of times when I arrived at the office early; he hadn't gone home the night before. He seemed totally devoted to his projects, and I know the bosses were initially impressed with his diligence. But over the course of the year I worked there, I watched this man lose his temper over silly issues—like a letter whose margins were set incorrectly by a hapless secretary or a borrowed electric eraser that was returned to the "wrong" corner of his desk. And when he got angry, he didn't display a quiet frustration. All forty of us were subjected to tirades that often lasted half an hour before he'd settle back down, snorting like an offended bull.

It appeared that in his life there was no such thing as a good day. And his projects, far from being well served by his apparent devotion, always seemed to be going badly. Eventually the company's owners realized the problem and insisted that he reduce the number of hours he was working each week. Only then did his behavior change. He no longer lost his temper all the time, and, despite his working fewer hours, his projects got done faster, and his clients were happier. So were his colleagues.

Everyone loses when people push themselves too hard or when they are pushed too hard by their employers, yet somehow we convince ourselves that ours is a good system and we are getting more things done by living this way. What we're really accomplishing is burnout. When things speed up to the point where you can't remember what you are doing or why you are doing it, there's absolutely no hope of being present in what you are doing. The energy that's wasted in the process is horrifying, and ironically, it takes significantly longer to accomplish the task at hand. When you are constantly pushing yourself, you feel exhausted, uninspired, and disenchanted with whatever career path you are on. I used to have a friend whose favorite phrase was "You don't get paid any more for liking it," a sad testament to the state in which so much work is performed.

If what you do for a living doesn't inspire you and doesn't allow you to flourish, then why are you doing it? When you listen to what your body and your intuition are telling you and when you slow down a bit so that you can be more engaged, tasks that seemed stultifying when you were overtaxed can reveal themselves to be of a very different character. They can be stimulating and enthralling when you are well rested and in a more peaceful state of mind and thus in a higher or more open state of being. It's not the task that's the problem; it's the speed at which you are trying to do it and the lack of presence as you engage.

I was taught an important lesson along these lines by one of my early clients, a medical doctor. To provide the best service possible for everyone I worked for, I set self-imposed deadlines and expectations that defined how fast I should complete the various aspects of a project. The process of creating the final drawings can take months, and there's always a big push as the blueprints for a house near completion. At the time I was working on the project for the doctor, we had only one employee, and he was busy drawing up another project. I therefore had to do all the work on this project myself, and I worked long hours to get the drawings completed according to the time line I'd set for myself.

I'd told my client I'd have the drawings to him on a Friday afternoon. But by midmorning on that Friday, I realized there was just no way I could complete them in the time allotted. I needed another couple of days. I called to tell him how sorry I was. "No problem," he replied. "Next week will be fine." But I was still a woman on a mission, so I didn't pay much heed to his response. I had a deadline, and I'd missed it, but I was going to get the project completed as soon as I possibly could.

I pulled an all-nighter, worked all day Saturday, got about five hours' sleep Saturday night, and finished up the drawings at 11:30 a.m. on Sunday. After printing out a set of copies of the completed drawings, I hopped into my car and drove to my client's house without even stopping for coffee or a bite of breakfast. I'll never forget standing on his doorstep with the roll of drawings in my hand. I was exhausted, but I felt that I had done a good thing. I was about to deliver the promised drawings to my client, and although I was late, I wasn't all that late. I rang the doorbell, and he opened the door a few moments later.

"What are you doing here on a Sunday?" he asked. I thrust the drawings toward him, but he stepped back. "I don't need these today, and I told you as much," he said. "Take a look at yourself in the mirror." He pointed to a mirror, and I looked. "You look terrible," he observed. He was right—there were dark rings under my eyes, my face was pale and haggard, my hair disheveled. "You've worked yourself half to death to bring me these drawings today, and I don't need them right now. Now take your drawings back to the office with you, and send them to me sometime next week." He paused. I was absolutely crestfallen.

"Let this be a lesson to you," he said. "Nothing is worth jeopardizing your health for. Nothing. And certainly not a project with an artificial deadline created by you. There's no honor in speed for speed's sake. Go home, eat a decent meal, and get some sleep." I did, and although I heartily resented him at that moment, I have been grateful ever since for a lesson that couldn't have been more profound or more life-changing.

From then on, every time I believed I had a deadline, I looked at it carefully in order to distinguish the real deadline from one I'd arbitrarily named. And what I discovered—and continue to discover as I strive to meet the deadlines created by others and as I attempt to see through my own—is that deadlines are only lines in the sand. If a deadline is unreasonable or unattainable without causing major disruption in your life, it is absolutely okay to ask for more time. The setter of the deadline may not be happy about giving it to you, but if you explain that the results will be dramatically better and that you are unwilling to sacrifice your health for the appearance of speed, some deadline setters will understand. Those who don't will have to live with the consequence—a project done less well. The choice is in the hands of the deadline setter, but the premium you place on your own health and sanity should be nonnegotiable.

This approach to time and deadline management is antithetical to what we are taught is appropriate workplace behavior; yet if you, like me, are a time-obsessive type, when you begin to adopt it, the results in your life will be dramatic.

There's an entirely opposite but equally intractable problem with deadlines for those who resist or ignore time. Time resisters consider a deadline arbitrary and so do not take it seriously. They often see planning and structuring time as huge and impossible tasks, chores that can result only in frustration. Whereas the time obsesser overplans, the time resister is baffled by the idea of taking action now to make sure that something is completed at a particular point in the future.

If you recognize yourself in this description, avoiding deadlines is only feeding into your personality's preference for no schedule, so for you, too, it will be beneficial to do the *opposite* of what you would typically do. Instead of resisting a deadline, give yourself a schedule to follow that will allow you to meet it with ease. Then pay attention to your resistance and avoidance patterns as you go about implementing the schedule, without getting down on yourself if you find you've misjudged the amount of time required for a particular task. It will take a while to learn how to prioritize, plan, and follow through, but once you do, you'll notice a dramatic decrease in the number of emergencies that arise. Over time you'll find that there's a lot less panic and frustration in your life as a result.

Burnout is the result of our conditioned patterns. Those who resist scheduling often find themselves just as burned out as their overscheduled counterparts. If you always blow deadlines, your challenge is to learn to meet deadlines. If you always make deadlines, your challenge is to learn to ask for more time when you need it. The medicine that's right for you may be one of these solutions, or it may be somewhere in between. Practice going toward the opposite of your typical behavior pattern and building in opportunities for coming to presence. When you are neither obsessing nor resisting, the mind finally relaxes and you can actually be here, fully engaged in what you are doing.

Life Juice

Anytime you feel that you are fighting or pushing to get something done or resisting what needs to be done, there is separation between you and the task, and so by definition you are not present in what you are doing, your judgments and reactivity in effect locking the door. You are also expending much more chi, or life force, than is necessary.

This Chinese word—chi—provides a useful clarification of the dynamics of consciousness because it not only refers to the life energy that flows through all things but also indicates the importance of balance in order for a system or body to be healthy and vital. When we're forcing or resisting, we're pushing the whole system—our bodies and everything around us—out of balance. It's just as wasteful to burn chi this way as it is to drive a car that gets ten miles to the gallon. It's not that you can't do it. You can. But the gas-guzzler's cost of operation, its effect on the environment, and its contribution to the depletion of natural resources are all unnecessary and ultimately damaging.

When you conduct your daily activities in a state of presence, there's no waste. In fact, you feel invigorated by the activities because being present is like an energy faucet. No matter what you are doing when you are present, you are like the football player immersed in the game. You don't need a gas tank, and you don't need to worry about running out of fuel. The fuel is always ample as long as you remain present.

The key to changing your experience of time is to become present by slowing down and staying aware of your surroundings. This doesn't mean stopping everything you are doing; you don't have to switch careers or leave your job. Neither does it mean becoming lazy; on the contrary. It simply means taking the time to engage fully in whatever you are doing, whether that is writing a memo, answering e-mail, washing dishes, or cleaning the bathroom. When your mind and heart are open and engaged in what you are doing, that's when the life juice of the present moment flows unimpeded.

Your Turn

If you slow down your body but find that your mind is still racing, you may want to implement the following practice. It is a way to perforate your day with mini-pauses that remind you of what's going on beneath the story line of your waking dream. It works the same way as a fifteen-minute break from work, but these breaks are shorter and more frequent. Here's the practice: Every fifteen minutes, take ten seconds to pause and notice what is happening in your body and your mind.

You'll need a timer with a repeat function to alert you to the fifteen-minute intervals. There are all sorts of watches and vibrating clocks available in the marketplace these days; a number of them are featured on the Not So Big Life website. You can even use an egg timer in a pinch, though if you are around others much of the day, it might drive them crazy in short order, so the silent variety of reminder is preferable.

Although this exercise sounds simple, its effects can be profound because it will bring you into the moment over and over again. If you'd like to learn more about its uses and potentials, look for the detailed description on the Not So Big Life website.

The Unfolding Moment

Although we believe we are in control of our lives, when we let go and let things unfold, everything moves more smoothly, often in ways we couldn't possibly have imagined. There was a wonderful example of this experience at a gathering I went to a year ago. We had been asked to bring flowers with us, but beyond that we hadn't been told what to expect.

As thirty of us sat in a circle waiting for the proceedings to begin, the teacher handed out small vases to everyone and then instructed us to silently make an arrangement in the vase using any of the flowers we'd brought, all of which had been placed in the center of the room. One by one, as the spirit moved them, attendees selected flowers and returned to their place in the circle to make their arrangements.

Once everyone had completed the assignment, the teacher passed around a bowl filled with folded slips of paper. Silently he indicated that each of us should select one slip at random. We understood without words that we were each to give our vase to the person whose name we had drawn. As this process proceeded in silence, the sense of presence began filling the room as we became increasingly engaged in experiencing the exchange of flowers. When Louise gave her vase, filled with white roses, to Marion, Marion broke into tears; none of us knew why, but we sensed that something profound had happened. Brad, who was sitting next to me in a wheelchair, turned and gave his vase to me. He had pulled my name from the bowl by chance, yet that chance allowed him to participate fully in the experience without having to ask someone to deliver his flowers for him. As he gave me the vase, everyone gasped. We could all see the perfection of the flow of creation at work, which was all the more beautiful given that we had done nothing to orchestrate it. It was outside our control but more perfect than we could possibly have made it if we had planned it.

Once the exercise was over, we discussed it, and story after story was told of a particular vase being absolutely perfect for its recipient. The most notable story involved the exchange between Louise and Marion. First Marion told us of an internal dialogue she'd had with herself while she was selecting the flowers for her vase, before any of us knew we'd be giving them to someone else.

She has a particular love of roses, so she instantly fell in love with a bouquet of white roses that had been brought to the retreat, but they had long stems, which would have made for a precarious arrangement in her diminutive vase. She had briefly considered cutting the stems but felt that to do so would be inappropriate. She also thought it would be selfish to take what to her were the most beautiful flowers in the room, so she decided to leave them for someone else. But Louise had no particular love of roses yet felt inexplicably attracted to these. She moved decisively to the bouquet early on in the process of flower selection, took all twelve roses, efficiently trimmed off their long stems, and arranged the shortened stems in her vase. Then, as she realized that most people were taking fewer flowers than she had taken, she started to second-guess herself. Had she done something wrong? Should she have left some of the white roses for someone else? She ended up feeling embarrassed and awkward and became convinced that she'd screwed up.

Then came the name drawing, and Louise realized, with some relief, that she would be giving her vase away. She stopped feeling so guilty, but when she gave the vase to Marion and Marion burst into tears, she again wondered if there was something wrong with what she had done. It was only during the ensuing discussion that she came to understand Marion's tearful outburst and the absolute perfection of her actions. Marion, who had so wanted the white roses, received them—all of them—and from someone who had had no qualms about shortening the long stems. The universe had provided in a way beyond Marion's wildest imaginings, and her worries about her selfishness and the propriety of cutting the stems had been rendered irrelevant. In fact, had she taken the roses in the first place, she wouldn't have ended up with them.

This experience allowed all of us to see vividly the embodiment of the saying "Ask, and you shall receive." With her love of roses, Marion had asked—not with words or wishes but through her actions and her consideration of others—and the universe had provided. It had required nothing from her other than to love their beauty. And Louise was able to see that she had been an instrument in a larger process and that there was no "wrong" action. The flow of moments and synchronous happenings occurs whether or not we are present, but it is only when we are present that those dynamics are observable. Otherwise, we are lost in the dream and lost in our thoughts about what is going on.

One of the other participants in the flower exercise dubbed this experience "the Flower of Now," which struck me as particularly appropriate, given that the word "flower" can also be seen as flow-er, that which flows. The whole process, from start to finish, was extraordinary because it unfolded so effortlessly and because so many of us were completely engaged in the moment. We were given, with the exercise, a lens through which to see the flowing of presence—of Now—as it happens, moment by moment, and, like an actual flower, every petal, every movement, was a reflection of the perfection and beauty of the whole. We were the movement and flowering of Now.

Being Present in Your Experiencing

There's a wonderful saying that my current teacher, Al, uses all the time to help his students appreciate the value of presence:

Life is the experiencing of the experience.

This statement is both simple and profound. The only place where anything happens, where anything comes into manifestation, is the present moment. So the only way life can be known is by experiencing what is happening in the present moment. Past is past. Although we may remember an experience of a moment before, the remembering is not the experiencing. And the future never comes: The future is a present moment that has not yet been experienced.

So Now is the only *real* time that exists, and paradoxically it is outside linear time. It has nothing to do with yesterday, which is memory, and nothing to do with tomorrow, which is conjecture. It simply is. It is the "is-ing" of everything, and it's all happening right *now*. Stop and consider this. Allow it to permeate the way you think things are.

This moment of experiencing is the only time there is. What are you experiencing in this moment? This is where life is happening—in the experiencing of Now.

What is Now?

Now I'm seeing the pattern of spectrums produced by a piece of beveled glass moving across my desk, across my hand.

What is Now?

Now I'm sensing a light fluttering in my heart, a thrill at becoming more aware of this moment.

What is Now?

You answer. No editing. There are no wrong answers. This is where your life is happening. Right now.

What is Now?

Every time you ask yourself this question, you'll see more of yourself, more of what you experience and how you experience it. When you are in the midst of your daily routine, ask yourself this question every once in a while and you'll start to see yourself in a completely different light. When you implement the "Your Turn" exercise with the pauses at fifteen-minute intervals, ask yourself this question with every pause and you'll become aware of what's actually here in the moment instead of what's going on in your head.

Because you can't automatically turn off the thoughts running through your mind, you must use inquiries like this to help you return to what's actually here. In this way your busy mind will gradually loosen its grip, and you'll start to see through the content of your waking dream. It will no longer be defining you; instead, the experiencing in the moment—what's really happening in the midst of all that content—will become your Light to Walk Toward, like a lighted painting at the end of a hallway. The experiencing of the moment is so much more alive than the story lines going on in your head that once you've experienced it once or twice, it will be impossible not to want to experience it again and again. Over time, as you keep tuning in to what is happening right now, even the phrase "my life" will start to change its meaning. Try it, and you'll see what I mean.

When you are really at one with the unfolding of every moment, when you *are* the Now-ness, the experiencing of time itself is very different from the way we usually think of it. Real time seems neither long nor short, neither instantaneous nor eternal. In fact, it defies description because it isn't related to linear time, or quantitative time. All linear time passes within the Now, but the Now cannot be defined by the terms we use to describe linear time. Now is experienced not as time but as presence, and though we are aware of flow, it's as though its duration is incidental; it barely touches us, much as a leaf floating along on a stream would barely be aware of the water's movement.

The exercise that follows has the ability to reveal this doorway to *real* time—to the Now: All that's required is that you eat a favorite food very slowly so that you completely experience its taste and texture. If you've ever tried a multicourse tasting menu at a fine restaurant, you've already experienced one variation of this exercise—though with a much larger dent in your wallet! Tasting menus are designed to bring you to a state of presence, the small, beautifully presented portions encouraging you to focus all your senses on each bite.

Another version of the same art is the tea ceremony. In Japan and China the tea ceremony has been refined over centuries to awaken an exquisite awareness of every movement and every sensory stimulus throughout the process. Although in this country it is rare to find a place where you can engage in the experience completely, I was fortunate enough to do so while visiting a wonderful tea shop in Berkeley, California, the Celadon Tea Room.

On the occasion that I visited Celadon with a group of friends, the tea master performed his magical art before us, and we were transported to a timeless, placeless perfection of sensory delight. The scents of the various teas, the pouring and repouring of hot water into lovely porcelain cups and saucers, even the process of cleaning up—everything was conducted in presence, and those who could be there as completely as the tea master enjoyed total immersion in the unfolding Now. This may sound overblown. All that was happening, apparently, was the drinking of tea. But when you are completely engaged, what's really happening is the dance of life and light, taste and color, and it seems to be presented just for you. Once you experience it, you'll never again wonder where to find meaning, because it expresses right through the experiencing itself.

If you've ever tried to watch a movie on fast-forward, you'll know that though the story may be vaguely discernable, the meaning is entirely invisible, and all you see is blur. In our own lives we're simply not aware of the real meaning of our personal movie because we're going too fast to notice and worrying too much about how we'd prefer things to be. We think we know where we are supposed to be going and what we are supposed to be doing, so when our plans are foiled we get upset, which takes us completely out of presence. To live in full color and experience directly the vibrant meaning of what surrounds us, we must show up completely in the Now that is actually happening, no matter what its content may be.

Our activities are just clothing covering each particular moment of Now. That which informs the Now, the "is-ness" of everything, is always here, and it's always completely new. However hard it may be to remember this, life is not about the content of our waking dreams. That content may stay the same from day to day, or it may "act up." What matters is that every moment is an entirely new moment and an entirely new unfolding, filled with the potential for entirely new experiencing in the Now. That's where the source of the more-ness is, in the experiencing itself, and that's where we become what we have the potential of becoming. By experiencing completely, we are always and inevitably becoming more.

What you'll find is that as you begin to live in the moment-to-moment unfolding, your life will change. It will morph from too big, too fast, and too frustrating to the vastly more manageable pace and clarity of Not So Big. And time will no longer be a foe to do battle with but will start to flow and open in unexpected places to allow your full engagement in the things you really love.

EXERCISE
experiencing presence

Being present is often shrouded in misunderstanding. It doesn't require that you retreat to a cave on a mountaintop to contemplate the meaning of life. Presence can be combined with your daily routine because it's not about the content of your life; it's about the attention with which you engage it; you can practice being present in your life just as it is. What most of us crave is a feeling of calm and delight in what we are doing. Being present is the doorway to that vitality we're longing for.

This exercise is an experiment in stepping outside all your frenetic activities for a bit so you can recognize what presence is firsthand. Allow at least twenty minutes, and make sure you are in a place where you won't be distracted. You can do the exercise alone or with friends or family members. But while you are doing it, don't talk or otherwise interact.

Take one of your favorite foods, whether a piece of fruit, like a strawberry or a peach, or a particular type of chocolate or a brownie. Put the food on a plate in front of you. For the next twenty minutes, you are going to become completely involved with this piece of food. The only things in the world will be you and your favorite delicacy. Look at it, touch it, smell it, taste it, and then consume it—very, very slowly. When you taste and then slowly eat, close your eyes so that your surroundings don't distract you.

An alternative first step for the extremely overcommitted and overtaxed: If in reading this exercise, you think to yourself, "There's just no way. Where am I ever going to find the time?" then start with something simpler. Eat dinner like a civilized human being: Turn off the television. Don't answer the phone. Tell your kids that you want to find out who among them can be the quietest for the longest. And eat—slowly, quietly, and without thinking. Look at the colors, taste the flavors, and enjoy the process of feeding your body. You can work up to the twenty-minute engagement with the favorite food over the next few weeks, but for now, this is a good beginning.

After you've completed the exercise, write down your experiences in your notebook so you won't forget them. What you will have experienced is presence, at least partially. You probably found yourself experiencing some intrusive thoughts, such as "I bet I look really stupid right now" or "I wish I'd picked a riper strawberry." In those moments, you are not present. When your mind is commenting on what's going on inside your head or around you, that's a clear indicator that you aren't fully engaged in what's happening right at that moment, and so you are not completely in the Now.

But when you tasted that first morsel of food, when the flavors exploded and the texture was experienced—perhaps with some surprise or delight—then you were totally present. You were so completely engaged in the experience that there was no boundary between you and the food. You and it were one, and the feelings it evoked were in all likelihood revitalizing and deeply fulfilling.

I conducted the tasting experiment once with a group of friends and a plate of brownies. Although each homemade brownie was only about two inches square, by the time the exercise was completed, I could have sworn my brownie had been three or four times that size. It was, without a doubt, the most delectable brownie I'd ever eaten. But what struck me most is that all my friends, who had never before had a way to gauge what it felt like to be truly present, immediately understood. As a result, they could also recognize other times in their lives when they'd been fully present, because they could use the exercise for comparison.

The point, of course, is not to eat brownies and drink tea all day but to do everything with this same total engagement. Although it won't happen overnight, with practice you can live more and more of your life this way, and the results in terms of quality of life will astound you.

The food-tasting exercise takes only twenty minutes. If you put the exercise off because you don't have twenty minutes to spare even though something inside you knows it might be valuable, you are most likely putting off a lot of other things that would be valuable to your development as well.

If you decide to put the exercise off and come back to it when you have more time, keep in mind that in most cases later never comes. Here's a question for you: Who or what is it that is deciding there isn't time? What would happen if you overrode that decision and simply did the exercise anyway? Sure, someone who is expecting you to behave in the same old ways might be put out by the break in your pattern, but it's amazing to discover that everyone can manage just fine without you for a little while.

PRINCIPLE
point of focus

This principle works in much the same way as the Light to Walk Toward, described at the beginning of chapter 7, except that here the thing we are attracted to is not light per se but an object or form that creates an implied center for the space we're in. The most commonly recognizable point of focus in a house is a fireplace. It roots the room it inhabits, providing a hearth or "heart" for the room's activities when it's lit and an identity for the room as a whole.

You can use almost anything that has meaning for you as a point of focus for a space—a beautiful work of art centered on the wall above the bed in the master bedroom, a glass sculpture on the buffet in the dining room, or a tile design above the cooktop in the kitchen.

What you'll be learning about in this chapter is the value and importance of creating a single point of focus in your own life—a place and time each day when you are simply by yourself with yourself, with nothing else going on. It is in this place and time that your true identity can begin to reveal itself—when you aren't trying to accomplish anything and you aren't worrying about how to make things happen or how to make them go differently than they are. It's in that stillness that your own point of focus becomes apparent.

Whereas Light to Walk Toward is focused on a source that's apparently outside ourselves, Point of Focus is directed toward a source that's apparently inside. Both are related to becoming more present in our lives, but the experiencing of this presence differs according to whether you are engaged in your everyday activities or are quietly focusing inward. When you create a point of focus for yourself, you are slowing your movie down to the point where the sequence of its frames shows almost no movement, revealing a scene that contrasts dramatically with the rest of your movie. This chapter will introduce you to the value and meaning of stillness.

EIGHT

Creating a Place and a Time of Your Own

Submit to a daily practice.
Your loyalty to that
is a ring on the door.

Keep knocking, and the joy inside
will eventually open a window
and look out to see who's there.
—RUMI

Time-out

Your remodeling is well under way now. You've identified a lot of the problems with the existing infrastructure, and even though the new construction hasn't been implemented, you can at least begin to envision your life with these improvements in place. But how can you find the time to make them happen? You may well be asking yourself, "Even if this is my movie I'm watching and I'm in fact watching it on fast-forward, how do I find the remote control to slow it down?" The answer is that change doesn't happen through a click of a button. It happens by making small, almost insignificant changes in your behavior. And the most important of these changes is taking time for yourself each day.

This is the remodeling equivalent of making a place of your own, like the attic I gave myself permission to include in the design of my first house. As we remodel our lives, designating a time of your own is just as important to the expression of who you are and who you are becoming as giving yourself a place of your own. This one small shift will ripple through the rest of your life. Once your behavior changes in this minor way, much bigger changes will be set into motion. And just as the participants in the flower exercise described in chapter 7 were not responsible for the outcome of that exercise, you will not be in charge of these bigger shifts. They'll happen of their own accord.

This may sound a little unlikely or scary, but your job right now is simply to suspend disbelief and remain open to the possibility that things aren't as fixed and unforgiving as they appear and that somewhere in all the busyness you'll be able to find the time you need. What you'll discover is that as you take time to get back into balance, the content of your movie will start to appear less chaotic because it will be reflecting your state of inner balance. Once you've established this new pattern of behavior, you'll find that when life events get crazy you will simply insist on stepping back from the situation and taking a few minutes for yourself. These moments will allow you to regain some objectivity, and when you reenter the situation, it won't seem so overwhelming. You'll have a new perspective. You'll be looking down from the upper levels of the amphitheater rather than from the soaker seats.

So the move you're implementing here is a way to slow down the speed of your movie so that you have time to look at it objectively. This may not seem very significant, but in fact it is the most important thing you can do in the remodeling of your life. If you were to make no other change, your life would still shift. And without this one change other remodeling would be much less likely to stick. Without time to yourself you're likely to forget your dreams, forget to see and appreciate what surrounds you, and forget that you are in a movie being drenched constantly by your own inner whales. So even if you think you know this stuff or don't need it, don't want it, or can't do it, read on. This is the big key that can unlock the door to your true nature and to your own Not So Big Life.

Throughout this chapter I'm going to use a word that has, in some circles, become the poster child for being way out there. The word is *meditation*. I've used it a few times already in this book, and some readers, I know, have met it with a sinking heart. There are so many mistaken meanings attributed to the word and so many assumptions made about it these days that it has become almost meaningless, so I'm going to attempt to redeem it and put it back into circulation in a clear and demystified way. But if you find yourself unable to read the word "meditation" without a knee-jerk reaction, substitute the words "still time." A word is just a label; what matters is the principle it conveys.

There are those who think meditation is only for the far, far out crowd, a crowd on the fringes of society. There are those who think meditation is something practiced primarily by emaciated yogis who twist themselves into unnatural body postures and drop out of life as we know it. There are those who think meditation is trendy and cool and they'd like to do it too but don't believe they can because it requires sitting still for extended periods. There are those who believe that meditation isn't real meditation unless they experience an inner light show like a laser light display at a planetarium. And there are those—legions, in fact—who believe they can't meditate because they can't shut their mind off.

But meditation is none of those things. It is very, very simple—even simpler than prayer, which is addressed to some higher power outside oneself. Meditation focuses internally. The reason it has become so misunderstood is that it isn't something you do at all. It's about *being* rather than *doing*. Yet, because we are so preoccupied with action in our culture, we can't imagine the value of something that isn't action- or goal-oriented. How can *that* be useful? The problem is that when we think that way, we are cutting out exactly half of our lives. We need both being *and* doing, and if we don't learn the being part soon, we're going to do ourselves right out of existence.

So what is meditation, really? And why is it important? What good can it possibly do? As many regular meditators can attest, and as I've come to know firsthand, it can help enormously with developing that more relaxed awareness that allows you to observe and engage what's happening in your life in a new way. Not only does slowing down occur in the act of meditating itself, but its effects linger and change the tone of your whole movie. By focusing inward for a short period each day, we can truly become human *beings* rather than human *doings*.

Still Time

My first experiment with meditation came at a time in my life when I knew I needed to make some changes but was afraid to do so—afraid to lift the lid off what I knew to be a mess of unspoken and apparently irresolvable discomforts in a relationship. I was in my late teens, and I kept a journal, mostly documenting my thoughts and feelings. One day while rereading the previous month's entries, I noticed a pronounced fluctuation in my perceptions from day to day. One day everything was wonderful and perfect and I was deeply in love, and the next day I'd be ready to give up on ever being understood or appreciated. There was nothing in between. Things were black or white, good or bad, happy or sad. I was swinging back and forth from one side of the seesaw to the other on a twenty-four-hour cycle. I remember putting my journal down with a sense of dismay. I hadn't been aware of these dramatic ebbs and flows, but the entries left no doubt about them.

What I know now, looking back, is that my childhood conditioning had taught me to focus on the bright and happy side of things in order to avoid any possibility of confrontation. So the fact that I was admitting, even if only every other day, that things were not going well for me was an indication that something of major significance needed my attention.

As I sat with my journal that day, I knew that I needed to do something, that I couldn't deny my feelings of distress any longer. But what to do? I wasn't sure. I felt the desire to hide away, like an animal that's wounded, but I knew that wouldn't solve anything. For a week or two I struggled, not knowing what to do next. Then Providence pointed the way, as it so often does when you truly desire help with a dilemma.

At the time I was living in Oregon, in a community that was planning to build a new town on about twelve hundred acres of as yet uninhabited land—an eco-village with a variety of dwelling types ranging from small homesteading farms to cluster housing in a densely knit village center. For an architecture student this was an ideal lifestyle—it allowed me to share my ideas about better ways of living with a group of eager idealists who were willing to entertain alternatives to the conventional three-bedroom, two-car-garage vision of existence. As part of the planning process for building the community, there were any number of group activities to attend, including frequent potluck dinners and meetings.

One of the community members was a young man who had been a serious practitioner of meditation for years. I often noticed him sitting below a huge oak tree on the property, the very picture of stillness. There was a serenity and calm surrounding him that made me want to learn how to meditate too. Something about those minutes of quiet solitude each day seemed to fill him and focus him, and I could feel the difference in the way he lived.

At one of the potlucks, I asked him to tell me more and found out that not only had he been on a number of spiritual retreats but he also taught meditation. I asked him if he could teach me, and he gave me an impromptu lesson right there in the middle of the floor of the old barn on the property where we were gathered. He instructed me to sit cross-legged on a firm cushion in order to raise the tailbone a few inches above the knees. He explained that the key ingredient to a good meditation posture is a straight spine, so if it's necessary to sit on a chair, you should choose one that allows the spine to be as straight as possible, with no slump in the back or shoulders, as though a rod were extending from the crown of the head to the tailbone. The next step, he told me, was to close your eyes and breathe slowly and fully, first deeply in, then deeply out, but without forcing it at all. Then, simply follow the movement of each breath with your attention. He explained that when you do this, the mind and body calm down and give way to a sense of stillness.

He also told me not to focus on any thoughts that came up but simply to let them go by refocusing on the breath, no matter how fascinating, frightening, or frustrating those thoughts might be. "Thoughts arise," he said. "That's the nature of thought. But you don't have to engage them. Just focus on the breath, and leave them alone." He told me that by taking twenty minutes each day to meditate in this fashion, I'd be able to observe significant changes in my life.

It sounded simple enough, and I was eager to go home and try out the technique even though at the time I wasn't sure what it would accomplish. I hadn't told him anything about myself and hadn't asked him for any help beyond teaching me how to meditate. But somehow I knew that this practice would help me with the relationship problems I was experiencing.

So my first lesson in meditation took all of ten minutes, but it was exactly what I needed. By sitting still each day for the prescribed twenty minutes, I found I was able to see the nature of the problem I was having with my relationship much more clearly than I had before. Note that I was not sitting there thinking about the relationship—just focusing on my breath, in and out, and returning to the breath whenever a thought intruded. I wasn't sure how it happened, but by simply breathing and letting my mind become more still than it usually was, in the hours after I meditated an understanding of what I needed to do next would arise as if out of nowhere. It was clear as a bell.

From that point on, whenever things got overwhelming for me or whenever I felt caught up in a dilemma, I knew that the solution was to meditate. Though I hadn't at this point made meditation a regular part of my daily life, I was certainly aware that the practice was capable—almost miraculously—of helping me identify what I needed to do next. Even though these thoughts and understandings came about sometime after I'd meditated, not during the process, it was pretty clear that the practice had allowed the insights to arise. So for many years I used meditation like a medicine you might take for a cold, except that I took the medicine whenever I was encountering problems, whenever my waking dream started to act up.

I was fortunate to have learned this relationship between finding stillness and the character of my waking dream when I was so young. It meant that I rarely stayed stuck in problems for extended periods of time. As long as I continued to meditate regularly, the problem, whatever it was, would gradually unravel itself, and things would return to a new state of equilibrium—not the version of reality my fears had me believe was inevitable, but a new and better place than before. It seemed that meditation allowed me to see things from a different perspective, so that what once had looked like problems were no longer problems at all. I could conclude only that the problem had been the way I was looking at things.

You might be asking yourself how meditating could possibly help, especially when the very practice precludes the brain's thinking mechanism. The answer can be glimpsed in this now-famous quotation by Albert Einstein:

> The significant problems we face cannot be solved at the same level of thinking we were at when we created them.

Another way of saying this is that when you think about potential solutions to a problem, those thoughts are all generated by the same mechanism—your personality—that perceives the situation as a problem in the first place. So thinking can only keep you locked in a hall of mirrors in which every option ensures the continuation of the problem or the birth of a series of related and equally unsolvable new ones.

Our problems arise from our limited understanding. What appears to be a problem at one level of awareness can be seen at another as just the way things are. As I was planning this chapter, I couldn't think of any metaphors that would adequately get this point across. Then my dream-world came through for me again.

In my dream I was surrounded by black-and-white stripes wherever I looked. It felt almost claustrophobic. Then suddenly the perspective changed, and now I was up above the stripes, looking down on them. I realized that I had been in a herd of zebras packed so close together that it was impossible to distinguish one from another. From inside the herd I could see only a sea of stripes. But from above, the individual bodies instantly became clear. The understanding that came with the dream was that even when things look black and white, right and wrong, good and bad—in other words, when things are part of a world of polar opposites—that appearance is true only from one perspective. From a higher vantage point the entire frame of reference shifts.

So it is with our everyday problems. Things that we are having trouble with in our lives will usually present themselves as polar opposites, such as a disagreement with a friend, in which we feel "I'm right" and "he's wrong." We identify with one side of this polarity and then get upset with anything that supports the opposite side. To resolve the tension, we need to move beyond this limited frame of reference. We have to see the zebras before we can understand what the situation requires of us. That's why things beyond our understanding almost always strike us as paradoxical. They don't make sense because we don't yet have access to the understanding that stripes and zebras are actually two views of the same thing.

What meditation does is introduce stillness into the equation so that a higher, more expansive perspective can make itself known. Although we are firm believers in our brain's ability to solve our problems, when we are trying to solve a problem that's outside the current paradigm, the mind becomes the obstacle, for there is no solution at the level at which we can think it through. That's why we'll go round and round in our mind, imagining every possible permutation of how something will play out but never finding the answer we seek.

From a higher perspective we can see that the problem isn't what we thought it was at all. This perspective comes not from thinking but from the relaxed awareness brought about by stillness and from the wider aperture it provides for viewing our waking dream. With our new blueprint, differences disappear, and the paradoxical makes perfect sense. We see clearly what we could not distinguish before.

The Monkey Mind

Buddhists describe the state of not being in the present moment as "monkey mind." The mind is running crazily from tree to tree, like a monkey, tasting one piece of fruit here, another piece there, without ever finishing any one. In meditation you can often see your mind doing the same thing, restlessly leaping from thought to thought, before you return your focus to your breath. We're usually unaware that this is our state of being, but in meditation everything slows down sufficiently for us to watch the process in action.

Remember the evening I described in the introduction, when I was reading in bed one night and woke up to the understanding that despite all of my apparent accomplishments and productivity, I was moving through my life on automatic pilot? After that night I wanted nothing more than to stay awake, spiritually speaking, and to find out more about what life has to offer and what is here to be experienced if you are truly awake, as opposed to just rushing from one thing to the next on automatic pilot. I knew, because of my earlier experiences with slowing down my movie when things got out of balance, that the solution would come through meditation, but this time I wanted to integrate the practice completely into my everyday life. I wanted to make it as habitual as brushing my teeth.

I decided, with a certain amount of embarrassment, to attend a session at the local Zen center, where I'd been told that members of the general public could go to learn the practices of meditation and mindfulness. I didn't want to get involved in anything that might be considered New Age, so with trepidation I called to find out when there were classes that I'd be allowed to attend. The woman who answered the phone told me that she was an assistant and that I'd need to talk to one of the priests in person. She gave me another number to call and then a piece of advice: "Let the phone ring for a while. They don't always pick up right away." I asked her why, and she explained that as part of their practice, they often listen to the ringing for a while. "For them it doesn't require the automatic response of leaping into action," she explained. "A ringing phone is simply a sound that repeats itself and is there to be experienced."

This struck me in a profound way. I'd never considered that a ringing phone could be heard as just a sound and not as a demand. I called the number. It took about twenty rings, but by waiting patiently while listening to the sound of the ringing in an entirely new way, I found myself speaking with a very gentle but firm female voice. She provided the information I needed regarding when to attend, where to go, and what to expect once I got there.

Shortly before the class was to begin, since I was early I took a walk around a nearby lake. And as luck would have it, I ran into one of my clients, who wondered what I was doing there. I decided, somewhat sheepishly, to tell the truth, to admit that I was about to take a class in meditation at the Zen center. Far from being put off, she was intrigued and told me that she'd wanted to learn to meditate for some years herself. My discomfort evaporated, and I realized this wanting to know myself better wasn't all that odd and was nothing to be embarrassed by.

I remember vividly that first visit to the Zen center, which was actually just a large house in a pleasant residential neighborhood. One of the first things I noticed were the handwritten signs posted around the building, signs that said things like "Take time to experience the washing of the hands" and "Be mindful of your stepping as you make your way upstairs." At the time I thought that the reminders were a little odd, but I also realized, as I tried to follow them, that they brought me to a greater awareness of what I was doing and to a dawning appreciation of the brilliance—the vibrancy—of the simplest activities. These were my first tastes of the Now and of beginning to see that activity is a veil over the vitality of the unfolding moment.

About six of us that evening were new to meditation and new to the center. We silently stepped into a large room on the third floor, together with some obviously old hands, who were taking their seats on the round black cushions laid out in rows across the floor. My experience with meditation all those years earlier had given me a taste of what it was all about, but I wanted to know more. I wasn't sure I was doing it correctly. My mind was filled with questions as I selected a place to sit and tried to look proficient at sitting in the cross-legged position that was clearly de rigueur at this center. There wasn't a chair to be seen.

In the practice of mindfulness, I learned, you simply focus on what you are doing, but you focus without thought, without your brain's constant labeling and commenting on everything you encounter. By stilling the mind through this process of mindfulness, you can "*be* in your doing" in a whole new way, a way that positively overflows with vitality once you've practiced the technique for a while. Because when the monkey mind is hushed, you have the time and the awareness to experience what's right in front of you.

Your Turn

Mindfulness versus Labeling: Look around you right now. Wherever you are sitting as you read this—whether in a subway car, on a park bench, or in your armchair at home—lift your eyes up and look at your surroundings. But look without naming things for a moment. Just take in the colors, the textures, and the quality of your environment. Listen to the sounds, not with their conventional associations but just as they are. If there are scents in the air, smell them as if for the first time. After doing this for a few minutes, change the way you are engaging what surrounds you by labeling everything you see—door, window, plant, yellow leaf, lamp shade, and so on.

Afterward, record in your notebook the difference between the two experiences. What were your observations of the period of simply experiencing versus your observations of the period of labeling? What can you learn about yourself and your engagement in your everyday activities from this difference? Did you have difficulty with either process? When you use labels, are you really experiencing what's there?

You may want to repeat this process a few times in the days and weeks to come. The more you develop a relaxed awareness, the more difference you'll experience between the two experiences.

Every experience of our day has within it the power to move us, but because we think we know our surroundings, we remove our attention from looking, listening, touching, tasting, and smelling. It's another version of conditioning. We believe we're in the same old same old. But we're not. It is entirely new when we meet it with mindfulness and as an integral part of this very moment.

The Buddhist priest who taught us that evening was the same one I'd spoken to a week earlier on the phone. She slowly and patiently explained the process of meditation, telling us that no matter how often we'd been taught before and no matter how often we'd meditated before, the student learns best when he or she understands that the mind is a beginner, that everyone in the room is a beginner, herself included, and that when you engage in anything whatsoever, if you engage as a beginner, experiencing an activity as if for the first time, then you are truly able to learn, truly able to receive. But if you believe that you know and that you've done this before, then your mind and heart will be closed, and you will not be able to learn, to receive or be nourished by the practice.

The process of meditation, she explained, is simply to show up, become alert, whether sitting, standing, or walking, and with an open mind allow whatever arises in the mind to arise and then simply let it go. Everyone has thoughts, she told us. But they're not "your" thoughts. They're simply thoughts, and, just like bubbles, you can let them go without becoming attached to them, identifying with them, or being drawn into them. It takes practice, she explained, to learn to let go of thoughts, and for some it is useful to follow the breath with your attention, just to give the mind something to do instead of thinking.

She told us that it is a common response to judge oneself for having thoughts, but she reminded us that the judgments themselves are just more thoughts. If you pay them no attention and attach no meaning to them, simply observe them and let them go as if they were thought bubbles, then gradually, gradually, the mind will become quieter, and gaps will emerge between thoughts. Although it takes time to become aware of these gaps, she said, with regular practice and without expectation or goal, the spaces will become apparent, not only when meditating but at other times as well. It is in these spaces between the thoughts that the stillness resides, she explained, and as these spaces grow, so will your ability to be present in your life.

When you were doing the preceding "Your Turn" exercise, if you have an active inner judge, you may have noticed its commentary arising, perhaps telling you that you can't quiet your mind or that you've tried this sort of thing before and it doesn't work for you. Just as you do during meditation, simply become aware of the thought or the judgment when it occurs, but don't identify with it as your own. It's simply "the" thought, and there's nothing personal about it. Many, many people hear these kinds of thoughts all the time. By not attaching to them, you'll find that it's possible to experience things afresh even while the judgment sound track is running. It's as though there are thousands of radio stations broadcasting simultaneously and your brain can tune in to whatever channel it likes. The problems arise when it then believes it is creating the programming—that all these thoughts are *you*. But they're not. They're no more you than the radio stations you tune in to on your drive home from work.

Back at the Zen center, as I heard the teacher's words of advice about approaching everything as a beginner, I felt all the questions and worries about correctness that had filled my brain a few moments earlier melt away. It's not that there weren't still questions, but I was able to see them now as impersonal thoughts bubbling up, as arbitrary as stations on the radio dial. I settled into meditation, my spine straight and my hands resting in my lap.

Plenty of thoughts arose over the next half hour—the duration of that first Zen "sit," as the practice is described—but now I was able to let them go without worrying about why I had had a thought or why I couldn't get my mind to shut up. It helped immensely just to know that everyone goes through this kind of self-doubt and that it, too, can be released, just like any other thought.

Over the next few weeks of classes, I learned to experience the world around me in a very different way. I tried to remember the mindfulness encouraged by the Zen center. And though I was amazed at how frequently I forgot it, when I did remember, I could feel the newness of even the most familiar tasks. I'd always enjoyed cooking, for example. But now, as I made dinner each evening, every vegetable, experienced in a mindful way, presented a stunning array of colors, textures, and geometrical intricacies as I cut it up in preparation for cooking. Even the patterns I chose to cut the vegetables into took on added significance. I was entranced by the richness of just about everything I engaged in and marveled at the fact that I had missed so much of it before.

The new blueprint was really starting to function for me by this point. I was seeing in vibrant new colors what I'd only *thought* I'd been seeing in the past. Now I began to know these colors and textures and patterns like intimate friends. When in this state, seeing through the things we think we know to what's really there, the boundaries between that which we call "me" and that which we call "vegetable" dissolve, immersing us in moreness. This doesn't in any way inhibit our ability to function. I could still chop vegetables very efficiently. It's just that now I was seeing the entire process in vivid Technicolor.

I also made time to meditate every day without fail after I came home from work. Though it was a break from my usual pattern and I had to struggle to put off until later the glass of wine I liked to have upon my arrival home, by making the new practice nonnegotiable, it became just what I had wanted it to be: an integral part of my life. I had asked sincerely, and the universe had provided. Whereas earlier in my life I'd thought I wanted to meditate regularly, until this point I hadn't understood why it was so important. I hadn't appreciated that without the stillness that meditation gradually allows access to, there is no way to widen the aperture of one's understanding. Now I realized the connection between meditation and detachment from the process of image making and thought production.

As if to confirm that this was indeed the right thing to be doing, I found out, just a few weeks later, that I am quite allergic to sulfites and so could no longer tolerate drinking wine without getting pretty severe headaches. My waking dream was supporting the conditions for my own awakening, conditions that I certainly wouldn't have chosen if left to my own devices, yet of course they were perfect.

Although I didn't become a Zen practitioner and my engagement with this meditation center amounted to only a handful of visits, the brief introduction it gave me to a different way of engaging my world opened the door to an exploration of mindfulness and regular meditation that has continued to this day. The two practices, hand in hand, when engaged in every day, are powerfully transformative techniques that work quite apart from religious belief. You can be a member of any religion or of none at all and benefit from the practices because mindfulness and meditation are about your relationship with your Self, which is something we all have in common, no matter what else we believe in.

Making Time to Be Still

At this point you may be wondering how to implement your own meditation practice. Many people begin to meditate to solve some problem they're trying to cope with, as I did initially, but this is certainly not a prerequisite. What you'll discover is that the more you practice, the more you recognize the other benefits of meditation: the reduction of turmoil in your life, the clarity about what to do and what not to do, and the increase in synchronicities. Though it seems like a simple thing to put aside twenty minutes a day, and for a few diligent souls it will be, for most of us this key that opens the door to moreness can be elusive. Your waking dream may present obstacles to meditation that seem insurmountable, but it's incredibly important for you to realize that this is pure illusion. You *can* make time for meditation if you want to. But you really, *really* have to want to before the opportunity to do so will present itself. Remember Marion's simple love of those white roses and recall how all the forces of the universe had conspired to give them to her, and you'll begin to understand how the process works.

You must have a strong desire for this clarity that flows from the Now in order to receive what it has to give you. And you must watch for the opportunities that present themselves to pursue that which you long for. Faking it or even willing it won't work. You'll find reasons why it is inconvenient to meditate, reasons to put it off until another day. But if you are resolute in your determination, things will shift and the time will show up, although it may present itself in a way you don't expect.

Although this next story isn't about making time for meditation, it will give you a sense of the extraordinary manner in which shifts in the waking dream occur when you are ready to receive them. Some four or five years after I'd started meditating regularly, I wanted to take part in a meditation retreat in which I would be able to practice for longer periods than my everyday life allowed. But it was a four-week affair, and it seemed impossible that I'd be able to take that much time from my work. I was working on plans for a couple who were paying top dollar to get a wonderful house. They had asked me to focus my time exclusively on their home, and I'd cleared away all my other projects so that I could do so. A four-week hiatus in their home's design process would go down like a ton of bricks, I assumed.

But I kept feeling a deep longing to go on the retreat, and I kept wondering what would happen if I just asked my clients how they'd feel about it. This went on for a couple of weeks, and then one morning I woke up with a certainty about my desire. I was going to go. I didn't know how it was going to work, and I didn't even know whether my clients would fire me if I went, but I knew I was going to make it happen. I resolved to call my clients—the husband and wife—as soon as I got to work, to let them know of my plan and to apologize for the inconvenience it would cause them.

When I arrived at my office, I discovered that the husband had left word for me to call him, which I did right away. Before I could begin to tell him of my plans, he informed me that every summer he and his wife spent four weeks at their lake house in Wisconsin, and he wondered if their house design could be put on hold for that period so they could enjoy their time away rather than be distracted by the activities back in Minnesota. I nearly fell off my chair when he told me the dates they'd be away: They coincided exactly with those of the retreat I'd decided to attend.

Surely it must have been coincidence. But what is coincidence other than the synchronous, harmonic movements underlying consciousness? That perfect orchestration is invisible to us until something like this occurs; when it does, we become exquisitely aware of the magnitude of the dance we're engaged in. As with the flower exercise, each of us imagines that we are separate, that we have our reasons for wanting this and doing that, but when the underlying musical score is revealed for just a moment, we recognize that any meaning we are attributing to our own actions is like the nibbling of a mouse in a world made of cheese. Things are vastly more magnificent and coordinated than we ever dreamed possible. And when you long for something truly—a desire not of your personality but of your higher self—then the waking dream provides you with the nutrition you seek.

Though people who want to understand more of their inner world are often referred to as seekers, the act of seeking often gets in the way of receiving what is available to be given. Our seeking obscures and impedes the flow. As Einstein revealed, we can seek only that which our thinking can imagine, which is by definition limited to our present state. True growth comes from a fresh perspective, from seeing zebras instead of stripes, and for that we have to relinquish control of the reins and allow what arises in our waking dream to teach us. The first and most powerful step you can take in this process is to begin to meditate regularly. Just try it, and see what happens.

making a time and
a place for solitude

When you are first starting to meditate or take time to sit quietly by your-self, it helps enormously to set the conditions for uninterrupted focus. You don't have to have the "perfect" place. You don't need to put off meditation because you can't find a spot that's soundproof, decorated in your favorite color, and filled with your favorite things. If you are lucky enough to be able to create such a place, by all means do so, but as any experienced meditator will tell you, the place is secondary. Your entire life, over time, becomes the meditation, so the right place is wherever you happen to be.

It's worth noting that when you start out, you are creating a pattern for yourself that will make it easier to meditate regularly. If the place is desirable, you are more likely to want to go there. If the peace and calm you enjoy there put you at ease, you are more likely to want to keep that time of day sacrosanct. In many ways, you are conditioning yourself to a new behavior, much as if you were training a child to learn to eat prop-erly. There's a regular ritual to eating, and that ritual brings with it im-portant nutrition beyond what you introduce to the digestive system.

The process of learning to meditate is the same. First you accustom yourself to meditating at a regular time each day, and then you are intro-duced to various experiences of meditation as you sit. You don't have to do anything. They just happen. One leg might go to sleep while you sit, and you'll feel the pins and needles spreading upward. All you need to do is observe the experience. You might feel light as a feather. A thought about floating away might go through your mind. But it's all simply illu-sion, simply thought. You just let it go, as you do every other thought. You might see stars, hear or feel vibrations, or perceive an expansive space. Everyone is different, as is every sitting, and there are no right or wrong experiences. I went through a period of shaking all over as I sat. It lasted for a month or two, and then it stopped.

If I'd read meaning into this, it might have scared me or perhaps made me think I was special in some way. But it's all simply part of the process of waking up, and when you avoid attributing meanings to the things that happen to you, you allow the natural flow of your own unfolding. Every time you attach a belief to an experience or an event in your life—and this is as true of your everyday life as it is of meditation—you will experience a restriction to that flow. You never know what "food" you'll be introduced to, but just like the child, your job is simply to taste, and to avoid judging the new flavors as either good or bad.

Meditation ABCs

The process I'm recommending that you start with is the same one that I was taught. It's simple, and it gives you very little to worry about—a real asset for dealing with the multitasking, hyperactive minds that most of us are endowed with. In the following sections, I'll give you more tips, but first let's review what you are going to do.

Simply sit on a cushion with your legs crossed if you can, kneel on the floor, or sit on a chair if you prefer. It is important to keep your spine straight, so make sure that whatever you are sitting on provides the support you need to keep it so. Then rest your hands in your lap, or on your knees if you like, and close your eyes. You are going to stay in this position for the duration of the meditation, so make sure you are reasonably comfortable and not slouching or slumping.

As you sit, you'll become aware of all the thoughts bubbling up in your mind. Typically, when we're not meditating, we follow one thought with another and another in a linear way, associating ideas with each one and then listening to the stories they create. But here, in this still time, you'll now just let each thought go as it arises. For the purpose of understanding the process, bring to mind a cartoon character with a thought bubble over his head, and envision that thought being released and the bubble floating away in its balloon. That's very much like what you'll be doing. So, for example, this thought might arise: "I wonder if I locked the door." Instead of proceeding to another thought in which you try to determine whether or not you did and then another in which you think about what might happen if you didn't, and so on, simply let the thought pass as though it had been spoken by someone you don't know and have no involvement with. Remember, it's not your thought. It's "the" thought, floating around in the ether, but entirely without meaning in this calm interior space you are making. Thought after thought will come; let each one go in the same way.

Because of all the letting go you are doing, along with sometimes getting hooked into a thought sequence and then suddenly becoming aware of that train of thought and the need to let it go, the first few times you sit may not calm. In fact, thoughts arise in meditation all the time, even in people who've been meditating for years. But the more practiced you become, the less you pay attention to them; gradually they won't enter your awareness anymore. What frustrates a lot of new meditators is that they can't stop thinking. It's important to recognize that that's not the point. The point is instead to stop *attaching* to the thoughts and buying into what they are telling you. Let those balloons just float on by.

For some people this approach is all they need. But if you find you need something to focus on as you sit, let your mind pay attention to the passage of your breath in and out. You aren't trying to do anything at all here other than keep your mind occupied with something harmless. If your mind wanders, which it will, just let the thought go and bring your attention back to the breath. That's it. There are no words to repeat or sounds to make; no special way of breathing and no special positioning of hands, lips, tongue, or eyeballs. Keep it as simple and as unencumbered as possible for now. If you want to practice another variant of meditation later, that's fine, but start the process with an absolute minimum of things to get hung up on. Just sit and let those thoughts go. There's nowhere to get to, and there's no one—no one—who can't do this. If you follow these simple instructions, you'll be meditating.

DURATION
By setting a length of time to sit—I recommend twenty minutes to start with—you are conditioning yourself to remain in meditation even when

something inside you thinks it might be more enjoyable to get up now. Just as you can discipline a child to stay at the table during mealtimes, you can discipline yourself to stay put until the period of meditation is over. Although you may not appreciate the value of this to start with, over time you'll come to see that the part of you that wants to get up before the appointed time is the part that cannot recognize the nutrition that comes from meditation. But through the discipline of simply sitting, that part, too, will be transformed in just the same way that the child finally learns to finish dinner so that he or she may be allowed to go and play.

If you have already written off the idea of meditating because you can't imagine sitting still for that long, start with five minutes a day for the first week, ten minutes a day for the second, fifteen minutes a day for the third, and twenty thereafter. Regularity is more important than the length of time as you accustom yourself to the habit of sitting quietly. By increasing the duration gradually, you'll find that it's not as difficult as you'd imagined, and after a while you'll look forward to the time each day that you sit because you'll feel so replenished by it.

PLACE

The basic conditions for a place in which to practice being still are as follows:

- The place is relatively quiet and as free from interruptions as possible. If there's a phone close by, unplug it. If there's an inescapable noise from an adjacent space, get yourself a pair of earplugs. Use whatever tools you need to create a sense of peaceful sanctuary.

- The place is always available at the time of day you've selected to meditate. I've known people who've been exceptionally creative in finding a place for themselves, even when the house or apartment they live in is very small. One man set up a spot for himself on the floor of his walk-in closet. Another used his whirlpool tub—without the water in it, of course. It was just the right size for him to sit in cross-legged. He could lock the door of the bathroom, so there was no chance of surprise visitors, and the room provided a pleasant, light-filled ambience that was conducive to sitting quietly. Other good options are a corner of the master bedroom or a secluded or seldom-used room. A guest bedroom is often a good choice as well. You can even use a bed as your sitting surface if you need to, by sitting on a couple of firm cushions for support.

- The place gives you a sense of privacy. One of the very common obstacles to sticking to a regular practice schedule is the fear of being seen while meditating. In the beginning you may feel awkward or embarrassed. This is simply because you aren't used to the idea of meditation yet and perhaps you assume you'll be considered odd for adopting this new practice. The fear is your own, but until this is fully understood, it's best to select a place that guarantees privacy. A lockable door is a great help, but if that isn't a possibility, something as simple as a trifold screen set across the corner of a room can give you at least visual privacy.

TIME OF DAY

As for the time during which to meditate, this will depend a lot on your schedule. Meditating during a period when you have more physical chi—more energy—is definitely preferable. If you have small children who are with you most of the day, you may want to wake up early and meditate then, or you may want to wait until after the children are soundly asleep. If you work at a job that tends to exhaust you, meditating before you go to work will be much more useful than meditating after you return home. If you are very tired physically and mentally, meditation can be a lot more difficult because your body would much rather go to sleep than sit and remain alert. And if you have the luxury of working at home or have the option of picking a time during the day to meditate, you might want to select the time when you feel most vital and alive.

For those who believe there is simply no time available, there may be a part of your personality that wants to keep you from ever being still. It is invested in keeping you doing, doing, doing, so that you never have a chance to be and never have a chance to stop and look at what's going on underneath all that busyness. In these situations it's important to refute the belief. There are a number of ways in which to do this:

- Check to see if there are ever any times during the day when you are waiting for someone or for something to be completed:

Do you sit in your car and wait for your child to get out of school each day?

Do you ride the train to and from work every day?

Do you have a cup of coffee while you are waiting for a laundry cycle to end?

All these are opportunities for still time.

- Check to see if there is someone you could delegate to do something that you currently do in order to free up a few minutes:

    Do you have an older child who could watch the younger ones for a while?

    Could you ask your spouse to make breakfast or the kids' lunches every other day?

    Could you make an arrangement with your neighbor to take each other's kids for a walk every other day?

    These kinds of time-sharing arrangements can open up time slots that are currently activity-filled.

- Check to see if there are time slots that you are currently using in other ways that could be repurposed:

    Do you have a designated lunch hour that you typically use for eating out with friends or colleagues?

    Do you work through your lunch breaks because everyone else does or because you believe you get more done during the day that way?

    Do you have a habit of vacuuming the house each day whether it needs it or not because that's what you learned from your mother?

    Do you watch television for an hour each evening before going to bed?

    The time spent in these activities could be abbreviated or redirected to free up twenty minutes for sitting alone quietly.

Once you give yourself permission to consider your schedule creatively, you'll find periods that can be opened up and designated for solitude. It is the belief that such times don't exist that is the problem.

If you find yourself slipping from regular practice because apparently pressing issues are impinging on the time of day you've selected, it may be an indication that the time you've selected isn't ideal or that your personality is looking for a way to avoid meditating altogether. If it's not obvious which is the case, try a different time and see if this works better. If it doesn't, the cause is almost certainly a personality issue. Take this as a cue that what's required is a stronger inner parenting style. I've certainly been through periods when I had to fight the urge to do the hundred and one other things I could think of to do right then. Recognizing the similarity between me and the wriggling child at the dinner table helps keep me on task.

TIMERS

A timer is a useful tool to include as a part of your meditation practice when you are starting out because otherwise the monkey mind is constantly wondering if it is time to stop yet. As far as timing devices are concerned, you can use a regular alarm clock, of course, to signal that the time you've set aside for meditation has come to an end, but if you do, make sure the buzzer isn't too startling, or it will instantly shatter your calm state. You can also purchase meditation chimes or an ambient sound generator that will serenade you with breaking ocean waves, rain forest activity, and any number of other natural soundscapes. The choices are many. I like the sound of a chime because it brings me back from meditation peacefully and allows the calm of the meditative state to continue as I start to reengage in my daily routine. (You'll find some links for various products that are available on the Not So Big Life website.)

SEAT

Finally, but most important, the cushion or chair you sit on is an essential feature of your meditation practice. Everyone's body is different, so it's worth trying out cushions of different shapes and sizes before you settle on one. The Zen center I went to when I first started meditating had round zafus, which are the most archetypal of meditation cushions. Many people love them, but I find them uncomfortable. My legs go to sleep very quickly when I'm sitting on a zafu.

I was lucky enough to stumble on a type of cushion that's shaped like an overstuffed boomerang and allows you to place some of the weight of your body on your knees while keeping your back very straight. This style of cushion allows me to sit comfortably for hours at a time. There are also low wooden stools, which work well for those who have a hard time sitting cross-legged. And if all else fails, there's the common straight-back dining room chair. But if you do use a chair, remember to keep your spine upright and straight, your legs uncrossed, and your feet firmly on the floor. It is almost impossible to meditate effectively when you are slumped over or lying down. There's something very important about having the spine at a right angle to the floor. (As with timers, I've included some sources of cushions on the Not So Big Life website.)

COPING WITH DISTRACTIONS

Wherever and whenever you decide to meditate, you will face distractions. But remember that even when there are fire trucks passing by your window and the cat is trying to climb into your lap, it is entirely possible to remain in meditation. These are just sounds and movements, available to be observed as phenomena but not requiring your attention. Just like thoughts, let them go. It's really a very natural thing to do. It's the mind that wants to make it complicated.

Now give it a try, and see how easy it is to set the conditions for widening the aperture of your awareness.

PRINCIPLE
layering

A series of walls that separate rooms one from another can also be thought of as a set of layers that divide space. The walls can be solid, like stud walls sheathed with wallboard, or they can be much less dense, like beams supported by columns or a series of sliding glass doors. Thinking of walls in this way allows us to see the much broader potential of each vertical plane in question, from almost completely open to partially closed to translucent or even transparent.

A house composed of a series of layers of varying degrees of permeability and translucency creates a very different experience from one in which every layer is solid. A house with solid layers can feel constricted and seem uninteresting since all the spaces end up looking much the same. By contrast, a house with many different kinds of layering can feel spacious and more engaging—even when the spaces themselves aren't very big—because it offers a variety of spatial experiences. The variety of layers reveals the beauty of the entire composition of the house rather than limiting you to the experience of the room you are in.

In the waking dream those things that we take for granted or accept as just the way things are act like the solid-wall variety of house design. They don't keep us from performing basic tasks in the world, but they're not inspiring. What you see is pretty much what you get. When you start seeing through those standard fixtures of everyday life, however, you begin to live a life with more permeable and varied layers, a life that consequently is richer and more textured.

Perhaps you experience job layoff after job layoff, for example. You assume that this is your lot in life, and you resent it heartily. This is the equivalent of a solid wall in house design. But when you start to look at what a layoff allows, when you see it as an opportunity to pursue something you are passionate about instead of taking it for a slap in the face, then your wall is no longer solid. It transforms into a translucent sliding door that broadens the view from one phase of your life to the next. In this chapter we'll start to see more clearly the interconnectivity that's possible in the quality and character of your life as this translucency and permeability of layers is revealed.

NINE

Proceeding Through the Construction Process

The trick is to realize that the shit that falls on you is fertilizer.
—RON MANGRAVITE

Not a Problem

We're ready now to begin the construction of your life remodeling, and as anyone who has lived through the remodeling of a house knows, this is the most challenging part of the process. Although the blueprint seems clear enough and you've got a pretty good idea of how you'd like things to look when you're done, the act of implementing specific changes always proves more difficult than you can imagine before you begin. It's all very well to understand intellectually that the content and story line of your waking dream are shaped by your conditioned patterns, but what happens when you encounter situations in which those patterns kick in and your personality won't give up its grip on the reins? How do you integrate these new understandings into your everyday reality so that the underlying dynamics of your waking dream can change? These shifts can happen only if you start working with the new blueprint. You'll follow it as best you can and deal with what comes up as your hot buttons get pushed, just as you would if you were remodeling a house.

Remodeling of any kind can be stressful because you feel, for the period of the construction, that everything is unsettled and you cannot control the process no matter how hard you try. Even if you have an excellent builder and an architect who is observing the process and answering questions that arise, this is a time when home owners are most likely to become distressed. Whatever their hot buttons may be, those are precisely the ones that will inevitably be triggered. Someone who hates a messy house will find himself confronted daily with the dust and debris of the construction process. Someone who wants everything executed exactly according to plan will find small deviations from the blueprint each time she checks on the progress. Someone who wants to be helpful to the builder and make him feel right at home will find herself being moved to the sidelines while he does his job. Remodeling is guaranteed to bring up those conditioned patterns that most significantly stand in the way of your living a fuller, more satisfying life.

When I work with home owners, I prepare them for this unexpected aspect of the remodeling process. And as you move into the construction phase of your life's remodeling, I offer the same advice: Be prepared for some surprising reactions to what happens in your daily life as you begin to live these new understandings. They will challenge you, but by sticking with the new blueprint, you'll begin to see that things do in fact change. You'll start to see the new form of your remodeled life appearing through what seemed to be a solid everyday story line. And as you engage with the challenges that arise, you'll be able to observe firsthand the shifting of the whole. Just as with the remodeling of a house, once you get the hang of it, the remodeling of your life is quite exciting to watch and participate in.

But stay aware of the fact that you can't *force* changes in the story line. They happen because of the work you are doing with your conditioned patterns and not because of your efforts to change your movie's plot. If you were paying close attention at the end of the last chapter, you might have noticed a sentence with the potential to rattle your universe: "Our seeking obscures and impedes the flow." Stop and consider for a moment how much time you spend trying to make things happen the way you want them to. Most of us do it all the time. We do it without even thinking about it, firmly believing that if we don't strive, nothing will happen and we'll stay stuck in the predicament of the moment forever. It's a common fear, and just about everything we learn during childhood and early adulthood reinforces this belief. It is a fundamental principle of our consensus reality: no pushing, no change.

But it just ain't so.

In order to understand this section, make a list of the handful of occasions in your life when things shifted dramatically for the better. Perhaps you got a new job; perhaps you got married or moved across the country; perhaps you lived abroad for a while or developed a strong friendship. Once you've written down the dramatic shifts that come to mind, make a note beside each one, identifying the apparent cause of the shift. In the case of the new job, perhaps you'd unexpectedly been laid off from a job and were forced to look for a new one, or perhaps you'd been looking and looking for a new position and then something quite different from what you were looking for opened up at the company where you already worked.

After you've completed this task, take a look at how many of these changes happened according to your plans. In most instances you'll discover that the big changes in your life occurred when you were least expecting them, much less as you'd planned them. This is an earth-shattering realization for most of us. We just assume we're in charge. We believe wholeheartedly that without our striving, nothing good would ever happen, but in fact quite the reverse is true. Change happens with every passing moment. It is the inevitable result of the unfolding of everything we perceive and experience in time. Nothing we do will alter this. But our striving often slows down the amount of change we let into our movie. In essence, every time we see a "problem" in our waking dream, we are resisting the flow and saying that what is manifesting is not okay with us. We are striving to make it the way we believe it should be rather than accepting the way it actually is.

There *are* times, of course, when you have to move quickly to get yourself out of danger, perhaps by dodging a falling object or moving out of the way of an oncoming car, but you'll notice that in those situations, no thinking is required. Your body springs into action, and you do exactly what you are impelled to do under the circumstances. So although we might label each of these situations a problem in hindsight, in that moment it is simply what's happening, and your response is totally in the flow of what's showing up. It may not be fun to experience, but it's absolutely spontaneous, absolutely in the moment.

While we're on the subject of what we commonly call problems, the Not So Big show house I'd been preparing for the annual International Builders' Show was not going according to plan. The house was to be built using modular technologies, but due to an incomplete understanding of the costs involved in transportation and assembly, my team's vision of an entirely assembled house on the parking lot of the Orange County Convention Center in Orlando, Florida, just wasn't going to happen. The reason in a nutshell: It was going to cost too much money, and there wasn't enough time left to raise more.

So the key players in the project, including me, were on a conference call to figure out what to do. The options on the table were to abandon the project completely or postpone it until the following year's show, when we would have more time to get our ducks in a row. None of us would have wished to be in this position, and some of us were pretty crestfallen. But if we'd been totally focused on seeing the situation as a problem and had been kicking ourselves (and possibly one another) for not seeing it coming, we wouldn't have been open to what happened next. I asked, "What story are we really trying to tell with this project?" Someone responded, "We're trying to show how the house of the future might be made and what it might look like."

"Do we need a fully assembled house to illustrate that?" I asked. "What if we just had three or four of the modular boxes (the long sections of a house that are transported by tractor trailer) delivered to the parking lot and used these as the basis for our exhibit?" We'd toured the modular factory a few months earlier, so we all knew the surprising power of seeing all the sections of a house lined up across the factory floor. Why not create an exhibit that gave our visitors the same experience?

There was a moment's silence, and then voice after voice responded with "I love it!" and "That's perfect!" Five minutes later, we were all realizing that this was in fact a far more effective way of demonstrating what we'd planned.

As I write this, it's still entirely possible that our plans will change again, but the point of the story is that every moment brings change, and how we perceive that change has a huge effect on the quality of our life experiences. What if we'd tried to cut costs dramatically by building a less detailed house, for example, or if we'd all gone into eighteen-hour-day mode trying to force it to happen on a too-tight schedule? The results would have been much more unpleasant for everyone involved, and ultimately less successful.

If any one of us had become angry or vindictive, this new idea simply wouldn't have emerged. If any one of us had become hesitant or concerned about the trustworthiness of the other players, the new idea wouldn't have been given more than a moment's consideration. But by seeing what was presenting itself as an opportunity rather than a problem, things shifted—for all of us. Today we are working on a very different project from the one we were working on yesterday, but it's one that feels right and serves the goals of everyone involved—just differently.

Whether something is a problem or not is a matter of perspective. Using the wider aperture and perspective that the new blueprint allows, you can watch your problems become translucent, so that you can see right through them. If you are invested in having things turn out a certain way, then you have a problem on your hands when they seem not to co-operate, but if you are open to what's happening and willing to engage in whatever it is at the moment that it occurs, then *there is no problem*. There's only life experience. Now, this isn't to say that all life experiences are pleasant. We know that's not the case. But by not rejecting them as they present themselves, you'll discover that your experiencing of your own life becomes very, very different. Because you are in the moment, because you are fully engaged in everything that happens, without fixed preconceptions, inflexible preferences, or straining effort, everything contributes to your growth.

Learning to Recognize the Nutrients for Inner Growth

Every single event in our lives is a type of food that allows us to under-stand ourselves more completely. If we reject that food when it's offered, we're like children who don't want to eat their vegetables. Yes, it's true that children can survive without their vegetables, but they will grow more readily and with fewer health complications when they eat nutri-tious food. What our experiences offer us has just the same effect. They're there to help us to grow. Most of us are quite convinced that if we're living properly, every life event should be yummy and positive. So when things don't proceed as expected, we perceive that something is wrong, and we assume that we must fix it. If we were personally in charge of determining what is best for us, we'd be eating the experiential equiv-alent of ice cream and chocolate cake all day long.

What if we were to see all events as nutritious, whether they made us feel good, bad, or indifferent? Imagine for just a moment how much less frustrating your life would be. Something happens. Your dog bites your neighbor, or your child comes home with a badly scraped knee. Now, these things require no emotional outburst from you and no judgment as to why they shouldn't have happened. They are simply events. They've al-ready occurred. What you are looking at are the results of a moment now past. How much sense does it make to get upset about the conditions that created that past moment whose effects are now showing up in your waking dream? Can you start to sniff out that it is your own reactivity, your own thoughts about what is happening, that poses the primary obstacle to flow?

Your dog bites your neighbor. What do you do? Your neighbor is now on your doorstep, demanding that you put your dog down. While you are trying to calm your neighbor and apologize for this horrible situation that's occurred in his waking dream, observe your reactions. What are you feeling? Are you horrified by the idea of someone's wanting to kill your beloved dog? Are you fearful that perhaps this angry person will take you to court? Do you feel guilty for having been unaware that your pet was on the loose? Do you feel pain and empathy for this neighbor because he has been attacked by your pet? Are you furious at the dog for having escaped again? Are you angry with your neighbor for his extreme response?

The possibilities are endless, but every one of these responses has the ability to reveal you to you. First, observe your reaction. Do you reflexively move to defensiveness, anger, judgment, or empathy? If you watch yourself and the unfolding situation closely, you can start to see, in real time, how those responses affect the quality of your waking dream.

When your neighbor shows up at your door in a rage about your dog, the only thing you need to do is to listen to your neighbor, take a moment, and respond in the moment. All your thoughts and fears are completely imagined. You can't know from moment to moment what the outcome will be, but by dealing with what is there right then rather than creating imaginary stories and trying to control your waking dream so that those story lines don't play out, you will be engaging in the present moment, in the Now. It's our thoughts about what is happening that get us into trouble. And those thoughts simply don't reflect what's real. When you see the truth in this, your whole life will begin to change because you'll no longer be seeing problems everywhere. Instead, you'll be seeing what's actually there and what's in front of you to do.

The unfortunate fact is that we waste massive amounts of energy reacting to things that are already in the past. Most people spend a huge percentage of their lives frustrated about this, and hoping for that, implicitly rejecting the way things are at that particular moment. Years ago I watched a friend's boyfriend work himself into a frenzy over his inability to dial a phone number correctly during a call-in show on which free tickets were being given away to the tenth, twentieth, and thirtieth callers. He tried three times to dial the number, each time getting it wrong in his haste. After the first time he started yelling at the "stupid" phone, and by the third time he had hurled it across the room in a fury. No amount of rational observation would have allowed him to see that the phone was not the source of his frustration.

Reactivity is always the result of conditioned patterns and confused thinking and should serve as a red flag indicating the presence of a filter over reality. When you find yourself filled with irritation at circumstances, you are behaving just like the man railing at the "stupid" phone. You are reacting because you believe things should be different from the way they are. You want things to go *your* way in your movie, and events are not cooperating, so you become angry, upset, hurt, or show any number of other emotionally reactive responses.

The next time one of these reactions arises in you, consider that it is in fact food to help you see yourself better. It's not good or bad; it's simply an indicator that there's something keeping you from seeing clearly what is in front of you. And by exploring your reaction, you can reveal the filter and thereby eliminate the obstruction that's leading you to see problems instead of simply the contents of your waking dream. When you simply observe what's happening, feel what's there to be felt, and deal with what needs to be dealt with in the moment, you'll discover that everything is actually fine.

But doing something other than what you would normally do is not easy because your conditioned patterns assert themselves so quickly, especially in highly charged situations. So take a deep breath to give yourself a moment's space, remind yourself that this is not the dire circumstance that your personality is telling you it is, and notice what happens, for example, when you just listen. Or see what happens if you express sympathy for someone who may appear threatening.

It's important to understand that there is no right or wrong answer and to see that every variation in your response to a given situation can elicit a different counterresponse from the other person. Giving yourself a moment to choose a new response allows you to taste the relativity and the fluidity of what is manifesting. You begin to see how you shape the content of your waking dream through your reactivity and fear-based thinking and how you unnecessarily complicate and obstruct the flow as a result. By clinging to one interpretation of your waking dream, you become blind to the possibilities for your growth that lie buried within the contents of that dream. By learning to observe, learning to experiment with the plot of your movie, you can retrain yourself to focus most of your time and energy on the food rather than the superficial content.

Working Mind versus Thinking Mind

The term that I like best to describe the spontaneous response to situations in the present moment is "working mind," a label coined by the author and teacher Ramesh Balsekar. This is mind without baggage, without preconceiving and second-guessing. As soon as you find yourself planning how to cope with a situation or with an eventuality that might come about as a consequence of a projected sequence of events, you are in "thinking mind"—the mind that believes it is up to it to orchestrate reality. With working mind everything is much, much simpler because there's no planning, no projecting, and no imagining. It deals only with what is right in front of it to do. It's a whole lot easier and a whole lot less stressful.

Perhaps you come home at the end of the day feeling as though you've been beat up by circumstances. What makes you feel exhausted and frustrated aren't the situations and the interactions themselves but your reactions to them, your thoughts about them. In the discussion about meditation in chapter 8, I mentioned that it is important not to attach any meaning to what happens in meditation, and the same advice applies to your waking experience. If you avoid attributing meaning to the events of the day, the thinking mind has nothing to work with, and your movie becomes much, much calmer.

Let me give you an example from my day yesterday to show you just how quickly and stealthily the thought stream takes hold. My friend and assistant, Marie, and I are part of a group that was getting together at my house at 7:00 p.m., and I'd asked Marie to pick up a snack for everyone when she was at the store. Since it's my conditioned pattern to worry about inconveniencing others, I probably said something like "It would be nice if you could pick up some fruit or something for us to share at break. Just see if something appeals to you." Not wanting to inconvenience her, I'd couched my request in words that made the snack purchase, to her ears, sound optional. When Marie went to the store, since she hadn't registered the "or something" part of my request, she was looking for fruit that would appeal to her as a snack. Nothing did, so she didn't buy anything.

When I called a half hour before our meeting to confirm that she had indeed picked up a snack and she told me that she hadn't seen anything that appealed to her, I was not happy. How could she have decided not to purchase something when I was depending on her to help me out? (Notice that I had instantly and unconsciously attributed a meaning of my own to her not making a purchase.)

I'm sure Marie sensed my frustration, as she knows me well enough to see through my pattern of being very nice and apparently unflustered even when I'm put out. She responded with "Well, people should have eaten beforehand." What I heard her say was "People should not show up to such a meeting without having eaten beforehand, so I've decided not to buy a snack." But Marie was really saying, "Given that the meeting is at seven p.m., they will probably have eaten by then, so nobody will mind if there's no snack." The word should was being used and interpreted in very different ways.

Can you start to feel how quickly two people, even when they are practiced in the art of understanding that "all there is, is you," can start feeling judged and defensive, based on the interpretation of a single word? Without fully realizing that I was upset by Marie's not purchasing a snack, I responded, "That sounds like a should statement to me," pointing out that Marie was imposing on the world her view of how it should be rather than seeing it as it was. My own filter was looking for reasons Marie was wrong because I felt wronged.

Marie didn't miss a beat and came back with "It sounds like you're should-ing me." True to form, I made a defusing remark that pulled us back from the brink of confrontation. I told her not to worry and that I had some potato chips at home we could eat. She also backed down a bit, apologizing for not buying a snack and offering to pick up something on her way over. "No," I told her, "not to worry. The chips will work." And with that we ended our conversation.

But once we'd hung up, both of us felt uncomfortable about the interaction. I noticed that I was having a hard time letting it go. I kept thinking things like "It looks like I can't depend on her to do the things I need taken care of" and "How can she take it upon herself to decide whether people should have a snack?" These kinds of thoughts are red flags, indicators that instead of seeing things for what they are, we are trying to justify our own stance. We are seeing through filters, even if we can't yet see what the filters are. If someone has upset you, you are in thinking mind, flooded by thoughts and judgments. It's these thoughts and not the person's actions that are the problem.

I decided to use a technique described by Byron Katie in her excellent book *Loving What Is* to decipher the meanings I was attaching to Marie's words. Katie describes a simple process of inquiry that allows you to see almost instantly how you are arguing with reality when you judge the actions of others. In preparation for asking the four questions she prescribes, I wrote down my primary judgment of Marie's inaction:

I can't depend on her to do the things I need taken care of.

Then I applied the sequence of Katie's questions to this statement. The first question is "Is it true?" No, it wasn't. Marie is very thorough; she follows through on the myriad details that fill my calendar. I *can* depend on her. This situation was an anomaly.

Had it not been instantly clear from the answer to the first question that my judgment was off base, I would have proceeded to Katie's second question: "Can you absolutely know that it's true?" The point of this reiteration of the question is that when you look more closely at a situation, you realize that what you believe to be hard fact is only supposition and not what is really there.

The third question is a wonderful one: "How do you react when you believe that thought?" When I believe that I can't depend on Marie, I feel horrible. I feel sad, and I feel as though I'm losing a friend as well as a very valuable assistant. If I hang on to the thought that I can't depend on her, I can in fact bring that reality into existence, at a very high price to me. If I continue to distrust her, I will have to do a lot of the things myself that I currently depend on her to accomplish for me, and I'd lose a dear friend. My world would change dramatically by not trusting and depending on Marie, and I'd feel lonely and isolated. It would be awful.

And then, with the last question, comes liberation: "Who would you be without the thought?" If I let go of the thought that Marie was undependable, I'd have my best friend and trusted assistant back, and I'd be working with her with no preconceptions and no worries about whether she was or was not trustworthy.

There's a final step in Katie's simple formula for seeing through the dream, and that's to turn around what you have been thinking and apply it to yourself. Since all there is, is you, any thought you are having about someone else is really about something in yourself. So for me turning around the judgment on myself would mean "I can't depend on myself to do the things I need to do." Hmm—there's a lot of truth there. There have been many occasions in my life when I've put off things because I wasn't sure what to do. I've often come to my own version of Marie's assessment that there wasn't anything appealing available, and so I haven't done anything at all.

The upshot of this process, no matter what reaction you apply it to, is that you are able to see that the judgments you are making about how things should be and the conclusions you draw as a result are all in your head. You discover that you can choose not to buy into these thoughts, and in so doing you reduce the stress in your life by orders of magnitude.

It was interesting that as soon as Marie arrived for the meeting, she pulled me aside and told me how sorry she was that she had become defensive. She told me that she'd realized she had misunderstood me partway through our phone conversation, but instead of telling me that, she'd started to defend herself by justifying her actions. When she'd turned the "should" finger back on me, she had felt upset at herself. I told her of my inquiry into my own reaction, and we ended up laughing and wondering out loud how human beings ever succeed in getting along with one another.

It is remarkable to see how quickly things can escalate into a full-blown misunderstanding. If you stay with the content of the story rather than the underlying dynamics, you will remain firmly in the soup of reactivity that we call everyday life. That's what thinking mind does for us, and the results are not pretty. We are in a miserable prison of our own making, and the only way out is to understand just how much what we see deviates from what is really there. This is what becomes clear when we implement the new blueprint.

Think About It

The truth is that thinking is an enormously powerful tool, but it is no more than that. When thinking is used by someone who recognizes that he or she is much more than the thoughts themselves, it can be very useful. The problems arise when the thinking mechanism starts running the show—when we believe that we *are* our thoughts, when we identify with the thinking mechanism itself.

Just because a particular thought passes through your mind doesn't mean you have to identify with it. Thoughts float around in consciousness like bubbles in seltzer water. Thoughts like "I'm too fat" or "I'm not good enough" or "I've been abandoned" or "I'm a lost cause" pass into and out of billions of minds on this planet all day every day. They don't belong to you—or anyone else, for that matter—and once you realize this you begin to recognize that you don't have to buy into them. You can simply let them go by.

With this understanding comes an enormous sense of liberation. You are not your thoughts. They are the thoughts, completely impersonal, like so many stations on a radio dial. You can tune in to any one of them and listen to it for a while; then you can turn the knob and tune in to another station, noticing how each different thought acts as a catalyst for a flood of personal associations.

Your Turn

Try thinking just one thing without associating it with anything else. Think "tree," for example. What happens? Close your eyes for a minute and see.

You may have conjured up a tree from your childhood, triggering a flood of memories. You may have brought to mind the names of types of trees that you know, or you may have recalled what you've read over the years about how a tree grows, from seed to aging giant. But you almost certainly couldn't stay with just "tree," because the word triggers thousands of associated thoughts and memories, which shape your experience in every waking moment without your even knowing they are there. One person I know even believes that she hates trees because one fell on her house once— for her this exercise can put her in a bad mood. But that emotional response is based on an arbitrary association she made sometime in her past, which she has continued to identify with, believing that she is defined by that thought. It is just a thought—no more, no less—and if she chooses, she can let it go.

This is how thoughts work on us when they're unregulated and when they aren't observed from a wider perspective. Because we've been taught to identify with the thoughts that float through our minds and we believe they mean something about who we are, we continually get bogged down in our emotional associations with those thoughts, not realizing that *we* are shaping the content of our waking dreams and therefore we are responsible for making them so uncomfortable. As Walt Kelly's famous cartoon character Pogo so wisely observed, "We have met the enemy, and he is us."

You, too, can let go of thoughts that make you reactive. A good way to do this is by implementing some of the practices we've been discussing: observing yourself in action by developing a watcher, meditating regularly to develop the reflex of letting go of thoughts, and learning not to identify yourself with those thoughts. You'll learn more about how to do this in the exercise at the end of this chapter as well.

Peace Training

Peace is a state of mind and a state of being. Only when you are at peace within yourself can you see what is actually here and that nothing about it is wrong. *Nothing* is wrong. It simply appears to be wrong because of our confusion, our thoughts about how things should be. That's a tall order for most people to grasp, but when you start to grasp it, you'll see that the only way to change the world is to change yourself. You are it.

When we bemoan the state of the world, we're saying that the ocean surface shouldn't be choppy—that there should be no whitecaps, no storms, that they are disturbing the peace, negating the possibility of heaven on earth. We are rejecting what is happening, not understanding that heaven, or bliss, or whatever name you care to apply to that which is truly meaningful, lies beneath what we see, under the story line of our waking dream. The new blueprint for the remodeling of our lives allows us to see other dimensions of what's going on.

There is absolutely no way to make what we are seeing perfectly still and tranquil, at least not unless we step out of duality. Everything that we see is the embodiment of a constant process. We are most familiar with this notion as it is stated in Newton's Third Law of Motion: For every action there is an equal and opposite reaction. A less well-known scientist and mystic, Walter Russell, called this giving and regiving. But in essence both Newton and Russell described the same situation. Everything is, in fact, in a state of constant equilibrium. It's only the waves that make it look otherwise—only the surface conditions. What lies beneath is peace itself.

For many years I had a list posted on the wall of my office, under the heading "The Symptoms of Inner Peace." Although when I first received it from a friend, I knew I wasn't able to live completely the qualities described, I recognized that they were certainly something to aspire to, something that could serve as a guide for my journey through life. I share the list with you here:

THE SYMPTOMS OF INNER PEACE

- A tendency to think and act spontaneously rather than act in response to fears based on past experiences
- An unmistakable ability to enjoy each moment
- A loss of interest in judging other people
- A loss of interest in judging oneself
- A loss of interest in interpreting the actions of others
- A loss of interest in conflict
- A loss of ability to worry (a very serious symptom)
- Frequent overwhelming episodes of appreciation
- Contented feelings of connectedness with others and with nature
- Frequent attacks of smiling
- An increasing tendency to let things happen rather than make them happen
- An increased susceptibility to the love extended by others as well as the uncontrollable urge to extend it

Today this list makes more sense to me than ever. When we understand that free-floating thoughts and their associations are essentially meaningless and impersonal, and when we understand that the appearance of things is only the clothing that covers the experiencing that allows us to grow and flourish, then all the "symptoms" in the list spring into existence unbidden. There is nothing wrong. Given the consensus-reality vision of the world—that we are on the way to Hell in a handbasket—this understanding puts everything in an almost shocking new light.

But stop and consider this for a few moments: What if there were nothing at all wrong with anything? What if all the waves, whitecaps, and storms were simply there to wake us up to who we really are?

An almost instant objection arises from deep inside us when we hear this. How can all the disasters and all the suffering in the world *not* be a mistake? This notion is worth examining more closely, because embedded in the question is a mystery that will help you meet adversity in your life in a new way.

Shock and Awe

Often the most uncomfortable circumstances bring about the greatest growth because they contain the highest-grade nutrients for inner development. When something awful happens, all your defenses and accepted ways of orienting yourself to your waking dream are unceremoniously ripped away. Remember the looks on people's faces along the Gulf Coast after Hurricane Katrina in 2005? Remember the despair in the eyes of the children who survived the tsunami in Southeast Asia in 2004? Remember the incredulous horror you felt as you watched—on television or in person—the airplanes flying into the towers of the World Trade Center on September 11, 2001? Remember the surreal experience of watching those two huge structures collapse? That was a shock to everyone's waking dream, with dramatic results. People began questioning whether they really wanted that bigger house, that better-paying job, that longer commute. Suddenly those things paled in comparison to family and other loved ones.

In the face of such tragedies, we are stripped bare, left vulnerable and disoriented, not sure who we really are. Like newborns, we have nothing to hang on to, nothing that defines or contains us anymore. We have no choice but to start over. And though it is immensely painful, just as it must be for the newborn suddenly assaulted by light and sound and touch, the process allows us to breathe in life in an entirely new way.

Profound shock can bring about an experience known in spiritual literature as cosmic consciousness, a sudden and complete understanding of the boundlessness and unity of all existence. People like Eckhart Tolle today and William Blake and Walt Whitman in the past have recounted experiences in which they suddenly and profoundly understood the inner workings of the universe. They couldn't explain how or why. It simply happened, often thanks to events that completely destroyed the familiar mechanisms with which we all orient and define ourselves.

Although this phenomenon happens only very rarely and cannot be orchestrated into existence, smaller shocks do happen to all of us all the time. Usually we heartily resent them, not realizing they are all gifts designed to wake us up. Every automobile accident, every physical injury, every personal loss, and every death of a loved one is a wake-up call. The universe is saying, "Stop sleepwalking through your life! Look. Look at how you are living, at how you are being. Is this what you really want? Is this who you really are?" And of course the answer is usually an emphatic "No!" When these things happen, it doesn't take long to realize that you *are* more and that you just needed a little course correction in order to start living more of your potential and more of who you are realizing yourself to be.

Typically, a week or two after a major shock we've all but forgotten what we knew in that moment. The experience is so otherworldly, so devoid of familiar and recognizable content that we can't hang on to it. We can't re-member it—we can't put it back together in our mind. But if you are alert to the way in which life sends signals, you'll be able to hang on to the new awareness just a little longer by asking yourself what changes need to be made in your life that you have been ignoring or not been paying sufficient attention to. The more you resist the promptings of the waking dream, the more insistent they will become. All you can do is remain present in what you are doing as much as possible and pay attention to what is being asked of you. If you do this, you will learn and grow swiftly. It's when you think you know better and when you decide to shut out the signals by racing back into the fray of the waking dream without pausing to ask what's out of whack that you'll find your life beset with more—and similar—obstacles.

Keep in mind that if you are trying to think your way to understanding, you are bound to get stuck, and you'll only end up confusing yourself further. The way to true understanding is through working mind—through simply doing what is in front of you to do. But how do you know what that is? How can you be sure? Open your eyes, experience the moment in its completeness and its newness, and do whatever it is that is required of you right then. Honestly, there is no one right answer. From this perspective anything you do is the right thing because that is in fact what you are doing. The common way of saying this these days is "It's what is."

When you are trying to figure out the right thing to do, you are in thinking mind. You have set up a duality between what is right and what is wrong, with the implication that if you don't pick the correct option, you'll be screwing up. But in reality, you can't screw up. Whatever you pick will produce a set of life experiences that will continue to reveal you to you, whether the content of what happens is pleasant to go through or miserable. All of it contains food for your growth. The part of you that's trying to determine what's correct is lost in appearances, whereas the nutrients for self-understanding lie in that vast ocean of peace beneath the surface.

Rest assured that the lessons you need will present themselves, requiring absolutely no effort on your part other than your attention. As Woody Allen so astutely observed, "Eighty percent of success is showing up." But I'd increase that percentage to ninety-nine, leaving aside the one remaining percentage point for that mysterious ingredient in life that can't be named.

Trust in the Moment

There's an ingredient in this process that I haven't described yet, but it is now of paramount importance. The ingredient is trust. When we first come into this world, we are fully trusting, but over time this changes.

I remember watching this erosion of trust happen right in front of me when a cat of mine had a litter of kittens. For the first four weeks all six kittens seemed equally trusting and equally adorable. Then one day, quite by accident, one of the kittens—the only completely black one— fell out of the big cardboard box that was its home and scampered off. It didn't make a sound, and the mother cat didn't seem to notice it was gone. I looked high and low but couldn't find the wayward kitten until late that evening, when I heard a single plaintive meow emanating from the dusty recesses of the stove's underbelly. With the long handle of a broom, I was able to fish the kitten out and slide it back into the world of daylight and open spaces, but it had been permanently traumatized by the experience. It no longer trusted.

After that, while the other five kittens would race all over the house in wild abandon, the little black one would sit alone. That early event in the kitten's life gave it a way of engaging in life that was very different from that exhibited by the other kittens. But it wasn't a bad thing necessarily, although I thought of it that way at the time. It was simply different.

As you read this, you may be recalling the first event in your life when you were aware of losing trust—in an adult, in a friend, or in your circumstances. These things happen to everyone. It's inevitable, part of being alive. But those events aren't who you are. Like the black kitten, you are still who you were before those events. You simply received a shock that changed your experiencing of life. But it also fueled your growth, allowing you to become who you are now. We are so used to thinking of things in terms of right and wrong or good and bad that it's hard to fully appreciate that your experiences don't define you. You are much, much more than their sum. Those experiences are nothing more than what happened in a past scene in your movie. They are memories, and so by definition they are not here and now. When you can truly see this, you can begin to reconnect with your original trust, the belief that no matter what happens you are always supported; you are never abandoned. And the way you know this is that you are still here now, still experiencing life, and still aware. That awareness never goes away—at least not while you are awake.

The black kitten wasn't abandoned either. It was adopted several weeks later by an older woman who instantly liked its shyness and who knew intuitively how to coax it toward her. It was an amazing scene to watch. They took to each other immediately, recognizing a similar way of inhabiting their lives, and each was a perfect companion for the other. Without the kitten's experience of falling out of the box, the kitten and the woman probably wouldn't have fallen together in this way.

Nothing happens by accident. There's an unbelievable orchestration going on that is completely outside our control (remember the flower exercise), and recognizing this is what allows trust to return completely. Once it does, you stop reacting to things as though they shouldn't be happening and start automatically seeking the gifts they contain, without judging the relative correctness of what is taking place. It's happening; that's all that matters, and you simply trust that this moment contains everything you need. It may not be what you want, but it is always, always what you need.

Doing What's in Front of You to Do

By this point, you may well be starting to see that you aren't in control of the events in your waking dream and that your being present and having an interest in growing are the only things that make a difference in the quality of your experience. "Can it truly be that simple?" you may ask. It really can.

I remember the day I completed the final revision of *The Not So Big House* and now had nothing to do but wait until it was published—an event scheduled for six months from that day. Of course, my mind turned immediately to the next major item on my to-do list, the task of organizing advance promotion to ensure the book's reception and success. A week later I was traveling on the West Coast with my friend and teacher Jan, and as we drove through the misty green fields and forests of the Pacific Northwest, she told me that what happened next would not be up to me, that all I needed to do was respond to what came my way, and that it wasn't up to me to arrange any promotional activities in advance of the book's release.

This was absolutely counterintuitive to me. I had always believed that if I didn't take action to promote my work, it would remain invisible. When Jan saw me squirming in response to her observation, she suggested an assignment. She told me that with the release of the book, I had an opportunity to see exactly how perfectly the universe provides when we don't intervene by trying to manage and control the process. She suggested something that until that moment would have been unthinkable to me: to leave the orchestration and the planning for the promotion of the book to others. The only thing I needed to do, Jan explained, was to respond to whatever came to my doorstep. So if a reporter called me, by all means I should talk to him or her, responding fully to the inquiries. But I should make no calls and write no letters to alert anyone to the book's release. I gulped and let the impact of what she was asking me to do sink in.

And then it happened. I felt all my worrying about how to get the job done dropping away. It was almost a physical release, like tons of weight that I was unaware of carrying sliding off my shoulders, leaving me feeling light and free. Although writing the book had easily been the biggest venture I'd undertaken to date and I felt I had a lot invested in it, something inside me surrendered in that moment. I knew somehow that Jan's assignment was exactly what I needed and that in following it religiously, I would see things unfold in an extraordinary way. I can't explain how or why I knew this, but I did. Every cell in my body was on fire with excitement and anticipation, but there was no longer any fear and no longer any striving. All I had to do was show up for whoever and whatever came my way.

The results were nothing short of miraculous. As weeks and months went by, I was filled with continual wonder as complete strangers, reporters, friends, and clients found out about the book through all sorts of unexpected means, often writing to tell me their stories via the book's website. There's no way on earth that I would have dreamed up (let alone orchestrated) the script for that year. In fact, if I'd decided not to take Jan's suggestion and tried to *make* things happen, I'm quite certain I would only have created obstacles and barriers to the natural flow of events. Ever since that day I've known unequivocally that what you need will be presented to you. Your obedience to the promptings of your waking dream will provide the most nutritious food for your development imaginable.

One side effect of this realization is that you can lose interest in doing much of anything. A personality fragment will sometimes arise and say, "So what's the point of doing anything? If everything I need will be presented, I can just tune out." Although, strictly speaking, that's true, the part of you that is asserting that it need do nothing at all is a part of your conditioning. What it's really saying is "From my perspective as a character in this waking dream, I've just been given permission to sit on my duff and do nothing. So that's what I plan to do." Obviously, this is not an enlightened part of you speaking. Experiencing the symptoms of inner peace does not mean doing nothing. It simply means doing what's in front of you to do and doing it with a lot less confusion and baggage than you otherwise would.

Change Happens

Early in this chapter I described the way that my current showhouse project had evolved into an exhibit showing how a Not So Big House can be built using modular technology. But the evolution didn't stop there.

Every moment is completely new, which means that things shift and change in the most unexpected ways.

Shortly after our breakthrough idea, our project team received a call from someone at the modular company, explaining that they didn't feel comfortable proceeding even if we exhibited only the modules rather than a whole house. For them, the reduction in work wasn't all that significant. Their company still had to have all its ducks in a row, and after due consideration it had been decided that the schedule was too tight. They realized that everything might go fine and the project would be a success. But it was also possible that it wouldn't, and the company didn't want to take that chance.

Do you see how the universe had taken the decision about what to build or whether to proceed entirely out of our hands? No matter how frustrated or upset we might have chosen to be in response to this set of circumstances, the result would have been the same. There was to be no showhouse project this year for us, and there was nothing we could do to change that. So at this point, rather than waste a lot of energy on being upset, we simply set about doing damage control, calling our sponsors and apologizing for the unexpected turn of events. Undoubtedly a number of the companies that had planned to participate were disappointed, but they saw, as we had, that there was no ready solution. Everyone involved was remarkably supportive.

Although I don't fully understand the reasons for the shift in plans, I can see that the experience provided me with a way to illustrate the point I'm making in this chapter: that things shift and change and that attachment to a particular outcome can become an obstacle to accessing the opportunity for growth embedded in the content of one's waking dream. Maybe that's reason enough, but I sense there's something more as well. The point in every such situation is not to solve the mystery but to live the questions and to stay open to whatever presents itself next.

As I close this chapter, I'm preparing to leave for this year's International Builders' Show, where my team's slot on the parking lot is being used instead to exhibit a truly Not So Big Modular Home, a house of just 400 square feet. Named Katrina Cottage by its architect, Marianne Cusato, and the group of builders and developers who created it, it offers an alternative to the standard Federal Emergency Management Agency (FEMA) trailer and is intended to demonstrate a better way of responding to the need for reconstruction in the Mississippi Delta and Gulf Coast. This is what the behind-the-scenes orchestration of events for which none of us is responsible has made possible, fulfilling a need for a new vision to replace our outmoded thinking about temporary housing.

I can't know what will happen next in this aspect of my waking dream. Will this be the end of showhouse projects for me? Or will it be the beginning of something similar—or something altogether different? Every moment brings forth an untold number of alternative possibilities, each of which has the potential to give birth to a multitude of life experiences. There is no *one* way in which things need to unfold. All possibilities are alive in the field of consciousness, and we, who are here to experience what unfolds each moment, are being fed by every permutation.

EXERCISE
"i am not that thought"

This exercise is as simple as telling yourself, "I am not that thought," whenever you find yourself getting attached to a particular notion and then associating other thoughts with it. But it takes practice. Although you may understand the process intellectually, to apply it when you are in the middle of reacting to something will severely test your ability to stay present. Even people who've been practicing for years fall into the trap and forget all the things that can help them remain objective. It is much like learning to ride a bicycle as a child: When you fall, you must pick yourself up and start riding again, without self-judgment and without self-recrimination.

The challenge is to metabolize experience—both external and internal experience—as it happens. As you become attached to a thought stream, take a moment to observe what happens. How do you feel as you attach to it? What's the point of attaching to it? Have you done this before with this same kind of thought? Where did the process of attaching to this thought begin? Where does it go? All these questions are food for you to metabolize, nutrients for your development. Every thought you have has something buried in it that you can use to learn about yourself.

Many years ago, when I went to my first meditation retreat, the teacher told all of us that for the next four days we would be doing a lot of sitting. Although we were encouraged to walk slowly from time to time around the grounds of the retreat center, we were directed to keep other physical activity to an absolute minimum. I remember one young woman's immediate protest. She asserted that she had to run for at least an hour a day. The teacher calmly explained that this would not be happening over the coming days. The woman protested vehemently. It was clear that she was completely possessed by the thought that she must run for at least an hour a day. It had become her identity—who she believed herself to be—and without that thought she couldn't imagine herself.

All of us have such thoughts; but they are so much a part of our inner fabric that we don't even know they are there. But by watching for the places in your life where you become reactive, you'll be able to root out some of your own beliefs.

Ask yourself: "What conditions do I believe are required in order for me to function?" For example, do you believe that without a cup of coffee or tea immediately upon rising, you can't face the day? Or do you believe that if you don't work through lunch every day, you won't be able to get everything done? Or do you believe that unless you watch an hour of television before going to bed, you won't be able to calm down sufficiently to sleep?

Once you've identified two or three such conditions of your own, ask yourself about each one: "Where did I get this thought in the first place?" and "What makes me believe it's true?" Then look for a way to test the validity of each thought or belief.

If you believe you absolutely have to have that cup of java to get your engines going, try abstaining for one or two mornings just to see what happens. You aren't being asked to give up this habit forever—just for a couple of days, so that you can experience what life is like without that stimulant. You may discover that your world will in fact keep going without the caffeine jolt—in other words, it's not an absolute necessity for survival. If you believe you must always work through lunch, take yourself away from your desk at lunchtime for a day or two and see if it makes any noticeable difference to your productivity. If you can't imagine calming down enough to sleep without the help of Letterman or Leno, try turning the television off an hour before going to bed and see what happens. Unless you try something new, you'll never test your beliefs, and they will continue to define your existence.

Here's another question you can ask yourself, to get at other thoughts that limit your life experience: "What do I believe to be true about myself?"

A friend of mine used to believe that she couldn't tell what colors went well together, so whenever she was about to make a home-decorating decision she'd ask my advice. When I pointed out that the color combinations she chose for her clothing were never timid and always excellent, she began to see that she *could* tell what combinations looked good to her eye and in fact loved to play with color. With a little inquiry into the roots of this thought about herself, she realized that her mother had been tentative about color choices and she had simply followed suit. Once she recognized the historical source of her feeling of inadequacy, she became much more adventurous with her color choices and no longer looked to me for recommendations. Her apartment is now a veritable blaze of color. It makes her feel right at home and expresses much more about who she is than it would have if she'd had someone else select the colors for her.

Or do you think of yourself as weak—a thought common to members of both sexes? Another friend, who'd always seen himself as a wimp and a weakling, when asked to probe the validity of this belief, decided to take a self-defense course. He was amazed to discover that not only did he enjoy the class immensely but he was much stronger than he'd ever imagined. Refuting his belief changed his life in many ways. Once he knew he was strong, he no longer perceived himself as a wimp and began to engage in all sorts of activities that he would never previously have entertained. His favorite pastime nowadays is rock climbing, a sport that would never have crossed his mind before he put his weakling notion to the test. More important, the way he conducts himself in the world has changed; I noticed a difference the last time we met for lunch. He is still sensitive and thoughtful but also more assertive; after asking my permission, he made menu choices for both of us, something he would never have done in the past.

If you have any suspicions that a belief or even an idea about yourself isn't real, it's worth investigating responsibly. You'll learn a lot about how you've created your own prison of unexamined limitations, all of which are keeping you from much of what life has to offer. In a very real way, we are what we think and what we believe, so when we change or shed those thoughts and beliefs, we change our life experience. The fewer limitations we have on what we can and can't abide or do, the more life can teach us about ourselves, and the richer our experiences will be.

If you employ this exercise over time with any thought that causes a reaction or to which you feel particularly attached, you'll be setting the conditions for your own flourishing. Very gradually you'll find that the barrage of free-floating thoughts that fill your mind will no longer plague you when you're not watching. There will still be thoughts, of course, but they won't be constantly pestering you, and you won't be associating them with particular meanings and conjuring up imaginary problems in every corner of your life. That's what inner peace really means. It's freedom from the constant chatter of thought—not *your* thoughts, but *the* thoughts.

PRINCIPLE
pattern and geometry

A pattern, when applied to a monolithic surface—a flat ceiling, for example—breaks the surface into bite-size pieces that make the big surface more intelligible to the eye while giving it a sense of human scale.

In many of our culture's most famous historic buildings, a key ingredient of the design is the use of a geometric pattern to help articulate and decorate the surfaces. Think of almost any building by Frank Lloyd Wright, for example, and you'll recall that he developed geometric motifs inspired by nature that he then used in the stained-glass windows, in the rugs and carpets, and often in decorative concrete blocks and woodcuts as well.

It's no accident that many architects draw their inspiration from nature. If you look deeply into any natural form or system, you'll find patterns created by geometric formations everywhere. Cut through a cucumber, and you'll see the quality of three-ness. Look at the composition of a violet, and you'll see the quality of five-ness. Compare it with a lily, and you'll see that the petals are organized into a pattern revealing the quality of six-ness. No matter where you look, geometry is the underlying informing process.

In our lives, which are also natural systems, we use patterns of behavior in a similar way. Most of us tend to get up at about the same time every day during the workweek. We eat at around the same time each morning and each evening. And we engage in the same habitual patterns each night to prepare the body for sleep. As we go through our familiar routine, we count on it to take care of our physical needs, to keep us on task, and to give our day a sense of order.

In a Not So Big Life there's an additional set of patterns—another kind of routine that must be put into place to ensure that the benefits of the remodeling endure. In the same way that a flower's growth pattern determines its geometrical formation and in the same way that our daily routine provides a structure that allows the body to flourish, these patterns of behavior will provide a structure to allow for our continued unfolding toward our true nature. This chapter describes the rules of engagement that constitute that routine. If you learn to integrate them seamlessly into your daily life, your full potential cannot help but flower.

TEN

Moving Into Your
Not So Big Life

Let yourself be silently drawn
by the stronger pull
of what you really love.
—RUMI

The Importance of Repeatedly Waking Yourself Up

There's always tremendous excitement the day you move into a house that's just been remodeled. Everything looks new and different, even though the spaces that were there before the construction started are still apparent when you look for them. But now they have a new face and a new feel, and it's clear that living in this new version of your home is going to be a delight.

Yet, if you could fast-forward a year or two to see how the remodeling has altered your life, you'd be surprised to find, in many cases, that old patterns of living will have reasserted themselves. Though the space is better designed than it used to be, allowing easier communication between rooms, perhaps, or a greater sense of spaciousness, without something more built into the design to keep you alert and aware, it's easy to revert to ho-hum living. You can lose sight of the new aspects of the remodeled house and once again function on automatic pilot.

This is why architects will often include in the blueprint for a remodeling features intended to bring the home owners to a greater awareness of their environs. They may design a window seat—a perfect spot from which to look out over a beautiful garden while reading the newspaper in the morning. They might arrange the location of the kitchen eating area to allow a glimpse of a long diagonal view from one corner of the house to the other. Or they might design a spot for a stained-glass window that will receive direct sunlight during the morning hours, filling the living areas with reflected colored light. All these features can cause a sudden shift of state as the home owners experience what is there before them. It's the architectural version of the "Experiencing Presence" exercise we explored in chapter 7.

Your remodeled life must have similar wake-up features that remind you to be present and to stay aware that your everyday engagements and activities are not what they appear to be. No matter how well you have understood the preceding chapters, you will forget that this is your movie and that you can be its director only if you are present in what you are doing. This chapter provides some suggestions for how to stay aware, not just at the time you move into your newly remodeled life but for the rest of your days.

Some Rules of Engagement

When you move into a newly remodeled home, in order to make the most of the physical changes, you need to establish new patterns of behavior. If you've added that window seat in the family room, for example, you might decide to sit there every morning and look out at the garden for a few minutes as you sip your first cup of tea or coffee, so that you start the day calmly rather than in the fast-forward mode you're accustomed to. The window seat supports the new pattern and so has the ability to shift the way you start every day, which affects not only that period but the rest of the day as well. But it works only if you *use* the window seat.

The same is true of your Not So Big Life. In order to make the most of what you've read and understood so far, you have to start to integrate your understandings into the way you engage your everyday activities, or the changes will not last. There *are* some basic strategies for living Not So Big that can help precipitate maximal growth. So what follows are some simple tools that you must learn to implement reflexively, in everything you do. In this way the blueprint will continue to inform your life and help you to become more of who you know you have the potential of being.

1. FOLLOW YOUR PASSIONS
The first rule of engagement is to identify and engage in those things that you feel passionate about. This is the real meaning behind Joseph Campbell's encouragement to "follow your bliss." When you are passionate about something, you have more of your heart and soul involved

in whatever that thing is, and as a result you are more alive in its engagement. This doesn't mean you can pursue whatever your passion is only if you can make your living at it. And it doesn't mean that you can pursue it only if it is considered valuable by others. This is *your* life, and this is *your* passion. It is a doorway that allows you to experience more of who you really are, and as such can be engaged just for the pure delight of it. The only thing stopping you from exploring it is you.

So many of the world's greatest discoveries have been made by someone who has worked on something passionately, usually without the support of institutions or sources of funding. Think of Marie Curie and her search for radium. Think of Charles Darwin and his fascination with living things. Think of Einstein and his struggle to find a general theory of relativity. Each was totally immersed in passionate inquiry.

Einstein was very nearly alone in his attempt to find a theory that would unite the disparate models of the laws of physics, each accurate for its own scale but inaccurate for another. In the process he had to overcome not only errors in the scientific canon of the day but also his own misconceptions. Yet something inside him knew, *knew* that there was more to find and that if he just kept at it, insight would come. His passion for the subject held his attention over many years, and eventually it was rewarded.

Whatever it was that Einstein touched in his search for a theory of relativity precipitated an avalanche of understandings about life as well, as we see in the following list of statements he made:

- "Reality is merely an illusion, albeit a very persistent one."
- "The only real valuable thing is intuition."
- "A person starts to live when he can live outside himself."
- "Sometimes one pays most for the things one gets for nothing."
- "Science without religion is lame, religion without science is blind."
- "Peace cannot be kept by force; it can only be achieved by understanding."
- "We can't solve problems by using the same kind of thinking we used when we created them."
- "The important thing is not to stop questioning. Curiosity has its own reason for existing."
- "As far as the laws of mathematics refer to reality, they are not certain, and as far as they are certain, they do not refer to reality."

- "My religion consists of a humble admiration of the illimitable superior spirit who reveals himself in the slight details we are able to perceive with our frail and feeble minds."
- "The most beautiful emotion we can experience is the mystical. It is the power of all true art and science. He to whom this emotion is a stranger, who can no longer wonder and stand rapt in awe, is as good as dead . . . his eyes are closed."
- "A human being is a part of a whole, called by us the universe, a part limited in time and space. He experiences himself, his thoughts and feelings as something separated from the rest, a kind of optical delusion of his consciousness. This delusion is a kind of prison for us, restricting us to our personal desires and to affection for a few persons nearest us. Our task must be to free ourselves from this prison by widening our circle of compassion to embrace all living creatures and the whole of nature in its beauty."

And this one, which I used to introduce an earlier chapter, that hung above Einstein's desk at Princeton:

- "Not everything that can be counted counts, and not everything that counts can be counted."

These are clearly the insights of a man whose understanding of what really matters in life clearly far surpassed the mathematics and physics that played such an important role in his waking dream. His theoretical investigations led him to the doorway of a much, much bigger discovery, one that great masters, sages, and mystics down through the centuries have been trying to catalyze in all humanity. This discovery, however, cannot be written down in the form of an equation. It's one of those things that counts but cannot be counted or quantified in any way. It can only be lived, and one extremely effective way in which to live it is by following your own passionate inquiry, your own search for the meaning behind the mystery.

Your Turn

Think back to your childhood, teens, or early adulthood, and recall what kinds of dreams you had for yourself. What did you enjoy most? What did you excel at? Did you have a vision of what you might become as an adult? Did you have a hobby or favorite activity? Take a few minutes to write down in your notebook all the things that come to mind.

Now recognize that it's not too late still to pursue those things. They may need to take a different form from what you imagined when you were younger, but if you are passionate about something, there's always a way. Simply paying attention to your passions will bring forth opportunities to pursue them.

2. CLEARLY EXPRESS YOUR INTENTIONS; THEN LET GO

The next rule of engagement is, in a certain way, optional, but when applied appropriately, it can be a very helpful tool on the journey. There's a lot of talk these days about the power of intention, the idea that by deeply focusing on an intended outcome, you can help to bring it into being. The difficulty here is that anything that is going to allow us to grow beyond our current boundaries can't be conceived by who we are today. We can imagine only variants on what we already have and what we already know. There's a saying by A. H. Almaas that beautifully describes this state of affairs:

An idea can only generate its own nature.

The intentions we set can only come from our existing paradigm. When considering the process of setting intentions, I often think of the song that goes, "Oh, Lord, won't you buy me a Mercedes-Benz. My friends all drive Porsches, I must make amends." Although the song is humorous and not intended to be taken seriously, it points at a common misapplication of intention. As observed back in chapter 3, our desires for expensive stuff are often surrogates for meaningfulness and fulfillment. If we were to explore the sense of incompleteness, we could express an intention rather than a wish, and it might be phrased something like this: "Help me to understand my own value and what I'm accomplishing through the living of my life." This is the type of intention that doesn't limit the form that the answer can take. Its open-endedness allows insight to enter and expand the aperture beyond the small self, and so allows an expanded understanding of who we are.

This is how intention can help you to grow. But it can't help you at all if you are trying to get specific stuff from life, like that Mercedes-Benz or a great new job or a slim waist, as though you were trying to milk a cow. That is a misunderstanding of how things work. Although you can focus on something and even once in a while bring it into being, it can't change your life in any meaningful way unless your intention has this more open-ended quality. You may get the Mercedes-Benz, but you still won't have the understanding of your own value, so you'll still feel incomplete, and you'll just focus on another object of desire and another after that.

I heard a wonderful story on Ira Glass's radio program *This American Life* on National Public Radio. A young woman was being interviewed for a story called "Seemed like a Good Idea at the Time." She was a singer for Riverdance, the successful dance troupe that has turned Irish folk dancing into an electrifying form of entertainment. She described how the troupe had decided to purchase collectively as many lottery tickets as there were troupe members for a lottery with a huge jackpot. They declared that they were going to win and then share the proceeds among themselves. Being just a little savvy about the process of setting intentions, they instructed one another to believe absolutely that they would win and to entertain no thought that contained any doubt in it.

Interestingly, they had all determined that when they won they would quit Riverdance and use the money to do whatever it was they really wanted to do: go back to school, buy a house, or whatever. Behind each of their wishes, you could read the longing for a change of direction in their lives. The young woman being interviewed admitted that although their shows were universally loved, it was in fact a huge challenge to stay engaged in them as participants because they'd presented the same set of dances so many times.

During the performance that took place on the evening the lottery winners were to be announced, the singer in Ira Glass's interview described a kind of ecstasy that swept up the entire troupe as they danced and sang. All the performers knew that this would be their winning night, the night they would be released from the repetitiousness of their lives. All of them knew as well, as they danced and sang, that it was the best performance they'd ever given. Afterward, the audience went wild. Something truly amazing had taken place.

In this case their collective lottery purchase produced not a single winning ticket, and this fact was initially difficult for all of them to accept. They had so convinced themselves they'd win that they couldn't believe they *hadn't* won. They scrutinized the ticket numbers, trying to find the mistake and reveal the presence of the winning ticket. But eventually they had to concede that their intention hadn't produced the desired result. The cow had refused to be milked, it appeared.

But had it really? Look at what happened that evening: The performers did in fact attain the longed-for release from their lives, at least for the period of that amazing performance. Through their collective intending they transcended the form of the dance itself. What had previously been a kind of unrelenting monotony became vibrantly new for the cast when they were engaged as if for the last time. So they *did* get what they were really asking for; but because the original intention was stated in a limited way, they didn't recognize it.

If you can learn to look in a more open-ended manner at both what is being intended and what is being delivered, you may well find that you *do* get what you are asking for. It simply comes in a different form from the one you've been envisioning, a form much better suited to your real needs and perfectly tailored to help you grow.

The young performer interviewed on *This American Life* had clearly been powerfully moved by that performance. She and her fellow dancers had been totally alive and present throughout it. That's the kind of moment that changes lives, and I'm guessing that for many dancers in the troupe, it had precisely that effect.

The Art of Living

The intention I've found myself expressing frequently over the past two decades is "teach me." It arises from somewhere in the depths of my being. It is a heartfelt longing to learn not the stuff we tend to focus on in academia but the means by which to metabolize more of life. I want to learn about living itself. I remember when this longing started to show up in my life. I read a book—a classic, I later discovered—by Erich Fromm, first published in 1956, called *The Art of Loving*. Though I can't remember it clearly at this juncture, I recall realizing that it was as much about the art of living as it was the art of loving.

Everything that has happened since that time has been a response to my intention to learn about being fully alive. And it's the source of my impetus for writing this book. I have become life's student, and looking back I see experience after experience that unfolded ever more of the response to my desire to learn. It is awe-inspiring to recognize the perfection of the process—to see the books that fell unexpectedly into my life, the chance meetings with people who led me to teachers, and the situations that taught me what I needed to know about living more of my human potential.

At one point not long after reading Fromm's book, I began to converse regularly with my then brother-in-law, who was probing some of the same questions I'd started to wonder about. Each conversation was driven by the question uppermost in his mind. "How do you live a life well?" he would ask. I could feel my mind trying to wrap itself around the question, trying to find a way into the answer. But it wouldn't open with thought. So I found myself just sitting with the question instead. "How *do* you live a life well?" I knew that I didn't really know. But I knew that I wanted to. I'd started to sense that when you are holding a question or an intention, clues present themselves in the fabric of your life. I realized I was beginning to taste the possibility below the surface of things.

Next came a book by Alan Watts called *Behold the Spirit*, through which I realized that I'd always known this inner passion for life and had always recognized it as my spiritual self, but I hadn't felt I had any authority to acknowledge it because I wasn't involved in any religious practice. Watts's book gave me permission to see that my inner experience was real and didn't require validation by a spiritual institution.

Then came an interview I heard on the radio about a process called active imagination, a Jungian technique for working with various aspects of one's inner world, through one's dreams. The technique proved to be enormously useful for accessing hidden and repressed life experiences and the conditioning that stemmed from them. The contents of my interior landscape presented themselves for review in a miraculous way during this period. There was even a point several months into the process when I had the distinct impression that some higher part of myself, some wider aperture of awareness, was saying to the "me" of that time, "All right. We're glad you are listening. Now we can really start the work of teaching you." I began to see that if I looked at all the happenings of my life with the eyes of a student, then everything could teach me. And once I started to see with these eyes, the lessons came fast and furious.

But none of this did I arrange or try to coax into existence. I didn't ever try to determine which was the right book to read next or the best radio program to listen to. I just let things come to me, which may sound trite, but it was the way things unfolded. For some reason I didn't go looking for answers; I simply engaged what arrived on my doorstep, and everything I needed seemed to flow out of those engagements. If you are sincere in your intending, what you need will show up at just the right moment.

Focus on What You Want, Not on What You Don't Want

A word of caution about intention: If you state an intention in the negative, such as "I don't want to fall in love with someone under thirty" or "I don't want to put my kid in day care," an odd thing happens. You'll find that the very thing you don't want keeps presenting itself. This is because you are focusing on what you don't want, and it's the focusing itself that attracts the response. The *don't* in the intention disappears, so what you pull toward yourself is the subject of the statement—in this case, a person under thirty and day care. This is one of the key mechanisms at work in shaping the content of our waking dream. When you find yourself constantly presented with what you don't want, check to see if this kind of unintentional negative focusing is happening.

I received a wonderful lesson in the workings of this dynamic when I was helping to teach my stepson to ride a bicycle years ago. My ex-husband had just removed the training wheels from his son's bike, and we decided to take him to an empty parking lot to practice riding. He was already able to stay up but was still learning to steer. Luckily, there were absolutely no obstructions in the vast parking lot except a single lamppost in the middle. As he set off across the asphalt, my husband laughingly admonished, "Just don't run into the lamppost."

Well, you guessed it. The kid, trying hard to please his father, must have been repeating those last words over and over in his head. "Just don't run into the lamppost. Just don't run into the lamppost." As he rode, he made ever-diminishing loops around the lamppost until eventually he was almost brushing it with his shoulder, and then *bam*—he ran right into it and fell off his bike. By intending *not* to run into it, he couldn't have been more focused on that lamppost if he had tried.

Anytime you don't want something to happen, focus on the positive intention. So instead of "I don't want to fall in love with someone under thirty," you could focus on "I will fall in love with someone over thirty." Or, better yet, you could do a little inquiry into why you don't want to fall in love with someone younger and completely reframe the intention, which might sound something more like "I long for mature companionship" or "I will be with someone who is interested in knowing more about who they are."

Even these intentions are limited, because they are still about something outside yourself. The most effective intentions of all are those that are stated in terms of a desire for something within your own self. The desire for mature companionship is ultimately a desire for your own maturing. So in this case, you might decide to hold this simple intention: "I want to understand who or what I really am." That statement alone will bring about tremendous transformation as you work with each of the responses delivered to you by the universe. And those responses won't be restricted by your current limited view of what they should look like.

Don't Push the Rope

There's a saying: Don't push the rope. A rope is fabulous for pulling, but it's useless if you try pushing it. So it is with longings and intentions. If you cast these intention seeds upon the good soil of your life, their inherent vitality will draw them slowly but surely into existence. But try to force them open, and you'll kill them. There is a season for everything.

It helps to see this dynamic on a larger scale. Think of the earth's rotation around the sun or the moon's orbit around the earth. We know that these cycles have specific lengths. There's nothing arbitrary about them. We know that the gestation of a human being takes roughly nine months. No matter how much a mother might like that fetus to develop faster, we know the cycle can't be sped up. It's the same with our longings. They must live the length of their natural life cycles before they can be harvested, and the only way to help bring them into being is to set the conditions and then get out of the way. So as you go about your daily life, watch for rope pushing, and as soon as you notice it, cease and desist. This is how you can get out of your own way most effectively.

I mentioned earlier that the use of intention is optional. It really is. Even with no intending at all on your part, life will present you with a steady supply of food for growth. But most of us can't believe that we can just let things unfold without directing them. So if you do decide to use intention in guiding the exploration of your inner world, keep the intention succinct and make it something heartfelt, something that is closer to a longing than a wish for something in particular and ideally something that is oriented toward the higher self. In this way you'll be setting the conditions for what you really need for growth to arise without forcing, manipulating, or orchestrating anything at all. Try it, and prepare to be amazed.

Your Turn

Write down in your notebook any intentions you've been aware of over the last couple of years. Have any of them been negatively stated, as in "I don't want . . ."? What has been the result of each of your intentions so far?

If you are not aware of having had any explicit intentions recently, is there some longing you're aware of that could point toward your heart's true desire?

Once you have identified your intentions or desires, pick the one you consider most important, and look for ways of widening the perspective from which the intention is stated. As you do this, attempt to make it only about you rather than a wish for something or someone else.

That's all for now. In the next chapter you'll learn how to use what you've written down to observe opportunities that come your way in response to your intention.

3. BE OBEDIENT TO THE SITUATION

Every situation contains within it the food and fertilizer for our flourishing, but the only way we can find this out is by being obedient to each set of circumstances that present themselves—to fully engage whatever arises to the best of our ability and to process any reactions and judgments as they come up, without editing or suppressing anything. When I first grasped the significance of this, I was stunned by the magnitude of the task. For years I thought I'd been the model of obedience to life, but suddenly I was confronted by the realization that I'd been obedient only when I liked the general direction of what was happening.

Whenever something arose that contained the ingredients of confrontation—my hot button—I would automatically discount it, deciding there was another, better way to proceed. For most of my adult life, I had avoided expressing what I was feeling in the moment if I thought it might make someone angry or upset. I would edit my speech even if there was something I really wanted or needed to say.

While running my architectural practice, for example, I needed to address a personnel situation directly on several occasions but avoided doing so until it became more uncomfortable not to act. In retrospect I am truly amazed that I didn't understand what was being asked of me by each situation, but at the time I wasn't aware of my avoidance behavior. I simply felt that I was in an increasingly untenable situation, and finally there was nothing else to be done but the thing I hadn't wanted to do from the start. After watching situation after situation play itself out to its thorny end, I started to recognize the pattern. It goes something like this:

1. Someone does or says something that evokes a reaction in me.
2. An internal judge decides that giving voice to the reaction would cause the other person to become angry.
3. I edit my response, couching it in terms that will avoid upsetting the other person.
4. The other person thus doesn't get the message.
5. The other person continues to do the same thing that evokes the reaction in me, and I continue to respond with a watered-down version of what I want to say, still trying to avoid confrontation.
6. The cycle continues until the lack of real communication causes others to be drawn into the fray.
7. I finally realize that not speaking directly is causing more turbulence than simply saying what needs to be said.
8. The dreaded communication is finally delivered, and the flow can finally resume.

The difficulty here lies in the long delay between my original desire to speak and the delivery of what needed to be said. As a result, the final delivery of the statement involves a lot more tension and angst than it would have if it had been spoken the moment the desire arose. This may also be an example of negative intention at work. Like my stepson and the lamppost, I was focused on what I *didn't* want—an emotional confrontation—so what came through for me was exactly that, amped up by the delay and avoidance.

Now I know that whenever I'm having a reaction to anything or anyone, it's there to be inquired into, so that I can find and refute the underlying hidden belief that's buried in the situation. This is the way to become obedient to life. You won't be able to recognize every reaction and identify every pattern right away. Clarity takes time. But you can be constantly open to looking more closely at what's happening below the surface of your waking dream and to remaining obedient to what is being asked of you in each moment. You'll gradually become more and more capable of metabolizing what is put before you, expanding increasingly toward your full potential, without getting in your own way all the time.

When you see one of your own behavior patterns clearly for the first time, it's common to believe that you've fully integrated what you see. You assume that the pattern will not happen again—or at least, if it does, that you'll be capable of remaining objective in it. And that's how I was feeling about my understanding regarding my confrontation avoidance pattern. But just in case I was feeling too pleased with myself, this morning presented me with a perfectly tailored lab test. I was sitting on my back porch, talking with one of my closest friends, Ben, discussing some of the intricacies of the way he runs his business. He'd been trying to refine a particular part of the production process for some months, and certain aspects of the solution kept eluding him. As we talked, it seemed that things were getting clearer, and then I felt something arise in the moment that, as I spoke it, I knew had the potential of upsetting him. Interestingly, though, my usual edit function didn't kick in. I spoke without prescreening, and no sooner were the words out than my fears were realized. He *was* upset by my comment.

Normally in the past I would have seen his reaction as confirmation that it is unsafe to speak everything as it arises in the moment. But underlying this "proof" is a belief that no one should ever get upset, and I'd come to understand that this belief was neither realistic nor healthy. This time I watched myself wanting to apologize to Ben, and I watched my impulse to rush in and try to make things better. But instead of acting according to my conditioning, I simply sat there, feeling the discomfort, feeling the awkwardness and my fear. Ben pulled back from me and from the conversation, and I could feel a sense of abandonment. I suddenly saw how I would do almost anything in order not to feel what I was experiencing now.

Your response to similarly charged situations will be different, of course, and will depend on the specific conditioned pattern you are working with. Your patterns may be the opposite of ones I'm describing in my own examples. Regardless, the important point is that long after you've identified them, the pull can still be incredibly magnetic.

I could not have experienced the sense of complete abandonment I felt with Ben if I hadn't stayed put and sat there as all the uncomfortable feelings arose. I also needed to stay with that feeling after Ben left in order to really experience what I'd always avoided before. That's what it takes to be obedient to a situation. You must implement what you know as best you can under the circumstances, knowing that you'll grow if you do. Sometimes an opportunity will arise, and you won't take it. Sometimes you'll try to live the new understanding and fail. But all you can do is try your best in each situation. One thing you can be sure of: The opportunities will keep coming until you finally get it.

It's never comfortable going through one of these life-lab tests, but afterward, if you've stayed with the tension and metabolized what's there, there's a powerful sense of release. Partway through writing this section, I felt a wave of calmness and inner strength wash over me. I recognized it as the release that comes with fully metabolizing a fear underlying a conditioned pattern. Just then I heard a knock at my door. It was Ben. He looked me straight in the eye and told me that he was sorry for his reaction and that although what I'd said had been upsetting to him, it wasn't fair for him to take his frustration out on me. Here was confirmation that inner and outer worlds are indeed perfect reflections of each other.

Your Turn

Name some situations from your past in which you were not obedient to the situation, when you were determined to get your way or refused to do something that was being asked of you. (I'm referring not to dangerous, painful, or hurtful things here but to things you felt you knew better about, on principle.) How did these situations turn out? Can you imagine what would have happened if you had simply done what was being asked of you? Have you ever asked yourself how you can know what would have happened?

Are there any situations in your life right now in which you are being asked to do something that you really don't want to do (again, omitting dangerous or painful activities)? If so, how do you know what would happen if you simply did what was being asked of you? What is stopping you from being obedient to the situation?

Try doing what is being asked of you, and write down, over the next few days and weeks, what happens as a result.

4. GO TOWARD THAT WHICH YOU ARE REJECTING

Whenever something happens in your life that you find yourself strongly rejecting, you are being provided with a tremendous opportunity to learn. But unless you understand this next rule of engagement, this opportunity will almost certainly pass you by.

You can get a sense of this by asking yourself to name something that you absolutely refuse to do. One mundane example is that you refuse to take out the trash on principle because you believe that's your spouse's job. Another example is that you won't ever eat mushrooms because you hated them as a child and you believe you still hate them, even though you haven't actually tried them in twenty-two years. A bigger example is that you refuse to call your sister because of a fight you had with her years ago, and you believe it is she who owes you the call. Or perhaps you are avoiding going to see a doctor about a pain in your left foot that you've been living with for weeks. You get the idea.

I have a theory that some of the so-called trash houses—houses filled from top to bottom with years' worth of refuse—that stun viewers of the evening news every few years are the result of a feud between spouses, where one or both refuse ever to take out the trash, so that it builds up and up until the situation becomes completely unmanageable. In maintaining their refusal they turn their home—the place that most closely reflects their inner state—into a trash dump. This is the power of rejection. It stops flow so that nothing can be resolved, nothing gets metabolized, and nothing can grow—except mold.

When I was in college, I rented a room in a house owned by newlyweds who were at war over dishwashing. I was grateful to have a meal ticket at the university cafeteria so I didn't have to involve myself in the fray. The couple had agreed that they'd take turns washing dishes each evening, but it became clear that neither one of them was enamored of the process, so after each meal the dirty plates would sit in the sink soaking. The next day's dishes would be stacked on top, and so it would go until one of the newlyweds—usually the wife—would break down and in a fit of ire wash all of them. She would then seethe at her husband while the next load of unwashed dishes accumulated.

If this were a situation in your life, what would you do? Remember that if this is happening in your waking dream, however much it might seem like the other person's issue, you have to look at it from the perspective that all there is, is you. The only way through this issue is to go toward the thing or things you are refusing to do—in this case, doing the dishes, speaking up for yourself, or both.

By going toward what you are rejecting, you set the conditions for the flow to resume even though the way to that flow may include some difficult discussions. In the dishwashing situation, you may already have sided with the wife, who seemed the more reasonable one on the surface. But there are always reasons why people feel justified in their point of view. In fact, the impulse to refuse to do something almost always indicates that there's a hidden belief lurking in the shadows and can be used as a tool to track that belief down. In this case, the husband worked fifty hours a week and his wife had a part-time job. The husband believed the wife wasn't pulling her weight. The wife believed both people in a relationship should do an equal amount of housework, since housework is a chore that no one enjoys. She also believed that her husband shouldn't put in such long hours at work and that he was doing so intentionally, to avoid being with her. You can see how all these beliefs got in the way of any real engagement.

How could either spouse possibly be present in the experience of washing dishes when both of them were so busy nursing their particular flavors of resentment and righteous indignation? This is how most of us spend our time: rejecting what's in front of us to do, believing wholeheartedly that we are in the right and that the person we're disagreeing with is completely unreasonable and clearly in the wrong. This is how we create our own suffering.

Your Turn

Make a list of your rejections and refusals. The following question may help you to access them: "What are the things in my life that I absolutely refuse to do?" (Once again, we're not including dangerous or hurtful activities.) Can you identify the hidden beliefs that fuel these refusals? How would your life change if you went toward the thing or things you are refusing to do? As opportunities to do so present themselves, try embracing that which you are rejecting, and see what happens.

---

5. DO ONE THING AT A TIME

Multitasking and overcommitting are excellent indicators that we are sleepwalking through the waking dream. As we saw in chapter 3, our addiction to adrenaline gives us the illusion of getting things done, but what we're really doing is eating up vast quantities of time and energy, racing around in fast-forward mode without awareness. In the movie Click the lead character is given a universal remote control with the magical power to fast-forward through the boring and uncomfortable parts of his life. His wonderful gift turns into a nightmare as he discovers that he remembers almost nothing about big chunks of his life because his awareness wasn't there. His body was moving on automatic pilot, and he was literally asleep at the wheel.

Many of us have become terribly efficient, but we have also become increasingly ineffective. Efficiency is measured by output, whereas effectiveness involves the extent to which something actually works. In all our efficient managing of input and output, we lose sight of what we are doing in the first place, making ourselves quite ineffective at our primary task. When rushing is the hallmark of a diligent worker, it is difficult to value effectiveness. But rushing makes it much less likely that things are being done with presence. Speed often precludes it. Effective people, by contrast, have a much greater opportunity to be present in what they are doing because they tend to be moving more slowly and doing only one thing at a time. And being present is what gives real value and meaning to the person doing the job. Without this it's all just busyness.

The remedy is not complicated. What is required is a commitment to single tasking—the radical notion of doing one thing at a time—and a willingness to experiment with the way you engage the tools you use to communicate and stay informed. For example, instead of interrupting a task to answer your phone or responding to e-mails as they come in, try setting aside incoming communications until you are finished with the task at hand. Then check for messages, respond to those that need immediate attention, and designate a time to follow up on the others after you've completed what needs to be done next. This simple prioritization is rarely considered possible anymore in our rush to deal efficiently with everything that's flying at us. It's as though all the communication droplets are raining on us, and we're jumping this way and that in a fruitless attempt to avoid getting drenched, leaving ourselves no time to open our umbrellas and manage the downpour effectively.

If you are one of those people who believe they need to be totally accessible, the only way to test your conviction is to go toward that which you are avoiding. Turn off your cell phone and your BlackBerry, and see what happens. I suspect you'll find that the world can, in fact, survive quite nicely without your constant attention (you may need to adjust to that fact), and you will almost certainly discover that your attention is most needed for the task at hand, something you've been overlooking because of the stream of distractions.

The situation is made even worse by instant messaging. It is now normal practice to send instant messages during conference calls and meetings. When you ask a question of someone exchanging instant messages, it's usually followed by a pause and an awkward silence as he or she tries to reconstruct what was being discussed while the separate electronic conversation was taking place. It's the adult version of exchanging notes during class in grade school. Remember how much you learned during those classes? The same is true of the meeting you are supposedly attending. There's no point in showing up if you are not really there.

This kind of multitasking is a highly addictive behavior pattern because it's brimming with adrenaline and it makes you feel wanted and important. Your attendance at the meeting is desired. You are also answering e-mails as they arrive, which makes you feel a bit more important. Finally, you are exchanging instant messages with your inner circle, which buoys your self-importance even more. That's a lot of busyness, and busyness equates with importance, so you must really be someone special. But at the end of the day, you feel drained and dejected, and you don't know why.

It's because you are not showing up in your life. Nobody's home—there's just a lot of activity. Real communication is incredibly powerful and transformative, but it happens only when you show up completely in the activity—whether by talking on a cellphone, exchanging e-mail, or sitting across a table from someone. The vehicle for the communication is not the issue. It is your presence that makes the difference.

The problem with so much of what arrives in our mailboxes and shows up on our various screens is that it lures us into a dreamworld not of our own choosing. We opt for it only because it is right in front of us. Rarely do we stop and ask ourselves, "Is this really what I want or need to do right now?" Yet once we've turned, pushed, or clicked, we're hooked by the story line of the world depicted. This is the fundamental principle behind advertising, but it's happening in more ways than we imagine—not just through those messages that we recognize as commercials. Everyone is trying to get our attention and have us focus on his or her take on the dreamworld. With all the devices available to do this these days, if we aren't aware of what's going on, we are literally led by the nose from one mindless engagement to another, all of which ensures that we stay sound asleep in the middle of our waking dream. But there is an alternative. All it requires is your attention.

Unless we return to one thing at a time, in short order we'll be living a new form of self-inflicted schizophrenia: We won't be able to distinguish among the voices speaking to us, and we won't know what to do next. The tools we're inventing to help us cope will, in fact, be rendering us impotent, unable to engage in anything meaningful or truly satisfying. The illusion will be complete, and we'll be completely lost in a nightmare of our own making. The antidote? Turn off the screens and see how quiet it gets. It's amazing.

Your Turn

Stay aware of multitasking behaviors. If you are used to keeping your e-mail in-box open all the time and answering every message as it arrives, try something different. Open it every two hours and set aside twenty minutes to answer the new messages before continuing with what you need to get done. Or if your job offers you enough latitude, you might open it only twice a day, once when you get to work in the morning and once shortly before you leave. Or, like me, you could open it only after you've accomplished your primary objectives for the day. If you frequently exchange instant messages, make yourself some rules, such as "I'll IM only when I'm fully engaged in the IM conversation" or "I'll never IM during a meeting or a conference call." The effects of any of these small changes will astound you. You'll find yourself starting to relax a bit. You'll feel less stressed and more centered.

Gradual Awakening

By using these rules of engagement as a guide for starting to live your own life in a Not So Big way, you'll find that the focus of what's important to you shifts. It's a strange and marvelous thing to discover that the blueprint you're using for your life remodeling is not a static thing. It continues to evolve, unfolding in the present moment, just as you do. The more you learn about yourself and the more you listen to what your waking dream is revealing to you through every experience, the more significance you'll find. You'll still be a productive member of society. You'll still be paying your bills each month, taking the kids to school each day, and buying the new couch or coffee table that you need. But instead of hoping that any one of these activities will bring more meaning to your life, you'll be *living* the moreness and the significance you've only *sought* in the past.

Once you acknowledge the desire within you for the full experiencing of being completely alive, and once you've had a taste of the creativity that's possible when you are truly present, you start to recognize that your whole life is a sort of canvas, and you are the artist. I've had a greeting card posted on the bulletin board above my desk for the past decade, and although it is dog-eared and perforated by innumerable thumbtacks, it still inspires me whenever I read it. Here's what it says:

> The most visible creators I know of are those artists whose medium is life itself, the ones who express the inexpressible— without brush, hammer, clay, or guitar. They neither paint nor sculpt—their medium is being. Whatever their presence touches has increased life. They see and don't have to draw. They are the artists of being alive. —J. STONE

This is what we all have the potential of becoming as we learn to see through eyes that are fully awake. You can make of your life whatever you want, but you can't start to paint anything that's more than mimicry until you find the freedom that comes with being present in the moment. Until then, though you may believe you are making decisions and choosing the best options for your own growth and evolution, the thing that is choosing is really the cluster of past conditionings that you've come to call "me." The more clearly you see that what you think of as your life is really only a movie with its true significance lying beneath the story line, the more freedom you have to become the artist of your life's canvas.

The important thing to remember here is that being present and becoming the artist of your own canvas cannot be seen as goals. As soon as you make them so, they become *things* that are separate from *you* and move beyond reach.

The experience of being completely awake is very rare, but becoming increasingly awake over the course of your life is entirely possible, and can vastly change the quality of your life experience. If and when you do recognize your own wakefulness, you'll realize that you've *always* been awake. I know this doesn't make sense logically, but from a wider aperture of awareness, it makes perfect sense. To use the arthropod eye as a metaphor, the awareness that perceives the truth in that statement sees through the entire compound eye, while currently you are seeing only through your single lens.

My friend Margo and I were discussing this the other day. For many months now Margo has been fascinated, as well as perplexed, by the word "awareness." Our teacher, Al, has often said to us that the only thing we take with us when we die is the awareness that you are aware. Margo has the kind of mind that seeks clear definitions, and she wants to know what awareness really is. Where does it come from, and why do we have it? Rather than try to figure it out using her thinking mind, she's been simply living with the question and seeing what arises in her waking dream to bring clarification. As she was pondering this last week, a phrase popped into her mind that provided an important clue to her inquiry. The phrase goes as follows:

> We are not humans having the experience of awareness. We are awareness having the experience of being human.

As soon as the words were out of her mouth, something inside me leapt. "That's perfect," I exclaimed. This simple phrase gives us a way to see what's going on from a completely different perspective. If, ultimately, we are awareness itself, and if our human form is nothing but a lens through which to see what is really here, then everything we experience directly is indivisible from the unity that we long to remember. We are awareness itself. But the only place from which we can know this is Now. The new blueprint provides a plan for your life and yours alone, despite the fact that by using it you begin to see from the universal perspective. It provides directions for seeing from the perspective by which the universal perceives itself in your life. Your physical senses are simply mechanisms through which that perception occurs.

So instead of trying to purchase and hustle our way to significance, as our current consensus reality would have us do, we just need to install these simple mechanisms within the waking dream for bringing us back to what is happening right NOW over and over again. We need to use what we know about conditioned patterns—about how to condition ourselves to new behaviors—to wake up within the dream, and to become "aware that we are aware" every moment of the day.

So, for right now, understand that even though you may be able to experience true presence, true wakefulness, only very occasionally, your actions in every moment set the conditions for your gradual awakening.

As you are confronted with options and decision points in your life, choose what makes sense to you right then based on the above rules of engagement, and as you go about living the results of those choices, know that your experiences will teach you what you need to learn. (This is the only process there is for becoming more and more free of your conditioned patterns, and so to become more who you really are.)

EXERCISE
changing your behavior

The following exercise will sound simple, but it's not an easy one to complete because it requires you to shift patterns of your behavior that may be unknown to you. When I first started working with Jan, my first teacher, she gave me this assignment, and it profoundly affected how I experienced my daily life. She identified three patterns of behavior that she asked me to change for a period of nine months. Once she had named these patterns, I recognized my attachment to them, but until that moment I had been unaware of how much each one defined who I took myself to be. These were the three patterns she identified and her requests for change:

1. You always wear long skirts. No more skirts.
2. You have worn your hair long for many years. Cut your hair.
3. You have a glass of wine when you return home from work each day. No more alcohol *after* 5:00 p.m.

The three assignments proved to be brilliant catalysts for change, not only in those patterns of behavior but in my entire self-image. When she first gave me the exercise, I didn't own a pair of pants. I had to go to a store that afternoon to buy a couple of pairs. I'd never really thought of it until that moment, but my self-image was deeply attached to its skirt collection. The hair assignment wasn't so easy. I went to a local hair salon and got my hair cut, but the thought of losing its length broke my heart. It became obvious that I was more than a little attached to long locks. In fact, although I had a good six inches cut off, I really didn't fulfill the assignment as completely as I could have. Knowing what I know now, I should have cut it really short, just to experience the full contrast.

But by far the cleverest behavior change Jan prescribed was the requirement that I drink no alcohol after 5:00 p.m. What she knew about me was that I was very busy and not likely to take a sip before 5:00 p.m., but telling me implicitly that I *could* meant that I wouldn't feel deprived. I'd been wanting to put a stop to the wine habit for some time, not because I drank too much but because I'd noticed that it dulled my senses ever so slightly. Her assignment provided a solution overnight, a result that both amazed and delighted me. The quality of my evenings changed dramatically simply because I became more alert.

All these changes allowed me to experience firsthand that my ideas about how I "am" are quite arbitrary and that by making even small changes in behavior patterns, big shifts will occur all by themselves. In this way we can turn the tables on our habits, transforming them into vehicles for significant personal growth. As you begin to identify your own habits, you may find that you perceive some as conscious, practical choices, while you have no good rationale for others. Either kind of habit will work in this exercise, since even those habits you think you've adopted for purely utilitarian purposes will in all likelihood prove to be more than that. What you'll discover, whichever habits you change, is that everything you do affects both how you perceive yourself and how others perceive you.

Without the ability to see yourself objectively, though, it's often difficult to know what behaviors to choose in order to effect the greatest shift, so I've devised a way to help you identify them when you don't have someone like Jan to select them for you. Before proceeding, write your answers to each of the following questions in your notebook.

Regarding clothing and appearance:

- Are your clothes all or predominantly one color? If so, what color?
- Do you always or predominantly wear a particular article of clothing or a type of clothing, such as jeans?
- Do you always wear your hair a certain length or in a certain way?
- If you're a man, do you have facial hair?
- Do you always or never wear makeup, perfume, or cologne? If so, which?

Regarding routines:

- Do you habitually read a newspaper, watch the news on television, or listen to the radio each morning or evening?
- Do you habitually check your e-mail or surf the Internet at certain times each day?

- Do you habitually have a cup of coffee or tea at certain times each day?
- Do you habitually sit in the same location when you eat?
- Do you typically eat the same thing at breakfast, lunch, or dinner? If so what is it?
- Do you clean up from meals right away or later?
- Are you typically late as you leave for or return from work? If so, why, and what needs to change so that you aren't?
- Do you typically feel frustrated as you leave for or return from work? If so, why, and what needs to change so that you don't?
- Are there other patterns of behavior that you are aware of that aren't covered by the preceding questions?

Now that you have your answers to these questions down on paper, identify the patterns you are most attached to by rating each one from 1 to 5, with 5 being most attached and 1 being least attached. Pick three habitual patterns and change them for six months.

The more attached you are to the habit, the more profound the effect will be on your waking dream. So if you pick three items with a "5" rating, prepare to be challenged, but know that by doing so, you'll be precipitating the most change in your life. If you pick three items with a "1" rating, you won't experience a lot of challenge; you'll still see an effect, just not as big a one.

If you have difficulty identifying behaviors you are attached to even after going through the list, I recommend that you ask a friend who knows you well and whom you trust to help you. Friends who can support you in the process of self-discovery are invaluable assets. A true friend is someone who will tell you what you need to hear, not what you want to hear. True friends are the people in your life who see your highest potential and not those who coddle your self-image even though that might make you feel better in the short run. The more you can be with true friends—the ones helping you to live into the realization of your true self—the more direct the journey will be.

Because everything we do is related to everything else, change in one part of our lives affects all the other parts as well. This exercise is the most effective way I know to start to see how the waking dream shifts as you change the way you act within it.

There are certain things in a home's design that we expect to be aligned with one another. If a house has a big gable roof, for example, it doesn't look right if the windows within the form of that gable aren't centered underneath the ridge. If they look out of alignment, the whole house ends up looking off balance. Or if the recessed light above the sink in the bathroom is a few inches off the sink's centerline, it simply looks wrong—like a mistake. So there are natural alignments that seem very obvious but aren't always apparent until the construction process is complete. In hindsight, it's easy to say that something should have been aligned differently, but if you haven't told the builder of your expectations ahead of time, he may not see things the same way you do. What to you may be obviously off, to him may be insignificant.

It's the same thing in our lives. There are certain activities—like finding time to be still and inquiring into reactions and judgments—that we can do every day to assist in aligning who we are now with who we are becoming. When we don't engage in these activities, the overall design of our lives becomes somewhat confused and disorganized—much like the effect of those off-center windows beneath the gable ridge. Without the interjection of these new activities, there's no order to the varied parts of our lives, no alignment with our real potential.

There are also things that our heart desires and that seem aligned with where we are headed but that won't happen unless we give voice to those longings—not to anyone else but to ourselves, so that we acknowledge what is stirring within us. Without trying to force the hand of the unfolding of our life but by simply stating a growing interest in a thing or a longing to start doing something that we've been putting off for years, we can engage the support of Providence. It isn't a matter of doing it ourselves, just as it isn't a matter of aligning the recessed light fixture with the sink below. We simply need to tell the builder that this is important to us, and lo and behold, it happens.

This chapter is about aligning yourself with your own unfolding, not through making things happen but by continually referring to the blueprints for your life so that you can stay on course as you venture ever closer to your true nature.

ELEVEN

Maintaining Your
Newly Remodeled Life

The breeze at dawn has secrets to tell you.
Don't go back to sleep.
You must ask for what you really want.
Don't go back to sleep.
People are going back and forth across the doorsill
where the two worlds touch.
The door is round and open.
Don't go back to sleep.
—RUMI

Capabilities of the New Blueprint

One of the greatest pleasures for an architect, after helping home owners through the remodeling of their house, is to be invited over for dinner
a few months later. The residents have by then settled into their home's
new form, and it is obvious that their patterns of behavior have been
changed and molded by the remodeled spaces. Almost always, the former clients will describe the surprise they experienced initially at discovering how easily activities flowed that had previously been awkward. And
often they'll describe the reduction in stress levels brought about by
something as simple as being able to see each other while dinner is
being prepared, for example, or having the option of closing a door to
contain the sound of a teenager's computer gaming while they are
watching the evening news.

But old habits die hard, and sometimes, despite the inclusion of
spaces for new functions, such as a mail-sorting place, a recycling center, and a place of one's own for each adult, the home owners have forgotten to make the necessary shifts in their behavior patterns that will
put these new spaces to their intended uses. The mail-sorting place is set
up neatly, as if for a photograph, but is not yet functional. The recycling
center patiently awaits the arrival of the first aluminum can or glass

bottle. And each place of one's own looks the way it did on move-in day: ready to provide solitude but not yet occupied. The problem here is that although the stage has been set for the desired shifts in lifestyle, the changes themselves have not been made. The blueprints were drawn up with the best of intentions, but without the necessary follow-through, these aspects of the remodeling could well be looked on as a waste of time, money, and space.

This is why it is often useful to suggest that home owners create their own "owner's manual" to remind them what they've invested in and why. By consulting the manual every so often, the residents of the house can make sure that every feature is being put to good use.

The same goes for the remodeling of your life. Throughout this book I've been using stories and exercises to provide you with the tools you'll need to engage this new way of living that I'm calling the Not So Big Life. Collectively they have the ability to offer you that new perspective for seeing beneath the surface of things and so for participating more fully in everything you do. But as you head toward the end of the book, you may be wondering how you can keep all of them in mind. And without establishing new patterns of behavior to support your new understandings, you'll go right back to sleep, all the time believing that you are now awake.

Let's review the primary features and capabilities of the new blueprint so that you have a bird's-eye view of the life remodeling you have just completed. Consider these features:

1. It helps to identify what inspires you, as well as what stands in the way of living the way you'd really like to be living.
2. It shows you how to identify and dismantle conditioned patterns and hidden beliefs that are no longer useful and that limit your ability to see what's here.
3. It allows you to see through the story line of your life to the meaning that lies beneath the surface by showing you how to read it in a different way.
4. It shows you the workings of your inner world through reflections in the outer one, revealing in the process that the content of your life is perfectly crafted to wake you up.
5. It allows you to see from two perspectives simultaneously: from your normal subjective perspective as a character in your waking dream

and from the objective perspective of the watcher, observing how you engage and what occurs as you do.

6. It depicts only the Now, looking neither backward to the past nor forward to the future, except when doing so helps with seeing the present moment more clearly.

7. It reveals the abundant synchronicities embedded within the events of your life, which are nothing more than indications of the harmony implicit in the movement of consciousness.

8. It allows you to see through a wider aperture—to see zebras rather than black-and-white stripes, for example, and to see that what seemed paradoxical now make perfect sense.

9. It allows you to remodel your life as you live it by making small shifts in the ways you engage your everyday involvements, bringing you to greater awareness within the experiencing itself.

10. It allows you to recognize when your personality gets in the way of the natural flow by trying to control things and make them go the way it thinks things should go.

11. It has the capacity to continue to inform your life remodeling, evolving as you do and helping you to become ever more of who you have the potential to be, of who you truly are.

12. It reveals a new dimension from which you can see that it is your belief in the separateness of the outside world that keeps you lost in appearances.

Just as we often end up using only one or two features of a newly installed computer program because those are the ones we master in the first week, so it is with our newly remodeled lives. But there's a lot more to the new blueprint than at first meets the eye. If you continue to explore its capabilities, it will continue to transform your life from this day forward.

The broad-brush changes—the ones that have removed some walls and opened up some interior views—will implement themselves automatically. Once you understand that everything is a reflection, for example, when your life experience gets stormy you'll immediately begin to ask, "If all there is, is me, what does this situation reveal about myself?" But other, less obvious changes in your interior scenery will need more intentional maintenance in order for them to work their magic.

So in the Appendix at the back of this book, I've included the

Owner's Manual for Your Not So Big Life. By taking the time to review this material at least once a year, as well as when you feel stuck in or frustrated by the story line of your life, you'll be able to put all its aspects to use, not just the ones you find easy to implement right now.

Consider where you'd be without an owner's manual. If all the things you've learned weren't written down in a place where they were easy to find and refer to, you'd be much less likely to go looking for the section you needed at a particular moment. In many cases it is the less obvious shifts—the ones that you may not even have noticed in a first reading—that will have the greatest effects and will allow you over time to uncover more of your potential. So the material in the Appendix will serve not only as a reminder right now of all the things we've discussed so far but also as a tool for your long-term life maintenance.

Here's another way to understand the function of the owner's manual. It's like sourdough starter. If you've ever made sourdough bread, you know that to give each loaf its distinctive flavor, you need this yeasty mix of fermenting flour and water. You keep the starter in your refrigerator and add a small amount to each batch of bread you make. By adding a spoonful of the ingredients from the owner's manual into each year of your life, you'll find that it continues to produce that Not So Big flavoring that helps you continue to grow into ever more of who you truly are.

The manual contains five sections:

1. Everyday Routines to Support Your Growth
2. Strategies for Revealing More of Your True Potential
3. Reminders to Keep You on Task
4. Questions to Keep Asking Yourself
5. Flags to Watch For

If you feel overwhelmed at any point while living according to the new blueprint, which will happen from time to time no matter how long you've been working on yourself, stop and focus on one thing. Just meditate, and let everything else take a backseat for a day or two or a week or two. When you get stressed out, everything on your plate seems to expand to unmanageable proportions. It's at these times that you need to keep in mind the one thing that's constant in life: change itself. Nothing lasts forever. Meditation helps move things along. By tapping into the stillness behind all the monkey-mind activity, as well as the openness and the allowing that meditation helps precipitate, you get out of your own way, and what needs to pass through the system can rise to the surface and be released. You don't need to do anything at all. Just sit and let the thoughts go, no matter how fast and furiously they are coming, and gradually the cloud over your life will lift.

Your Turn

Look over the sections included in the Appendix right now, to familiarize yourself with their content. As you read through the lists included there, keep a record in your notebook of the five points in each section that stand out most at this period of your life. You may also want to jot down the reasons each one strikes you as significant. In addition, take the time as you read to look back through your Not So Big Life Notebook and find any other points in each category that you've identified but aren't included in the following lists. They will in all likelihood have special significance for you and should definitely be included as points to remember and to keep track of.

Once you reach the end of this chapter, go back over your selections, type them or write them out for yourself, and place them where you can refer to them often. They will provide you with a road map of sorts for the coming year. The list will remind you of the things you want to keep focusing on in order to grow into more of your true self. Each year when you engage in the year-end ritual, you will reread this owner's manual to identify the most significant points for the period you are entering and update the list accordingly.

Inner Listening

There's one last tool for maintaining your Not So Big Life that is crucial to its long-term benefit. It's an annual review of sorts, much like a maintenance checkup for your automobile, except this one includes all aspects of your life—physical, mental, and spiritual—and both inner and outer worlds. The process presented itself in my own life in two distinct stages and turned out to be one of the most important ingredients in helping me find my way back to my first love: writing. The exercise at the end of this chapter describes the process in detail, but the description that follows will help you understand the role the year-end ritual can play in providing a compass bearing for your passage through life.

In 1996, the first time I traveled to North Carolina, I stepped out of my habitual patterns in a big way. I was on vacation with my family, and we were staying in a cozy beach house we'd rented on the Outer Banks. As we departed after a week of sand, sun, and surf and were heading back down the coast to Kitty Hawk, everyone wanted to stop at the Wright Brothers Museum. Everyone, that is, but me. Although I admire the Wright brothers for what they accomplished, I wasn't in the mood that afternoon for a tour around *any* museum. The break that the vacation had given me from my work routine had created a certain distance from the person I normally perceived myself to be. I felt introspective and could hear with some inner ear I hardly knew existed that ideas were arising concerning my heart's true longings. I wanted nothing more than to sit by myself for a couple of hours and listen more closely to these whisperings of my soul.

Ordinarily I would have gone along for the museum tour anyway, despite my personal desires, since I'd always believed that to do otherwise might be construed as rude. But on this particular day I didn't much care what anyone else thought. So while the rest of the clan went inside to look at airplanes, photographs, and historic documents, I got out a pad of paper, sat on the warm grass outside the visitors' center, and started to engage in a process that I now call inner listening.

I began by closing my eyes and asking myself, "What is it that I really want for my life?" I sat for a moment or two, and then, as if released by some invisible faucet, the wishes and longings started pouring into my mind. I wasn't thinking them exactly, although it was certainly thinking that allowed me to catch them by writing them down. Over the course of the next hour, I filled six pages with all the repressed longings of twenty years of adulthood, feeling a bit like a fisherman who has unexpectedly dropped his net into a school of fish that want desperately to be brought to the surface. When it was over, I was flushed with excitement. I had caught a glimpse of the possibilities that lay beyond all my beliefs about what adults are supposed to do with their lives.

I wish I could find that list now. I just turned my house upside down, in fact, looking for it, but it seems to be lost, at least for the time being. I remember a few of the items on it, though, such as the urge to start writing again and the desire to go on a retreat for a week or two. The specific longings that arose are less important than the fact that when given the opportunity to speak, my heart opened and its wishes presented themselves instantly and without hesitation. Until I'd made the commitment to listen, I'd had no idea that all this was bottled up inside me. By simply focusing with this largely unused inner listening capability that resides in all of us, we can provide ourselves with compass bearings for the journey to our true selves.

What happened after that is still more amazing. I didn't actually *do* anything. I read the list over a few times as we completed our travels and then put it away in the drawer of my nightstand when we got home to St. Paul. After a while I forgot that the list even existed. I simply went about my life. Looking back, I now realize that this was the year in which I started to make the time to write. It was also the year that I first built time into my schedule for engaging in whatever I felt moved to engage in that day. It wasn't until I was riffling through my bedside drawer for something a year later that I came across the list and was astonished to see how many of those longings had come into being. It was as though once they were allowed to surface, they'd been able to sprout in the ground of my life's event schedule even though I'd completely forgotten about the list or what was on it.

But at that point, the fact that so many of these latent dreams had come to pass just seemed like some sort of anomaly. I didn't recognize the power of what I'd stumbled across, and I hadn't considered the notion that I could weave the practice of inner listening into the fabric of my life. That idea delivered itself from the pursuit of something apparently unrelated—a desire to express my gratitude for the wisdom and vision of one of my favorite authors, Normandi Ellis.

I knew of Normandi through her books *Awakening Osiris* and *Dreams of Isis*. Each of my teachers has read aloud from Ellis's work on occasion, so her words have flavored some of the most profound moments of my life and will continue to do so for years to come, I'm sure. Both of these books are powerful descriptions of the process of awakening. The first is a new interpretation of the ancient Egyptian Book of the Dead, and the second is a record of her own process of self-discovery. Like Jelaluddin Rumi's words, the poetry and prose of *Awakening Osiris* reach far beyond the bounds of normal human experience and limited "small-self" identity. And by revealing the jewels embedded in her "spiritual sojourn," as she calls it, she gave me permission to look at my own with the same depth and intent.

Whenever I read the work of authors whose words touch me deeply, I feel connected to them and often wish that I could meet them and thank them personally. But I never imagined I'd meet Normandi or get to know her. Yet as if by magic she suddenly appeared in the life of Jan, my teacher at the time, and so in mine. The story bears telling because it so perfectly illustrates how easy it is to pass by the gifts to be found in the apparently "bad" things that happen to us.

Jan was attending a conference on the East Coast as a reporter for a Twin Cities independent newspaper. When she arrived, she discovered that in order to enter the cafeteria for lunch between sessions, she had to have a meal ticket. She hadn't bought one when she signed up for the conference because her media status typically allows her access to meals. Not so at this conference, however, and now, she was told, it was too late to purchase a meal ticket. There was no more room and no more tickets available. Jan, as you might imagine, was not pleased. Her opportunity to interview the people she'd come to the conference to meet was being substantially compromised, and try as she might, she could not persuade the woman at the registration desk to reconsider. So, attempting not to lose her cool but feeling deeply frustrated, Jan sat on the bench outside the cafeteria during lunch break and read a book, hoping that at some point the people she needed to talk to would emerge.

There was no one else around except one other woman, who was sitting on the bench across from Jan. As Jan read, she became aware of the woman's eyes on her, but she didn't look up. Then the other woman stood up, came across the room and sat next to Jan on *her* bench. Still Jan didn't acknowledge her presence, although by now she was feeling distinctly imposed upon. Finally, when the woman cleared her throat and said, "Excuse me," Jan looked up, now thoroughly annoyed. What on earth could this woman want? "Hello," the woman persisted, unperturbed. "I'm Normandi Ellis," she said, "and I have a feeling we are supposed to meet." Needless to say, Jan nearly fell off the bench and promptly burst into laughter, as she understood that here, right beside her, was a human being whose words had deeply moved her for years. Had either one of them been given a ticket to enter the cafeteria, their meeting would most likely not have happened. They talked for much of the afternoon and by the end of the day had made arrangements to meet again. Jan would organize a workshop to be led by Normandi in Minneapolis so that those of us who knew her work could meet her in person. I attended that workshop, of course, and so my longing to meet Normandi was fulfilled.

I tell you all this because there's an obvious moral to the story. Nothing is ever what it appears to be. The absence of a meal ticket was a ticket to something of far greater interest to Jan than the various speakers she thought she was at the conference to meet. And when we feel a deep connection with someone or something, we draw that person or thing toward us in ways that seem quite miraculous and certainly synchronous.

Normandi's workshop was wonderful, but the part of it that has had the most profound long-term effect on my life was a tool that she shared with us that had an obvious resonance with the work I had been doing a few months earlier. This tool is an exercise intended to develop inner listening skills by creating an annual ritual during which you intentionally turn on that inner faucet of unexplored longings, like the one that I'd accidentally opened up when I sat down in Kitty Hawk with my notepad.

She suggested to us that we set aside some time during the final five days of each year—a time that is typically pretty quiet anyway in the working world because of the holidays—and to make it a period of introspection and self-exploration. She gave us a series of questions to focus on and told us that we should allow ourselves to review the results of the previous years' explorations only during this period each year. Normandi's questions are reproduced for you in the "Year-End Ritual" exercise that follows, along with some additions that will allow you to integrate what you discover as you complete the exercises in this book. If you can possibly make some time once a year to engage these questions, you'll be astonished by their effect on your life.

When you review once a year all the questions presented in the exercise, supplemented by your review of the Appendix, you'll find that the everyday content of your life will begin to feed you in an entirely new and deeply satisfying way. As you review previous years' written records of

EXERCISE
year-end ritual

In the ancient Egyptian calendar, days 361 through 365 were considered feast days of the gods—extra days, if you like, completing the cycle of the year and the earth's rotation around the sun. This exercise is intended to give those same days an exploratory purpose in your own life here in the twenty-first century. If you engage in this yearly ritual, you'll find that the time spent greatly enhances the process of your own unfolding. Though you may forget precisely what wishes you articulated during the five-day period, when you look back a year later, you'll discover that many of the things you'd expressed an interest in came into being over the past twelve months, although not through any planning on your part. They came about simply because you allowed yourself to listen to the inner longings of your heart and then let them go.

The process is very similar to sowing seeds. When you plant a garden, you don't sit and stare at the seeds until they sprout. You know that some will germinate and some will not, but it is not up to you to make them grow. All you can do is set the conditions for their growth with good soil, adequate water, and the right amount of sun. In exactly the same way, all you can do for your own unfolding is to set the conditions by slowing down a bit (that's the good soil), giving yourself the gift of your own presence in your life (that's the water), and meditating regularly to help open to more of who and what you really are (that's the sun). None of this can take place, however, without sowing seeds. And that's what this exercise does—and while you are sowing seeds during this five-day period, you can be enjoying the fruits of the previous year's harvest at the same time.

You can design this exercise to fit your own time schedule, so there's really no one way to do it, but I'll tell you how I've practiced it, and then you can determine what works best for you. I designate two hours each day between December 27 and December 31—five days in all—to engage the questions below. During each two-hour period, I don't answer the phone or respond to e-mail messages, and I ask other family members not to interrupt me. Some years, if I'm going to work each day, I'll take these two hours in the evening; other years, if I'm on vacation, I'll take the time right after breakfast—the time of day when my mind is clearest. Before starting the exercise each day, I meditate so that I'm really open to what arises once I begin writing down my thoughts, memories and insights.

As you plan your own year-end ritual, it helps to make it happen at more or less the same time each year so that you'll remember to do it. Summer vacation might work better for you than the last few days of each year. Or you might prefer to designate one single day on which this exercise is all you do rather than spread it out over five days. That's fine too, of course. Just try to stick to ten hours and try to avoid interruptions. Hire a babysitter if necessary.

You may want to write your responses to the questions below in a blank book or journal similar to your Not So Big Life Notebook, or you may prefer to make an audio recording. The medium is up to you. The key is to make this an enjoyable process during which the faucet can simply flow unimpeded.

First, respond to these questions about the past year:

- How have I spent my time?
- What are the results of the actions I have taken?
- What events, realizations, and understandings have come into being?
- What has inspired me?
- What am I grateful for?
- What were my sorrows and disappointments, and how have I been changed by them?
- What were my enthusiasms, accomplishments, creations, and joys, and how have I been changed by them?
- What books have I read this year, and what impact have they had?
- What movies and other entertainments have moved me, and in what ways?

- What journeys have I taken?
- What patterns and themes have I noticed in my nighttime dreams?
- What have been my most significant dreams, and how have they affected me?
- What patterns and themes have I noticed in my waking dream?
- What conditioned patterns have I recognized, and what experiences have allowed me to see them more clearly?
- What hidden beliefs have I uncovered in working with these conditioned patterns?
- What previously unrecognized aspects of my personality have I discovered?
- What habitual patterns have I experimented with or changed?
- What new patterns of behavior have I adopted over the past year, and what effects have they had?

Then engage these questions about the present:

- How am I different now from the way I was last year at this time?
- How can I integrate the key lessons of the past year into my life?
- Are there any strategies, phrases, questions, or flags that have particular significance for me right now? If so, why?
- Are there any things I'm being asked to do right now that I am rejecting? If so, what would happen if I simply did them?
- Are there any things I'm trying to force into existence right now? If so, what would happen if I stopped trying to make them happen?
- Are there any new characters in my life who can reveal to me unrecognized aspects of who I am?
- What recent synchronicities do I recall? What do they appear to point toward?
- To what part of myself am I giving birth?
- What am I becoming?
- Who am I really?
- Has my experience of time changed at all since last year?

Finally, here are the questions about the future:

- Specifically, what is it that I wish to focus on or experience in the coming year?

- Looking far into the future, what wishes, longings, or creations will I be bringing into being or engaging in some way?
- If I could sum up all my desires and longings in one simple statement spoken from the highest aspect of myself, what would it be?

That's all there is to it. The more engrossed you allow yourself to become, the more potent this tool for transformation will be. When I engage in this exercise, my first step is to answer all the questions—which I usually do in the first three days. And when this part of the process is completed, I reread the previous year's answers. This is always the high point for me because, like my rediscovery of the forgotten list in the drawer of my nightstand, it is only then that the results of the previous year's planting become apparent. This is the moment when you can really appreciate the power of the entire ritual.

At the end of the five-day period—or however long you've designated for your own ritual—close your journal and place it in a locked file, safe, or somewhere else out of harm's way so that you won't be tempted to look at it until next year. Then forget about it and drop all attachment to anything you've written in this exercise, understanding that that part of the process is not in your hands. You are simply the gardener.

In house design the most all-encompassing definition of *home* is not limited to the structure and its contents. It also includes the home's surroundings: its garden and even the views beyond the property's boundaries. A well-designed house is one that allows the separation between inside and outside worlds to almost disappear. This can be done in all sorts of ways, but much of the art of eroding the boundary is accomplished through the placement of windows and doors. The more window area there is, the less distinction there appears to be.

In our lives we can also learn to see beyond boundaries. We typically think of ourselves as ending at the outer layer of skin on our bodies, but as we come to see that everything in the world is a reflection of our inner nature, we begin to recognize that what's inside and what's outside are not different. They are both part of one totality, one home—our home.

In a similar way to the process of merging inner and outer worlds in house design, we can lift the veil between these two aspects of our lives as we learn to turn walls into windows and doors. The very structure that we've always assumed is separating and therefore protecting us from the dangers of that hostile outer world turns out to be the obstacle to finding what we've been looking for our whole lives. There really is nothing that creates this separation. There is no inside and no outside. They are only imaginary constructs that allow us to know ourselves through the experience of contrast. Contrast is the way we know difference, the way we sense and perceive. It makes our world appear to be one of duality: light and dark, tall and short, big and small.

But where does something change from being big to being small? Where does darkness end and light begin? There's no solid dividing line. Dark and light fall in varying degrees along a spectrum, with the two apparent opposites located at either end, but neither one has an inherently independent existence. So whether we're referring to our houses or our lives, we are seeing only the appearance of difference, the appearance of duality, and not something real. Our perception of contrast is what convinces us that polarities exist, and that conviction is what causes us to feel separate, both from one another and from our true selves.

In the same way our experience of a world "out there" that is different from the one within gives us a convenient way to perceive ourselves through contrast. But just as we can begin to see beyond the walls of our house, we come to know that in our lives home is without boundary. Home is the entirety of our lives, and the more open we are to our experience, the fuller and more complete that sense of home becomes.

TWELVE

Being at Home in Your Life

The way the soul is with the senses and the intellect is
like a creek. When desire weeds

grow thick, intelligence can't flow, and soul creatures
stay hidden. But sometimes

the reasonable clarity runs so strong it sweeps the clogged
stream open. No longer weeping

and frustrated, your being grows as powerful as your wantings
were before, more so. Laughing

and satisfied, the masterful flow lets creations of
the soul appear. You look

down, and it's lucid dreaming. The gates made of light
swing open. You see in.
—RUMI

Growing Beyond Who We Think We Are

The more a house expresses the passions of its inhabitants, the more at home those inhabitants will feel. And the more your life expresses your own passions, the more at home you will feel in your life. The paradox is that you must learn to get out of your own way in order for that expression to take place. As I have intimated, the obstacles we encounter are always walls created by our small self, our personality, which is constantly on guard and trying to protect itself.

Gradually, throughout these pages, I've been encouraging you to chip away at your attachment to that small self, to reveal more of who you really are. The small self isn't real. Its apparent solidity is one of those imaginary polarities created to separate "me" from everything else, so that the "me" can have some sense of control and dominion over its existence. Seeing through this illusion is the work of a lifetime, and if you've just begun the process, it can seem both thrilling and overwhelming. Sometimes it will look deceptively simple, and sometimes it will seem more complex than learning a new language.

As you've seen, the one thing you must not forget is that in the midst of it all, your only job is to show up and experience what's here to be experienced in this moment. It is the direct experiencing of everything that happens that provides the key to your true nature. You don't have to change a thing. You just have to be here completely and then inquire into your experiences to find out why you react the way you do, why you think the way you do, and why you feel the way you do. It's through your being here now, being fully engaged in every moment, that those walls of isolation will come down. You don't have to go after them with explosives. They just crumble and fall away of their own accord as you see through your various filters and conditionings and realize that you aren't what you thought you were.

It is this self-observation and this questioning of the things about yourself that you've always taken for granted that will start building some windows and doors into the structure of your life. When we think we know something, all our searching will confirm only what we already know. As you've seen throughout these pages, conditioned patterns allow us to see only what those filters are programmed to look for. They *can't* reveal anything else. So the only way out of our limited, frustrating world is by looking for the filters themselves and inquiring into each one in turn, to find its roots, the hidden beliefs that hold it in place, and the characteristic reactive behaviors that indicate it's at play behind the scenes.

By being present in your everyday experiences, you'll find that the raw material for seeing through the filters is constantly being delivered to your doorstep for consideration. It's not a process with a beginning and an end. It's something that continues for many years, revealing more and more of who and what you really are. The more you are able to let go of the preconceptions about who you think you are and how you think things are supposed to be, the more you experience what's really here and the more possible it is for the vitality you've longed for to fill your world. In fact, the fuller your life becomes, the less you even remember how constricted and frustrating it once was. That's the real promise of a Not So Big Life. By implementing the recommendations in these pages, you'll be creating a life that becomes truly vast as the boundaries between inside and outside all but disappear.

Now you are no longer trying to buy your way to satisfaction, no longer taking risks, swigging gallons of coffee, or rushing from meeting to meeting to convince yourself that you are alive. Now there are space and time in your inner world, room created by your no longer running away from yourself all the time in an effort to fill the void you feel inside but don't want to look at for fear it will swallow you whole. You are coming to know, more and more, who you *really* are rather than who you think you are supposed to be.

On one level this may sound scary, because it implies you are undefended and not in control. But as I hope I've been successful in revealing, you never have been in control. You just thought you were. And all the attachments we have to our to-do lists, our schedules, and our familiar patterns are only walls of our own making to help hide this uncomfortable truth from ourselves. Once we can accept it, though, once we can cut a window or two in the wall and look outside, we find that things aren't nearly as frightening as we imagined they'd be. In fact, we discover incredible beauty that was there all along. We've simply walled off the view in order to create the illusion of boundaries and in order to give ourselves the impression that we know what our lives are all about, so we can direct them to our own ends.

But over time, as we live within our self-imposed limits, we lose contact with the vitality we felt earlier in our lives. A creeping numbness and discontent push us to search for that certain something that we know is our birthright. Almost all of us sense there's something wrong. We just can't figure out by ourselves what that is. The reason is becoming clear: We're searching within the confines of the walled enclosure of our own separateness when the moreness we long for awaits on the other side of this imaginary boundary.

So the scary message has a flip side that's quite thrilling: Punch out a few holes in those walls, gradually open the door to your *real* self, and you discover a life that's truly limitless. *This* world is full of possibilities that were previously invisible and unimaginable. Because you are now directly experiencing your life rather than holding it at arm's length, because you are now fully inhabiting your life instead of just going through the motions, you are now, finally, at home. Home isn't something to construct and hide inside; it's a way of being in the world without the walls that hold you back from being whole and full and completely alive.

If I'd said that on page 1, you might have dropped the book in terror.

"Of course I'm separate," you'd have said. "Of course I have to protect myself and make sure no one takes advantage of me." Now you are able to see everything in a new light. You know, at least in principle, that all there is, is you—you seeing reflections of yourself in the contents of your everyday life, your waking dream. It's just that the *you* you thought you were when you started reading this book is different from the *you* you are beginning to understand yourself to be here at the end.

One of the challenges I've had in writing this book has been that it presents tools for all manner of readers, from those who've never thought much before about their inner world to those who've been practicing some form of contemplation or meditation for years. The message that I want to impart about who and what we really are can be said in many ways, some appropriate for the beginner and others more suited to the longtime practitioner. To accommodate this wide range of readers, I've created an extension of this chapter that's available only on the Not So Big Life website. It is there for those who are ready to explore more deeply the terrain that lies beyond the boundaries of the small self.

It will probably be most helpful after you've been diligently practicing the exercises in this book for at least a year or two. You might want to ask yourself each year when you perform your year-end ritual, "Am I ready for the next level?" When your answer is a confident "yes," go to the chapter extension—but not before. It's not that reading it will do you harm, but it might not make much sense. And since some of its power to affect you resides in its newness, if you've read it before you're ready, it won't be new when you *are* ready, and so it won't have the same ability to shift your understanding of how things are. A good litmus test of your readiness lies in how you can absorb the next section. When you can really hear and consider the questions it poses about your true identity, you are ready.

Life Lessons

A few months ago, as I was listening to one of my favorite CDs of Coleman Barks reading Rumi's poetry, the letters of Rumi's name sprang to mind and formed themselves into questions. R-U-M-I. Say them out loud to yourself. "Are you? Am I?" I laughed as the perfection of their meaning hit home. In this world of reflections and imaginings, we perceive the separateness that we assume ourselves to be, but Rumi constantly asks us to consider if we've really got it straight or if we're simply players in some magnificent theatrical performance. Each of us plays a role we didn't choose and gradually comes to believe we are that role. Rumi is constantly imploring us to wake up from the play and remember who we *really* are. Remember that one thing he told us, back on p. 89, that we are here to do? This is it: We must re-member ourselves by gradually uncovering what's been hidden from view by all the walls that the small self has erected to protect itself from the great spaciousness of the *real* world.

So who are we really? Are you who you think you are? Am I who I think I am? And if not, then what? No one can do the discovering of these truths for you. We must each explore our own personal experience: We must each live the truth of every moment as it happens in *real* time.

And if we want to experience that aliveness, we cannot keep waiting for things to change, for everything to be just right. People set goals all the time, telling themselves that they'll be able to really live once the goal is achieved, but of course the goal is rarely, if ever, achieved, so real living is forever put off. That's one way in which we wait. Another is that we argue with what is placed in front of us to do. We don't want that food. We want something else instead. So we spend our time rejecting what comes to us and striving for the things we think we want. Again we are waiting—this time for things to go our way. Or we believe that we're inadequate, that we can't do what we want to do because we're not good enough, not talented enough, not strong enough. So for all these reasons we shy away from that which is in front of us and wait for the day when we are no longer inadequate. And then we wonder why life is passing us by, why we're always dissatisfied, always in a holding pattern.

The problem is that the self who is waiting for the goal to be accomplished, for the thing it prefers to show up, or for the inadequacy to go away is your personality, your small self. It will never, ever be satisfied because its very existence depends on your *not* being present and your *not* simply doing what's there to be done. We never question the prevailing paradigm; we believe unequivocally that if we stop all the striving and goal setting, we'll somehow get hammered, nailed—maybe even die. But it's all imagined. It's all part of the dream. Real full-octane living is happening right Now. It's just that you aren't accepting delivery.

This is the moment—this Now. This is the doorway to ourselves, and when we step through it, we discover the reason we've been in such confusion and distress. Once again Rumi transforms our disorientation through poetry:

> I have lived on the lip
> of insanity, wanting to know reasons,
> knocking on a door. It opens.
> I've been knocking from the inside!

There *is nothing* to find. There *is no place* to go. There *is no one* who can save us from our frustration and discontent. Like a fish in the ocean not recognizing the water it swims in, we are already completely immersed in the meaningfulness we're seeking.

So when we find ourselves tired and frustrated by the direction of our lives and wanting to make room for things that have more significance and more meaning, we must realize that our image of fulfillment looks entirely different from the actual experiencing of fulfillment. It turns out to be unbelievably simple, requiring no doing at all, only a great letting go as we quit hanging on to the character in the waking dream that we believe to be our self and become aware that our lives are perfectly crafted to reveal who and what we really are. All that's required is our presence. We just have to show up.

What's real must be experienced directly and explored personally. It's one of life's great paradoxes that what is universal can only be accessed by becoming completely who you are as an individual. Once you see that you are most present when you are engaged in things that allow you to transcend your small self's boundaries, you begin to understand the ingredients necessary for a life that's fully charged and fully vital. You become that point of experiencing that allows self to know the greater Self. If you never investigate the small self, the greater Self—the universal you—remains firmly beyond reach.

So our lives aren't really about our successes and failures, our possessions, or our mates and progeny. Those are only catalysts for the real living that is going on as we awake to whatever the world presents us with to be consumed each day to help us grow. Life is about playing our part in the concert of manifestation, simply experiencing firsthand the brilliant orchestration and choreography of the one who teaches us, "our music master," as Rumi puts it in the poem that introduces this book. Once you recognize the nature of the dream, you'll understand when I say that everything you have read on these pages is *you* speaking to *you*. It's time to make room for what really matters, and now you've had at least a glimpse of the fact that it's been here inside you all along, waiting for you to open the door and step out into the sunshine.

It's time to wake up. Wake up! As you set foot across the threshold, mark this moment for yourself in some way that is memorable, and keep alive the awareness that there is more to life than the story line of your waking dream—more by orders of magnitude.

That's what I mean by a Not So Big Life, and I hope that in sharing the blueprint for its design, you, too, will be able to enjoy the life you are living from this new perspective. If you do, you'll find that you are increasingly at home in your life and, in the true meaning of Gandhi's famous quotation, that you are *being* the change you wish to see in the world; and as you change, the world—all of it—changes with you. It is in this never-ending unfolding that fulfillment lies—not in the accomplishment of some goal but in the journeying itself. If you pay attention to what is entering your world, the teachers and teachings you need at that moment will be there, each of them manifestations of the one true teacher: life itself.

So now it's time. Open the door and begin the process of learning to participate fully and lucidly in this ultimate virtual reality game:

The Waking Dream
Location: Planet Earth
Era: Twenty-first century
Identity: You

Travel well, and don't forget your owner's manual.
Welcome to your Not So Big Life.

APPENDIX

Owner's Manual for Your Not So Big Life, Step by Step

As you read through the owner's manual and pick the five points from each section that stand out most for you in your life right now, you may also want to include a note that will remind you a year from now to reread and update the list you've created. Include the date of your next review, just as you might when you've had your furnace inspection or the oil changed in your car. You might even want to put a note in your calendar as well. Though this will be obvious to you now, a year is a long time, and it's easy to forget. Placing a note on your page of reminders will keep it in your awareness and will make you much more likely to follow through next year and the year after that. Imagine what shape our cars would be in if we forgot to change the oil periodically. Without this exercise, our lives will be in a similar state of disrepair.

ONE • Everyday Routines to Support Your Growth

This first aspect of the owner's manual is a continuation of a number of routines that are fresh in your mind right now but that you will need to revisit and reinforce over the coming months and years in order to remember their importance. These routines are listed, with their respective chapters and sections identified, so that you can go back and read about them if you've forgotten how to implement them effectively. You may want to reread the respective sections once a year anyway, since words and explanations tend to grow in meaning as you become more practiced in a particular discipline.

A. MAKING A TIME AND A PLACE FOR SOLITUDE

See chapter 8, p. 170.

You can meditate for twenty minutes, thirty minutes, forty-five minutes, or an hour each day. Whatever duration you choose, make it one that you can maintain and that you commit yourself to. Make it as automatic as brushing your teeth.

B. KEEP A LOG IN YOUR NOT SO BIG LIFE NOTEBOOK OF THE FOLLOWING INFORMATION:

- Significant moments and synchronicities
  See chapter 2, "Identifying the Significant Moments in Your Life," p. 39.
  As you start engaging in your life in this more active way, you'll find that you experience more moments of significance and more synchronicities than you used to. But if you don't record them in some way, you may well forget them. The point is not to become attached to or identified with these moments of significance but to use them as a lens through which to see changes in yourself over time.

- Observations made by the watcher
  See chapter 6, "Developing a Watcher," p. 123; chapter 4, "Revealing the Underpinnings of Your Personality," p. 79; and chapter 3, "Understanding Your Relationship to Time," p. 59.
  These include the recognition of hidden beliefs, patterns of reacting to things occurring in your daily life, rejections of or judgments about what is happening to you, and changes occurring in your orientation to time.

- Inquiries into any of the above
  See chapter 4, "Revealing the Underpinnings of Your Personality," p. 79; and chapter 9, "I Am Not That Thought," p. 201.
  These will help you better understand what lies at the root of your beliefs, reactions, rejections, and judgments. Keep in mind that all your observations about conditioned patterns are food for *you*. They don't have anything to do with the "other" that you are reacting to, rejecting, or judging. What you react to in your waking dream is there to help you see *you*.

- Dreams and dream expansion
  See chapter 5, "Exploring Your Dreamworld," p. 102.
  If you continue to keep a journal beside your bed for recording dreams and you designate ten to fifteen minutes after you wake up for jotting down what you remember, you'll find a continuous influx of nutrients for your growth and development. Don't forget that every character and image in your dream is an aspect of you. It's not about anyone else.

- Observations about meditation and other exercises in presence
  See chapter 7, "Experiencing Presence," p. 150; chapter 8, "Making a Time and a Place for Solitude," p. 170; and chapter 9, "I Am Not That Thought," p. 201.
  As with observations about significant moments, the objective here is not to attach to or identify with the experiences but to use the documentation process to help you observe the changes that are under way. When you are in the midst of your life, it is often difficult to notice changes because they happen slowly. Documenting your observations allows you to see what's happening.

- Experiences following intentional behavior changes
  See chapter 10, "Changing Your Behavior," p. 230.
  Whenever you feel stuck, bored, or frustrated, changing a conditioned pattern or two will move things along. The pattern you pick to change doesn't have to have anything to do with the place in which you feel stuck. A single change of behavior alters the whole picture. It can't help but do so because the entire system is interrelated.

TWO • Strategies for Revealing More of Your True Potential

This section of your owner's manual cites specific ways to proceed in your life, ways that will provide you with the most nutritious diet possible for your growth and evolution. You may want to refer to these attitude statements often, for if you don't have them readily at hand for certain situations, you'll find yourself doing the opposite of what is best for your growth. Again, I have added references to the sections in the book where you can read more about each attitude. You'll find it useful when you are faced with a dilemma or when you feel overwhelmed by circumstances to read through the section that most closely applies. A reframing of the issue can always help you see a different way of proceeding.

- Be on the watch for the things you are addicted to accumulating: p. 56.
- Let go, breathe, and allow the unfolding to unfold: p. 143.
- Experience, but do not attach to or identify with anything: p. 117.
- Follow your passions: p. 208.
- Clearly express your intentions; then let go: p. 211.
- Focus on what you want, not on what you don't want: p. 215.
- Be obedient to the situation: p. 217.
- Go toward that which you are rejecting: p. 221.
- Do one thing at a time: p. 223.

THREE • Reminders to Keep You on Task

Throughout this book I've provided phrases that are intended to be catchy reminders that will arise in your mind when you need them. As you do more of this introspective work, you'll find that the guidance you need for each situation will often come through these succinct commentaries. They'll pop into mind when you least expect it, and if you listen with the inner senses you've been developing as you worked through the preceding chapters, you'll find that the very thing you need to do next or the understanding you need to recall is contained within the phrase. When one of the phrases presents itself, by reading the section in which it occurred you may find additional insights to help you on your way. Here is a list of my top twenty of those reminders:

- The *only* way to change the world is to change yourself: p. 35.
- Live into the questions: p. 93.
- Everything's a reflection: p. 105.
- The world is not out there; the world is in you: p. 109.
- All there is, is you: p. 116.
- Never underestimate the personality: p. 124.
- *Be* in your doing: p. 133.
- Follow the synchronicities: p. 135.
- Ask, and you shall receive: p. 143.
- Life is the experiencing of the experience: p. 146.
- We can truly become human *beings* rather than human *doings*: p. 157.

- Everything is food for the journey: p. 183.
- There is no right or wrong answer: p. 185.
- You are not your thoughts: p. 189.
- There is nothing wrong: p. 191.
- You are never abandoned: p. 196.
- Do what's in front of you to do: p. 197.
- Nothing happens by accident: p. 196.
- An idea can only generate its own nature: p. 211.
- When you look with the eyes of a student, everything can teach you: p. 214.

FOUR • Questions to Keep Asking Yourself

As we've seen, the process of inquiring into the beliefs and conditioned patterns that we've previously taken for granted is a powerful method for waking ourselves up. But when we are in the midst of our daily lives, it is easy to forget that we are functioning on automatic pilot; it is easy to forget to inquire. So this aspect of your owner's manual is a list of questions that are intended to keep you aware. Every time you are about to make a decision of any kind, read through this list to see if there are any questions that leap out at you suggesting something to be inquired into before you proceed. These questions aren't intended to stop you from acting, but they will allow you to look more closely at your motivations and hidden beliefs before you proceed. Sometimes the inquiry will refine your decision making, and sometimes it may change the outcome of the decision making. But in either case, through the inquiry process you'll be learning more about yourself. Always keep in mind that the point isn't to arrive at a single fixed answer but to probe the underlying framework of your beliefs and expectations.

- How have you wanted to change the world? Can you identify the ways in which you have been looking for a related change in yourself?
- With each purchase that you make, what are you looking for? What does the purchase represent? Does it fill a need, or is it a substitute for something else?
- What could be done with your resources (time, money, energy) once your physical well-being has been accommodated?
- When do you know you have enough?

- Is there an interest or an alternative career that you've been putting off pursuing? If so, what keeps you from pursuing it?
- Who or what is deciding there isn't time?
- How many "extracurricular" events are you involved in? What are you getting out of them?
- What are the stories you tell over and over? Why do you tell them? What does each one represent?
- What conditioned patterns are you aware of in your behavior? Why do you do them? Where or how did they originate?
- What does your internal judge say about your behavior? About the behavior of others?
- Can you see that the events occurring in your life are there to feed you, whether they make you feel good, bad, or indifferent?
- As you attach to a thought stream, you have the opportunity to watch what happens. Ask yourself:
  - How do I feel as I become attached to it?
  - What's the point of attaching to it?
  - Have I done this before with the same kind of thought?
  - Where did the attachment to this thought begin?
- Whenever something "bad" or uncomfortable happens, ask yourself: If all there is, is me, what does this signify?
- What conditions must be in place in order for you to function?
- What would you do differently if all the waves, whitecaps, and storms of life were simply there to wake you up to who you really are?
- How do you live a life well?
- What is Now?

FIVE • Flags to Watch For

When you know how to recognize them, there are many behavior patterns that can allow you to see when you're stuck or functioning in sleep mode even when you think you're awake. This list of behaviors is intended as a reminder for your watcher. If you observe any of these flags in the content of your waking dream, take a time-out and read the section that's referred to. This part of your owner's manual is hugely important because it is most difficult to stay objective when you are feeling reactive. This list provides a method for noticing when you are not being objective and offers a reminder to pause while you inquire into the real issue at hand.

- Watch out for magical thinking and self-inflation. If you believe there's something magical happening just to you or if you are "being told" by some inner voice that you have a special mission, know that this is the personality at work. It is not real or true.
  See chapter 4, "Revealing the Underpinnings of Your Personality," p. 79.

- When you believe that something upsetting in your life is about someone else and not you, stop. It is about you, and it's happening so that you can learn more about you.
  See chapter 6, "The World Is in You," p. 109.

- Reactivity is always the result of conditioned patterns and confused thinking, and it's a flag indicating the presence of a filter over reality.
  See chapter 6, "What You Believe, That Just Ain't So," p. 119.

- The way things are is the way things are and no amount of wishing will make them any different.
  See chapter 9, "Not a Problem," p. 179, and "Learning to Recognize the Nutrients for Inner Growth," p. 183.

- When you are looking for the right way to go and you can't figure it out, remember, there is no right answer. Honestly. The part of you that's trying to figure it out is lost in the appearances.
  See chapter 9, "Doing What's in Front of You to Do," p. 197.

- If you try to think your way to understanding, you are bound to get stuck; you'll end up only confusing yourself further.
  See chapter 9, "Working Mind versus Thinking Mind," p. 186.

- When we bemoan the state of the world, we're saying that the ocean surface shouldn't be choppy. There is absolutely no way to make the appearance perfectly still and tranquil.
  See chapter 9, "Not a Problem," p. 179, and "Learning to Recognize the Nutrients for Inner Growth," p. 183.

- When you find yourself believing that you are in the right or someone or something in your environment is intolerable, you are experiencing your personality in an all-out fight for survival. Don't buy into its absolutism.

See chapter 9, "Not a Problem," p. 179, and "Learning to Recognize the Nutrients for Inner Growth," p. 183.

- Watch for rope-pushing behavior, and as soon as you notice it, cease and desist.

See chapter 10, "Don't Push The Rope," p. 216.

ACKNOWLEDGMENTS

Writing and publishing a book is a lot like having a child. It looks as though there's one person delivering this new life into the world, but in fact, had it not been for all the progenitors of the mother and her husband, and all her present caregivers, the child born of her pregnancy would not have come to be. At this point in the process, on the last day of this two-year gestation, it is eminently clear that this child-to-be is only the inevitable result of all the ingredients that have been poured into its incubation vessel. So what may look like one person's expression is in fact a weaving of the teachings and ministrations of some amazing human beings. The gratitude I want to express here is for the deliverers of the ingredients that have come to me over the course of my life, recent and historical, visible and invisible.

First there is the team of people who have helped me through the gestation and delivery process:

- My literary agent, Gail Ross, and her associate Howard Yoon, who helped me first to formulate a proposal, then to shop it around to publishers—quite a stable thereof—and finally, assisted me in selecting the one that would midwife me through this process, Random House.
- Susan Mercandetti, the person at Random House who brought this expectant mother into her publishing house for the duration of the pregnancy. Without her conviction that this was a message whose time had come, this book would have been significantly less accessible to those unfamiliar with the inner work of self-discovery.

- Peter Guzzardi, an amazingly talented editor who helped me craft and hone the text, and who became a dear friend over the gestation period. When you work closely together on a book like this one, you can't help but grow together in the process.
- Caroline Sutton and Jennifer Hershey, two wonderful and insightful editors from Random House whose expert wordsmithing capabilities have left their mark, each in their own inimitable way.
- My dear friend and assistant, Marie St. Hilaire, without whom this book would have been a very different and far less effective tool. Although I call her an assistant, that word does not even begin to reflect the role she plays—ally, colleague, right-hand woman, and traveling companion through the process of this inner work to understand ourselves.
- Two early readers, Alice Lutz and Winifred Gallagher, who were key in the shaping of the book, each offering advice part way through the writing process. Gallagher, who has authored books in both architectural and spiritual genres, was particularly helpful in showing me that readers expect an architect to point the way with architectural metaphors.
- And the fleet of associates both at Susanka Studios and at Random House who have helped to design, manage, publicize, and promote the book. These individuals are usually invisible, but their roles are incredibly important to a book's delivery into the world: Suzanne Fedoruk, who has worked with me on the publicity for several other books, is at my side for this one too, as are Irina Woelfle and Barbara Onieu. The designers and the public relations team at Random House, Carole Lowenstein, Sanyu Dillon, Sally Marvin, Tom Perry, Jennifer Jones, and Carol Schneider, to name a few, are all providing their knowledge and expertise to prepare for and announce this birth.

Then there's the other type of ingredient, the providers of the genetic material, if you will, without which I would have had nothing to say. These are the real heroes in this story. I have enormous gratitude for the work of four authors who have had a profound affect upon my understanding of the waking dream:

- Coleman Barks, whose beautiful and poignant translations of the poetry of Jelaluddin Rumi introduce many of the chapters in this book, has made the understandings of that great soul available to a new generation of lovers of life.

- Normandi Ellis, whose work with the teachings of ancient Egypt has likewise made the understandings and worldview of that extraordinary period accessible to us today.
- Ramesh Balsekar, whose lucid explanations of the teaching of Nisargadatta Maharaj have given seekers of truth the world over a way to see that that which is seeking is in fact the sought, and the only way to understand is to still the mind and appercieve the truth. No thinking required.
- and A. H. Almaas, whose writings on the explorations and discoveries of his own inner work have provided a clear path to self-understanding for thousands of attentive and disciplined students. Though he has not been a personal teacher, his words have had a deep and pronounced effect.

I am also immensely grateful for the three teachers in the art of living more consciously that I've had the privilege of working with directly, Jan, Ron, and Al. These individuals give their all to transform their students by using their everyday experiences to profoundly alter the understandings of those they work with. Such teachers are authors of a different type, shaping lives rather than words to convey what they know. The contents of this book are a weaving of the teachings that I've imbibed from these amazing human beings, translated through my own experience:

- Jan gave me many crucial assignments and lessons to help wake me up to what's always here. Because they were so effective I've passed several of these along, so they can work their magic on you too.
- Ron showed me how to look at things differently, and to begin to taste the mystery underneath surface appearances. He passed away in 1998, but his legacy lives on.
- And Al taught me to see through the waking dream by looking objectively at all the ideas I had about myself, showing me how to build in the space to disidentify from them so that they were no longer limitations to living fully. Much of what is written here comes by way of his careful study of the mechanisms human beings use to protect and defend themselves, but which ultimately restrict them to mere shadows of their true potential.

And I'm also most grateful for the early lessons of my parents, who encouraged me always to be curious and to pursue my interests and passions, no matter how unconventional they might be. They taught me both to love life and to know that anything is possible if you believe in it. That's an amazing gift.

For me, the joy and the learning in bringing this book into being have come from engaging each day as it unfolds during the period of its incubation. For you, the learning (and, I trust, some joy) will come as you engage the suggestions implied by the words of this new way of living, this new form in the world. But as you read, and as you engage what is written here, I hope you will remember, as I do, the immensity of what has preceded it . . . aeons of human beings living their lives in the pursuit of their own passionate engagement in that illusive quality of being that we know is our birthright—to be completely and unequivocally alive. That is truly, as Rumi puts it, the *one* who teaches us, the true mother of this new way of living life.

And so, I extend my final gesture of gratitude to you, the ones into whose arms this child is now being born. It is through your actions in each moment of your life from this point forward that the potential of this new form in the world will grow and flourish. Thank you for beginning the journey toward the truth of who you really are.

INDEX

communications, time management
    and, 224–25, 226
  exercise in, 225–26
compartmentalization, in
    architecture and life, 5
composition, in architecture and life,
    2, 4
  See also authenticity; remodeling
    process
conditioning, in social values, 25, 26,
    73
  See also behavior patterns
confrontation, avoidance of, 73–74,
    111, 113–14, 158, 218–20
connection. See unity
consciousness, dynamics of, 142
  See also presence
consensus reality, 87–89, 90
  on dismal state of the world, 192,
    193
  dreams and, 92
  on forcing change, 180
  illusion of time in, 127–28
  questioning the values of, 193,
    228, 255, 256
  See also reality
construction process, dealing with
    stresses of, 11
contrast, human perceptions of,
    250
control, illusion of, 197, 251, 253
cosmic consciousness, 193–94
creativity, in art and life, 9–10, 14, 31,
    33, 34, 70–71, 110, 227
crises, as moments of self-
    questioning, 26, 49, 50–51
Curie, Marie, 209
Cusato, Marianne, 199

Darwin, Charles, 209
deadlines, dealing with, 140–41

delight. See epiphany, moments of;
    inspiration
design. See balance; beauty; house
    design
desires. See passions
dreams
  active imagination technique and,
    214
  exercises for exploring, 102–3
  listening to, 8–9, 14, 21, 28, 84,
    85–86, 92–101, 105, 156, 160–61,
    261
Dreams of Isis (Ellis), 241–42

eating, and experience of presence,
    146–47
efficiency vs. effectiveness, 223–26
  See also busyness; multitasking
Einstein, Albert, 43, 160, 169,
    209–10
electric light, social changes and,
    43–44
Ellis, Normandi, 241–43
engagement, 14, 27, 28, 58, 70, 92,
    98, 106, 117, 121–22, 127, 129,
    130, 133, 142, 149
  basic rules of, 208–29
  postponement of, 255
  See also fulfillment; life; Not So Big
    Life; presence
"enough," definition of, 57, 89
entry sequence
  in life and architecture, 18
  as remodeling challenge, 4
epiphany, moments of, 20, 21, 30,
    90, 92
  See also inspiration
exercises. See Not So Big Life
    Notebook (exercises)
experiencing
  as essence of life, 252, 262

reflective surfaces and, 104, 236

as search for hidden meanings, 86,
90–92, 93, 101, 236

seeing through obstacles to,
105–22, 199, 252, 255

through direct experience, 252–57,
262, 263

See also awareness; behavior
patterns; change; insight,
dreams; meditation; Not So Big
Life; Not So Big Life Notebook
(exercises); presence; reality

self-neglect, dangers of, 54

sensory experiences, presence and,
146–47

September 11, 2001 terrorist attacks,
26, 50, 193

shock, spiritual effects of, 193–94

significance, identifying life
moments of, 15–16, 39–40, 260

See also fulfillment; synchronicities

size, in house design, 42, 49, 85

sleep deprivation, effects of, 108–9,
138–39

slowing down

difficulty of, 127–28

value of, 26–27, 39, 49–51, 57–58,
139, 142, 157

See also haste; meditation; quiet
time; time

space

de-cluttering of, 69, 70

enhancing sense of, 5–6, 68, 84,
120, 128, 178, 207

focal points for, 154

as matrix for self-discovery, 21,
23–25, 27, 70, 207–8, 253

quantity *vs.* quality of, 42, 129

spatial experience, power of, 20–21,
23–25

speed. *See* haste; slowing down

spirituality, religious practice and, 214

stillness, value and meaning of, 154,
167

See also meditation; quiet time;
retreat place

stress

daily sources of, 54, 55, 70

house design and, 235

improved ability to deal with,
13–14, 189, 238–39

See also adrenaline; busyness

stuff

See possessions

success, pursuit of, 51, 89

See also busyness; consensus
reality; productivity

Susanka, Sarah

architectural practice and, xi, 13,
19, 23, 29–30, 49, 52–53,
131–35, 137–40, 168–69, 218,
235–36

burnout and, 137–41

busyness and, 21–23, 25, 35–37,
39, 56, 70–71, 130, 162

childhood summers and, 128–29

conditioned patterns and, 25, 71,
73–74, 75, 82–83, 111, 113–14,
186–89, 218–20, 230–31, 240

effective use of time and, 134–35

hidden beliefs and, 110–11

hidden meanings and, 86, 91

inner listening process and,
240–41, 243

kittens and, 195–96

life teachers and, 113–14, 135,
143–46, 197, 198, 228, 230–31,
241–43

as life's student, 28, 213–15, 228,
240–43

meditation and, 24–25, 157–60,
162–67, 168–69, 171, 177, 201

Not So Big House promotion and,
197–98

ABOUT THE AUTHOR

Bestselling author, architect, and cultural visionary, SARAH SUSANKA is leading a movement to redefine the American home and lifestyle. Her "build better, not bigger" approach to residential architecture has been embraced across the country, and her "Not So Big" philosophy has evolved beyond our physical habitations and into how we inhabit our lives.

Susanka has shared her insights with *The Oprah Winfrey Show*, *Charlie Rose*, and HGTV. *Fast Company* named her to their debut list of "Fast 50" innovators whose achievements have helped to change society—an honor preceded by her selection as a "top newsmaker" for 2000 by *Newsweek* magazine and an "innovator in American culture" in 1998 by *U.S. News & World Report*. *Builder* magazine consistently ranks her as one of the "50 most influential people in the building industry." She is regularly tapped for her dynamic presentations by Fortune 500 companies, homebuilders, nonprofits and trade organizations.

Susanka is a member of the College of Fellows of the American Institute of Architects, and a Senior Fellow of the Design Futures Council. She is the author of seven books and lives in North Carolina. Join her online community at www.notsobig.com.

ABOUT THE TYPE

This book was set in Quadraat Sans, a typeface designed by Fred Smeijers. His first Quadraat typeface was serified, and he successfully adapted it to a sans version without sacrificing its lively and humane character. Quadraat Sans has display qualities, yet it is efficient, making it equally suitable for texts. Fred Smeijers (born 1961) was educated in typography and graphic design at the Arnhem Academy of Art and Design. He has been designing typefaces since the 1980s.